Communication
for Business

Communication for Business

a practical approach

Third edition

Shirley Taylor

 LONGMAN

Pearson Education Limited
Edinburgh Gate
Harlow, Essex CM20 2JE, England
and Associated Companies throughout the world.

Published in the United States of America
by Pearson Education Inc., New York

First published 1991
Second Edition 1993
Reprinted 1994 (thrice), 1995, 1996
Reprinted by Longman Group Ltd 1996
Reprinted by Addison Wesley Longman 1996, 1998
Third Edition 1999

ISBN 0 582 38164-9

British Library Cataloguing-in-Publication Data
A catalogue record for this book is available from the British Library.

Library of Congress Cataloguing-in-Publication Data
A catalogue record for this book is available from the Library of Congress.

Typeset in 11/13 Sabon
Produced by Addison Wesley Longman Singapore (Pte) Ltd.,
Printed in Singapore

Contents

Section 7   Reformulating and Summarising   265

Section 8   Comprehension   291

Appendix   313

About the author

Shirley Taylor worked as Private Secretary at director level for nine years. She has many advanced secretarial qualifications including the LCCIEB Private Secretary's Diploma (Fourth Level) and a shorthand speed of 170 wpm.

After obtaining teaching diplomas and the Certificate in Education, Shirley taught on business and secretarial courses both in the UK and overseas. She spent several years in Singapore as Training Consultant and Lecturer and was Head of Secretarial Department at a college in Bahrain, Arabian Gulf.

In recent years Shirley has put her considerable experience into writing. Originally published in 1991, *Communication for Business* was her first book. Since then Shirley has written *The Secretary in Training* (*Textbook* and *Answerbook*), *Practical Audio Transcription* (Workbook and Cassette), *Elements of Office Administration* (*Textbook* and *Workbook*) and *Gartside's Model Business Letters and Other Business Documents*.

Having lived and worked in Singapore, Bahrain and Canada as well as her native UK, Shirley now enjoys travelling to undertake consultancy projects and to conduct seminars and workshops. In addition to her writing and consultancy work, Shirley is an examiner in secretarial skills for a major examining board.

Preface to the third edition

I was asked to write this third edition of *Communication for Business* some time ago. At last it is here. In compiling this new edition I have taken into account many comments from current users of the book, to whom I send my thanks for kind remarks about the usefulness of the text and constructive suggestions for improvements. I hope you will feel that I have done justice to this third edition and that you will find it even more user-friendly than its predecessors.

This third edition has involved me in a huge research task which started in Singapore and Malaysia and finished in the UK where everything finally came together. I felt it was necessary to find out what really happens in business today, so I sent out a letter to many companies asking for samples of anything they wished to send me. I also collected material everywhere I went. I thought it would be so much better to include 'real' business documents and correspondence in this new edition and I was thrilled to receive such a fabulous response. I hope users will find this authentic material interesting and useful.

In compiling this third edition I thought some restructuring was necessary to ensure a more logical order. Part of this restructuring involved the creation of a new section which I have called Persuasive Communication. By popular demand the specimen layouts and What's Wrong? features have been retained and the unit on use of English has been expanded. I have also included some more recent examination questions which will be useful for students studying for a wide range of examinations from Pitman, RSA and LCCIEB as well as those studying GNVQ key skills in Communication.

A completely new feature of the book is the inclusion of illustrations. This light touch is intended to make the study of communication fun while helping users to assimilate the material in the text. Other new features which I hope will be popular are tips, things to discuss, suggestions for research and project work – all easily identifiable by ingenious icons. Improvements on earlier editions include a bigger page size, more attractive page design and a much improved overall appearance.

I hope this new edition helps you to achieve your objectives, whether they are to teach the subject of this wide and wonderful world of business communication or whether they are to develop and improve your own communication abilities – perhaps a little of both.

Shirley Taylor

Introduction

The third edition of *Communication for Business* will be helpful to anyone who is working or training to work in an administrative, managerial or secretarial role which demands good communication and business English skills.

This new edition is designed to be a comprehensive textbook, a workbook and a reference book. It aims to:

+ stimulate interest in the use of business English so that it can be written more accurately, clearly and concisely
+ provide specimen layouts of all business communications
+ discuss essential theory on each topic to help develop understanding
+ provide a wide range of authentic documents for interest and reference
+ supply a wide range of assignments to reinforce learning
+ help readers to develop confidence and expertise in composing effective business communications.

✦ Organisation

Each self-contained unit includes all the necessary theory, specimens, suggested layouts and explanations required to develop understanding and initiative. Units are flexibly organised so that you can choose an appropriate learning sequence. Assignments are provided so that theory can be put into practice; they can be worked alone, with a partner or in group discussion.

✦ Specimen layouts

The fully-blocked method of display with open punctuation is stressed throughout this book. This is the most up-to-date and attractive method of presentation which is widely used by many organisations. If you choose to adapt this style or use your company's housestyle just remember the main rule: be consistent in presentation of all your communications.

✦ Special features

Look out for these special features throughout this new edition:

TIP

Tips, advice and suggestions are given throughout the text to help you.

LET'S CHECK

Put your new knowledge into practice by answering some quick questions which test the theory you have just learned.

THINK

Suggestions are made about things to do, think about, find out about, discuss with your colleagues, find out from your company. It could also suggest research or project work which you could undertake.

WHAT'S WRONG?

What's Wrong? gives you an opportunity to criticise answers to some assignments. You can then rewrite the documents more appropriately.

✦ Examinations

This book should prove useful to students wishing to take the following examinations:

- ✦ Pitman Qualifications English for Business Communication
- ✦ LCCI Examinations Board English for Business
- ✦ RSA Examinations Board Communication in Business

It should be noted that the following abbreviations have been used throughout the text:

- ✦ Pitman EFBC1   Pitman English for Business Communication Level 1
- ✦ Pitman EFBC2   Pitman English for Business Communication Level 2
- ✦ LCCIEB EFB1 style   Assignments written in the style of the English for Business First Level examination from the LCCI Examinations Board*

✦　LCCIEB EFB2 style　　Assignments written in the style of the English for Business Second Level examination from the LCCI Examinations Board*

✦ Communication for Business Resource Pack

Teachers will find the resource pack very valuable. It contains answers to all the questions and assignments in this textbook. OHP transparencies are also available featuring some illustrations and extracts from the main text. It is hoped that this resource pack will help teachers to plan and present interesting and informative lessons while helping students to help themselves.

I hope you enjoy this third edition of Communication for Business and that it helps you to achieve your objectives, whatever they may be.

Shirley Taylor 1999

The names, addresses, post codes, and other details of individuals and organisations used in examples and assignments in this book are ficticious. Any resemblance to existing individuals or organisations is coincidental.

*The author wishes to make it clear that LCCIEB style exam examples are not copies of LCCIEB examination questions. They have been written in a style which the author considers to be similar to that of the examination and level stated, but they have not been approved by or used by the LCCIEB.

Acknowledgements

I hardly know where to start saying thanks to all those who have helped me with this third edition.

First of all, to the many companies who provided material, whether I used it or not, thank you for the opportunity to take a glimpse into your world.

I am very grateful to the following organisations for their interest and help in providing permission to reproduce copyright material:

Ameron (Pte) Ltd
Boots the Chemists Ltd
British Telecommunications plc
Cadbury Ltd
CISCO
Civil Aviation Authority of Singapore
Cold Storage Singapore (1983) Pte Ltd
Department of Health
Doctor Jean Emberlin, National Pollen Research Unit, University College, Worcester
Doctor Patient Partnership
English National Ballet School
Eurostar (UK) Ltd
Hays Montrose
Institute of Qualified Private Secretaries
John Wilson, ITSA Goal
Kodak Ltd
Lever Brothers Limited
Lichtwer Pharma UK Ltd
Michael De Kretser Consultants
Midland Bank plc
Midland Mainline
Mr & Mrs Anthony Morgan
Mövenpick Marché Restaurant Singapore
Nestlé UK Ltd
Prima Magazine, London
Sheffield Insulations Group plc

Sheffield Wednesday Football Club Ltd
Sheraton Towers Hotel, Singapore
Singapore Airlines Ltd
Singapore Broadcasting Authority
Singapore Computer Systems Pte Ltd
Singapore Exhibition Services Pte Ltd
Singapore MRT Ltd
The Body Shop International PLC
The Boots Company
Thistle Hotels
TIBS Holdings Ltd
Van Den Bergh Foods
Waterlow Business Supplies
YHA (England and Wales) Ltd

Thanks also to Pitman Qualifications and the Oxford Cambridge and RSA Examinations Board for permission to reproduce past examination questions.

Special thanks go to Peter Leggott and Tony Sidell who very kindly produced some examination questions for me similar in style to English for Business examinations First and Second Level from the LCCI Examinations Board. I am so very grateful for their help and expertise.

Communication for Business is very special to me. In the first edition I drew largely on my experience of teaching ambitious and conscientious students in Singapore and Bahrain. I thank those students for showing me that communication can be fun (I hope for them too).

Communication for Business might never have happened in the first place without the confidence and support of David Buckland and Peter Marshall to whom I shall always be grateful. Since then I have enjoyed a great deal of support and friendship from the Addison Wesley Longman teams in the UK, Singapore and Malaysia. I would particularly like to thank Ian Little for his enthusiasm and support in the preparation of this third edition.

My thanks also go to the editor, copy-editor, artists and designers involved in this project. Your valuable contribution, innovation, talent and creative flair is very evident and much appreciated.

I could not have put this new edition together without a little help from some special friends who provided advice on authenticity as well as lots of moral support throughout this project.

The greatest thanks of all go to the one person who makes it all worthwhile, who has supported me and encouraged me always. This book is for you Mum. With love.

THE NATURE OF COMMUNICATION

UNIT 1

An overview

By the end of this unit you should be able to:

❏   define the term 'communication'

❏   list and explain the different methods of communication

❏   discuss the factors to be considered in choosing appropriate
      methods of communication

❏   explain the key stages in the communication cycle

❏   give examples of barriers to communication

❏   discuss the various communication systems in an organisation

❏   list the guidelines to follow to achieve successful communication.

✦ What is communication?

Communication may be defined as *giving, receiving or exchanging information, opinions or ideas by writing, speech or visual means, so that the material communicated is completely understood by everyone concerned.*

All day every day we are communicating, whether it is talking to people on the telephone or in person, taking dictation and transcribing business correspondence, liaising with colleagues and staff, writing letters and other correspondence. The importance of developing good communication skills cannot be over-emphasised. You might ask 'I communicate all the time, so why do I need to study the subject?' The reason for this is because the process is not so easy as simply talking or writing. We need to make sure that we get it right – that our ideas and information are completely understood.

✦ Methods of communication

The main methods of oral and written communication, both internal and external, are shown in the following diagrams:

Internal communication

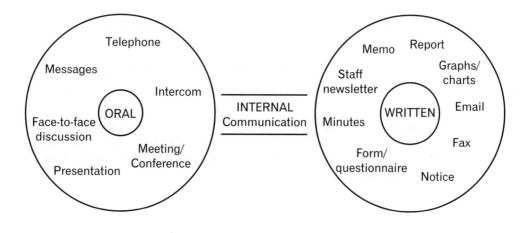

External communication

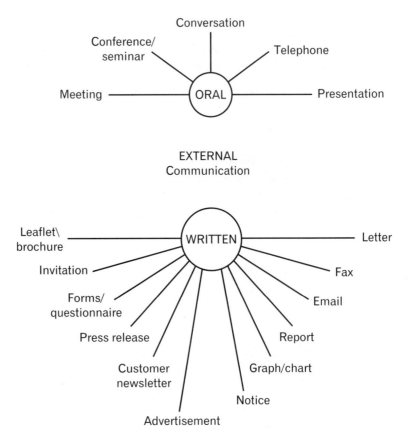

THINK

How many of these forms of communication have you had experience with so far?

✦ Choosing the means of communication

The medium chosen for communicating any message will depend on various factors such as:

Cost

- ✦ Consider how much the communication will cost in terms of the results expected.
- ✦ Can an internal message be handwritten or is a printed copy important?
- ✦ Is the postal service satisfactory, or is email or fax justified?

Confidentiality

+ Email or fax may not be appropriate.
+ A telephone call could be overheard.
+ An internal memo may need to be enclosed in an envelope.

Safety and security

+ Should a special Post Office service be used, e.g. registered or recorded delivery?
+ Would a courier service be justified?

Influence

+ To convey a certain impression, would a congratulatory telegram or invitation be suitable?
+ Multi-coloured letterheads on high quality paper convey a good image of a company.

Urgency

+ Choose the method which will produce the desired results in the time available.
+ Perhaps the higher cost of a fax will be justified by the results obtained through its speed.

Distance

+ Is the communication within the building, in the same town, or the other side of the world?

Time of day

+ This is particularly important when communicating with overseas countries.

Resources

+ Consider the equipment and staff available (sender and recipient).

Written record

+ Written communications carry more authority and are proof of a transaction.

Recipient

+ Consider who is sending/receiving the message.
+ Personal contact may be appropriate on certain occasions.
+ Verbal communication will not be appropriate where complex information or bad news is concerned.
+ Choose language appropriately, considering the situation and the relationship between sender/recipient.

TIP

A wrong decision about how a communication is expressed, and the method used to convey it, could have disastrous results. Think twice, and then think again!

✦ Key stages in the communication cycle

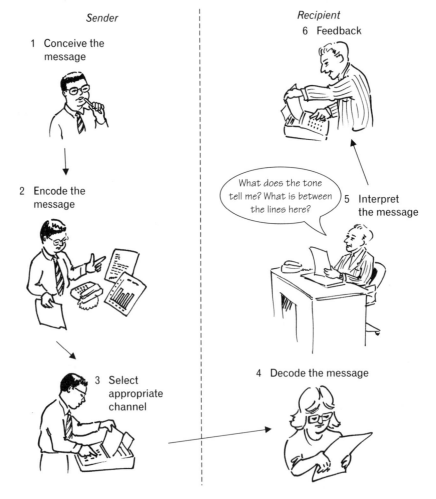

Sender

1 Conceive the message

'Don't open your mouth only to put your foot in it!' When you have something to say, consider the best means of putting your message across, and bear in mind that timing is important. Consider your recipient carefully and aim your message to suit their specific needs.

2 Encode the message

This stage involves putting the information into an appropriate form suitable to both the sender, the recipient and the aim. Think before reaching for your phone or putting fingers to keyboard. Decide first what specific outcomes you want from the communication. This will help you choose whether words will suffice, whether a printed record is necessary and whether graphics are appropriate. It will also help you choose appropriate language and tone.

3 Select the appropriate channel

This stage is where the message is actually sent and the information is transferred. The technological revolution has brought about a wide range of telecommunication methods. You must consider all aspects: speed, cost, quick receipt, printed record, confidentiality, etc., and make an intelligent decision before sending your message. Time and money can be wasted if the wrong medium is chosen.

Recipient

4 Decode the message

Because so many messages arrive in offices today, it is important to ensure that they are routed promptly and are given the attention they deserve. To achieve success at this stage it is also important to take the trouble to ensure that the recipient will understand the language and vocabulary used.

5 Interpret the message

Very often it is necessary to 'read between the lines'. It is always important to consider carefully the tone and register used in your communication so that the correct message is received. For example, you do not want to risk antagonising a good customer by using a harsh tone. Distortion of the message may occur if the sender has not carefully encoded the communication, in which case the recipient will interpret the message differently from how it was intended.

6 Feedback

The communication process cannot be successful without appropriate feedback. In oral communication this is often immediate, in meetings the audience may nod or smile to show understanding and agreement. But with written messages courtesy and discipline are important to acknowledge receipt of messages until a full and appropriate response can be given.

> **TIP**
>
> How well you communicate is determined not by how well you say things but by how well they are received.

✦ Barriers to communication

Many problems encountered in our business and personal lives result from miscommunication. What the recipient understands by a message may not always be the message which the sender intended. Several communication barriers exist between sender and recipient, and they may be responsible for a message not being understood correctly, or a message becoming distorted.

Communication may fail for a variety of reasons:

Non-verbal signals

Non-verbal signals, often referred to as 'body language', can provide valuable feedback where verbal communication is concerned. Such signals include facial expressions, gestures, movement, eye contact and nodding the head.

Language

Choice of words is vital to the effectiveness of any communication. Many words have different meanings. Our background knowledge and experience affect our understanding. Foreign languages, dialects, regional accents and the use of technical/specialist language should always be considered.

Listening

Anyone who has something valid to say deserves attention. Listening, however, is a skill. Careful concentration is demanded if a communication is to be understood. Success at gaining attention may depend on the words used, the way the communication is expressed, our interest in the speaker, our interest in the communication and various other factors.

Pre-judgement

What is understood is often conditioned by what we already know and by our background knowledge and experience. Often we hear what we want to hear, or what we think we have heard, instead of what has actually been said.

Relationships

The effectiveness of any communication may depend on our relationship with the person giving the message. If relationships between people are not good, communication may fail to be effective or may break down altogether.

Emotional responses

Communication cannot succeed if a person is highly emotional about the topic concerned. Problems may arise from insecurity, fear, anger, etc. If emotions are high on the part of the sender or recipient, then it would be better to wait for a while before trying to put the message across.

Systems

In any organisation there should be prescribed procedures for getting messages to the people who need them. Without such systems there can be no effective communication.

✦ Communication systems

In small organisations of just a few people there may be few communication problems. In larger organisations the process is more complicated. Most larger companies produce an organisation chart which makes lines of communication quite clear.

Aurora Holdings plc

Shirley Taylor
Chief Executive/Chairman

Joe Leighton
Managing Director

- Company Secretary
(Lesley Bolan)
  - Office Admin
(Rosehannah Wethern)
  - Computer Services
(Peter Nunn)
  - Legal
(Mark Farrelly)

- Financial Director
(Doug Allen)
  - Sales Accounts
(Louise Dunscombe)
  - Purchase Accounts
(Tony Morgan)

- Production Director
(Douglas Cowles)

- Human Resources Director
(Caroline Marshall)
  - Training Manager
(Candice Graham)
  - Personnel Manager
(Natasha Sirley)

- Sales Director
(George Freeman)
  - Customer Services
(Suzanne Sutcliffe)
  - Marketing Manager
(Ashley Ong)
  - Sales Manager
(Jack Daniels)
    - Australasia
(Keith Walker)
    - Far East Division
(Tan Lay Hong)
    - Europe
(Sue Gingell)

- Purchasing Director
(Angela Morgan)

THINK

Does your company have an organisation chart? Could you bring in a copy to show the rest of your group?

Organisation charts make it easier to see how communication can take place vertically (between levels), horizontally (between sections) and diagonally (between different levels and sections). It is important to keep all communication routes as open and as effective as possible.

Downward communication

This is by far the most frequent form of communication within an organisation, where higher levels communicate with staff below them. In this category are communications like memos, notices, in-house newsletters, company handbook, procedure manuals.

Upward communication

The upward communication flow is equally important as the downward flow. Communications are directed upwards to managers, supervisors or directors by using memos, reports, meetings, informal discussions.

Horizontal communication

This occurs between people of the same status – sales staff, departmental heads, directors, supervisors. As well as memos and reports, horizontal communication could include committee meetings, seminars and conferences.

Diagonal communication

Tasks frequently arise which involve more than one department and there is often no obvious line of authority. Diagonal communication often relies largely on cooperation, goodwill and respect between the parties concerned.

The grapevine

When the correct lines of communication are not used, the grapevine often results. This term describes an unofficial communication system which is constantly changing. The grapevine is a vehicle for distortions of the truth, rumour and gossip. An active grapevine can cause much damage to an organisation by spreading incomplete, false or exaggerated information. It results in low morale, cynicism, fear and an unsettled workforce.

Although the grapevine may never be completely eradicated, management should take steps to reduce its influence by considering carefully ways in which information is communicated, particularly in times of uncertainty within the organisation. The confidence of an organisation's employees is vitally important, and adequate and accurate information should always be made available to the people concerned at the earliest possible opportunity, through the correct channels.

THINK

Is there a grapevine in your organisation? Has any damage resulted from the spread of information through the grapevine? Discuss this with your colleagues.

✦ Principles of effective communication

Communication, whether oral or written, is all about understanding. Our aim should be to communicate a message successfully so that it is received as we intended, without any misunderstanding.

Effective communication can be achieved by having a thorough knowledge of the communication cycle, being aware of the barriers which exist and by considering carefully the following vital factors:

- ✦ *What is the objective of the communication?* Is it intended to give information, to persuade, to request, to inform?
- ✦ *Who will receive the communication?* What is the relationship between the sender and the recipient? What is the recipient's background knowledge and experience?

- *Under what circumstances is the communication taking place?* Why is the communication happening? Is it urgent, serious, dangerous, emotive, informative?
- *How will the recipient react to the communication?* How will the message affect the recipient? Is it important? Will the recipient be offended or angered? Will it achieve the desired aims?

✦ The impact of information technology

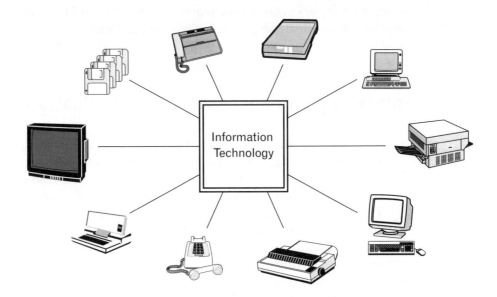

In recent years there has been an information technology revolution. While paper-based manual systems for processing information and communicating are still very much evident, more and more office functions and procedures are now being undertaken by computer-based technology. The implications of such information technology on communication methods cannot be ignored. However, the technology will always require people, and in communication it is the input of the operator that will ensure effective communication (or otherwise).

In the area of text creation, computer experts are trying to make the task of creating documents much easier. Programs are available that will produce standard layouts for most business documents when the inputs or variables are keyed in. In other words, the originator does not decide on the layout, the computer program does. Sadly, many computer programs are written by computer experts who may not be so expert in the modern display of business documents. Some of these standard layouts leave much to be desired.

The fundamental skills of structure, tone and composition will always be of vital importance in ensuring effective communication. As an originator of printed communications, you have control over these factors. However, while technological developments are making your role more interesting and challenging, the basic presentational conventions should not be allowed to suffer. No matter how technology develops in the future, high standards must be set and maintained in order to ensure that all your communications are not only appropriately worded and logically structured, but are also consistently and attractively presented.

THINK

How do you think information technology will develop in the future? Are there any dangers in our reliance on such technology? How will developments affect the process of communication?

✦ Top ten tips for successful communication

1   *Read.* Extend your knowledge of language by reading.
2   *Listen intelligently.* Remember that communication is a two-way process. Listening is just as important as speaking. Similarly, try reading your written message as if you were the recipient, and consider if it will be effective.
3   *Think and plan.* Think before you speak or write. Plan all your communications carefully, whether oral or written.
4   *Use appropriate language.* Use clear, simple language, and appreciate the same used by others.
5   *Be open-minded.* Consider other people's viewpoints, be willing to adapt and change methods or procedures if necessary.
6   *Select appropriate media.* Consider carefully the method to be used for communicating your message. It should be appropriate to the desired objective.
7   *Time your communication appropriately.* Consider the best time for the communication and how long it should be.
8   *Use appropriate language.* Use words which are relevant to the topic and which will be understood by the recipient.
9   *Obtain feedback.* Obtain feedback to ensure that the communication was effective. If the message is not understood, rather than blame the recipient, ask yourself why the communication failed and how it could have been improved in order for it to be effective. Some questions you might ask are:

  ✦ Did your expressions or language create confusion or misunderstanding?
  ✦ Was your timing poor?
  ✦ Was your message too long so that the main points were lost?
  ✦ Were your tone and manner appropriate?

10 *Aim high.* Set and maintain high standards in all your methods of communication, both in terms of language and presentation.

✦ Assignments

1 Which communication method would you use in each of the following situations?

   a) congratulating an employee on passing an important examination
   b) informing employees about an annual dinner and dance
   c) putting a nervous applicant at ease while waiting for an interview
   d) displaying the past 5 years' sales figures
   e) confirming a lunch appointment with an important client next week
   f) describing the location of a hotel where your company is hosting a seminar
   g) reminding staff of the security procedures at your company
   h) obtaining the reactions of staff to a new telephone system recently installed
   i) putting forward a proposal for a change in company policy
   j) sending an urgent message to an overseas client.

2 List the six stages in a two-way communication process, and briefly describe each stage.

3 Explain the importance of feedback in the communication cycle.

4 Illustrate the main communication systems in a large organisation by drawing a simple diagram. Suggest some methods of communication which may be used within each system.

UNIT 2

Oral communication

By the end of this unit you should be able to:

- ❏ explain the importance of oral communication

- ❏ outline the steps needed to structure effective oral messages

- ❏ discuss effective techniques used in speaking and listening

- ❏ identify non-verbal communication signals and use such signals effectively

- ❏ give examples of some types of interviews which may be held in business

- ❏ discuss preparations required by the interviewer and interviewee

- ❏ outline effective interview techniques

- ❏ discuss some guidelines for effective telephone technique

- ❏ complete a telephone message form effectively.

✦ Oral communication in business

If you aim to make a success of your career, your success will depend on much more than your practical or specialised skills. If you are a secretary, of course you need good shorthand, audio and typing skills, good knowledge of word-processing and other software programs, the ability to present documents attractively. If you are aiming to work in administration, marketing, sales, personnel or another area, then you will need knowledge specific to your particular area of specialism. However, no matter what field you choose to specialise in, you will not get far if you cannot get along with people. Problems will need to be discussed, information requested, instructions given. To achieve cooperation and effective teamwork, good human relations skills must be developed.

Oral communication is the life-blood of our personal and business lives. We do it so naturally and frequently that there is a danger in taking it for granted and not seeing it as something which needs to be practised and improved. Indeed, a number of fairly complicated skills are involved in oral communication. The essential ingredient is *you*, and it is important to recognise that you play two roles here – as a listener as well as a speaker. It is not sufficient to be someone who can communicate ideas effectively; you must also appreciate that it is equally important to try to improve your ability to listen.

✦ Oral communication in practice

In your business life you will probably spend much more of your time talking and listening to colleagues and clients than you will writing and reading. Oral communication can take a variety of forms. It can be over the telephone or face to face. It can be:

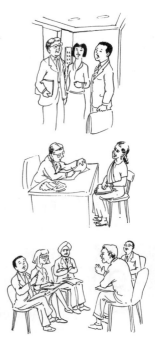

- ✦ a private discussion
- ✦ a conversation over lunch
- ✦ a gossip in the lift
- ✦ a telephone conversation
- ✦ a chance meeting in the corridor
- ✦ an informal gathering of staff
- ✦ instructing subordinates
- ✦ dealing with clients
- ✦ formal meetings
- ✦ interviews
- ✦ training sessions
- ✦ giving a presentation
- ✦ conferences/seminars

✦ Speaking skills

Most people find talking easier than writing because phrases can be used in speech which would be unacceptable in written communication. However, if understanding is to be complete and effective, language needs to be chosen carefully. Effective oral communication should be planned just as carefully as planning what you write. However, with oral communication there is the flexibility of being able to change your approach if necessary.

Here are some guidelines to follow in order to create a well-structured oral message:

1 Decide the desired outcome – what is the aim of your message?
2 Select the important facts and figures to support your message.
3 Identify the key points of your message.
4 Arrange the key points in a suitable order which will flow naturally from introduction to middle to conclusion.
5 Choose an appropriate style in which to put your message over. Its acceptance will depend very much on

   ✦ facial expressions (sincerity, warmth, assertiveness, diplomacy, fairness)
   ✦ body stance and gestures (ease, physical presence, enthusiasm, conviction, determination, respect, eye contact)
   ✦ articulation (tone, enunciation, emphasis, volume, projection).

6 When delivering the message, monitor the feedback constantly. Watch for unusual facial expressions, gestures, body movements. Be prepared to adjust your delivery or content in accordance with the listener's reactions.
7 Know when you have said enough and try to end on a positive note.

THINK

Do you use expressions like: um, er, you know, know what I mean, kind of, sort of?
Take note of any speech patterns like this and try to correct them.

✦ Listening skills

There is hardly any point in someone talking if no-one listens to what is being said. Listening is half of oral communication, and it is a skill that needs to be practised and taken equally as seriously as speaking. All effective leaders and managers realise the importance of acquiring good listening skills so if you aim to climb the ladder of success this is something which you will need to practise. The consequences of not listening carefully could be disastrous.

Here are some guidelines to follow if you want to be an effective listener:

1 *Prepare to listen.* Clear your mind so that your attention is assured. Concentrate on what is being said. Learn to listen, not just hear!
2 *Avoid pre-judgement.* Do not pre-judge the speaker because of appearance or occupation, or jump to any conclusions before hearing what is said.
3 *Be open-minded.* Hear what is being said, not what you would like to hear. Appreciate the speaker's point of view.
4 *Establish eye contact.* This shows that you are listening, as does your posture.
5 *Watch for signals.* Pick up aspects that the speaker considers important by watching posture and gestures, and listening to intonation in the speaker's words. This is like listening to the 'music' as well as the words.
6 *Extract main points.* Pick out and repeat to yourself the key words or phrases. This will help to fix in your mind what is being said.
7 *Give feedback.* Learn to give positive feedback non-verbally, by nodding, smiling. Be alert so that you can provide a suitable remark or ask a question to assist your understanding of the message.
8 *Make notes.* Record important conversations afterwards. Your notes will serve as a useful reminder. Develop your note-taking skills by jotting down the salient points of lectures or meetings.

LET'S CHECK

In pairs, present to your partner something that you did recently – a movie you saw, an interesting story. Your talk should last about 4–5 minutes. Ask your partner to tell you the content of your talk. Then change over and you do the listening. How good are your listening skills?

✦ Non-verbal communication

In face-to-face encounters non-verbal communication is often just as important as verbal communication. As you are speaking information can be conveyed non-verbally as well as verbally. The non-verbal signals of listeners will provide instant feedback. Non-verbal communication is often referred to as body language.

Non-verbal communication techniques are often used unconsciously, for instance while speaking we may throw our arms around; while listening a sudden shock may result in a sharp intake of breath. Such non-verbal signals add impact to a meaning, and they combine to provide an instant impression in a way that written communication or telephone calls cannot. Actions of this sort are an important part of the communication process.

Posture

The way people stand or sit can say an awful lot about how they feel. Someone who is nervous or anxious will fidget with their hands, tap their feet, drum the table with their fingers. Someone who is sitting well back in their chair, legs crossed at the ankle, may be seen as being relaxed and confident. Someone with a gloomy expression, head down and lifeless is probably feeling depressed or dejected. Someone sitting forward in their chair looking intently at the speaker, is showing a great deal of interest. The ability to interpret such signals and act as necessary is important in developing good human relations.

Facial expressions

Human faces are capable of communicating a wide range of expression and emotion. A smile conveys good humour, raised eyebrows denote questioning and disbelief, a frown denotes upset or worry.

Gestures

Many gestures are used as we speak, for example shaking a fist to denote anger, sweeping arms in excitement, using hands for emphasis. In listening, too, gestures are used, like nodding in agreement, shaking your head in disapproval, putting your hand to your chin in consideration, folding your arms in boredom. These are all valuable signs in communicating and you should learn to read such gestures carefully.

Eye contact

The importance of eye contact is paramount. Looking someone directly in the eye suggests openness, honesty, confidence and comfort. Looking away gives an impression of being conniving or sly, or perhaps just unsure and uncomfortable. When speaking to one person try to look them in the eye. When speaking to a group avoid fixing your gaze on one or two people – let your eyes roam regularly to all corners of the room to let everyone feel involved.

THINK

Discuss the body language/facial expressions which may be used to express: anger, love, jealousy, surprise, impatience, alertness, satisfaction, nervousness, assertiveness, friendship, hostility, sympathy, pain.

✦ Interviews

One very important type of oral communication is an interview. In the business world you may be involved in various kinds of interviews:

- ✦ *Selection interviews:* the kind when you consider someone for a job
- ✦ *Promotion interviews:* this takes place when you wish to be considered for a job at a higher grade within your organisation
- ✦ *Appraisal interviews:* this generally takes place annually to review progress and discuss the future
- ✦ *Counselling interviews:* this may be held to find out what has been troubling an employee or why someone has not been working to their usual high standard
- ✦ *Disciplinary interviews:* this is carried out when an employee has been accused of breaching company procedures
- ✦ *Grievance interviews:* this is carried out when an employee feels that he or she has been treated badly by another member of staff.

In discussing interview techniques we will look specifically at those that are held with applicants for a job, although many of the basic principles can be used in any of the above interview situations.

The interviewer

If an interview is to be successful effective planning is essential. If the interviewer makes thorough preparations, the rewards will be well-structured, enjoyable, informative interviews for both the interviewer and the interviewee.

Before the interview:

+ *Aim:* Think about the purpose of the interview and what you hope to achieve.
+ *Information:* Familiarise yourself with any relevant information – correspondence, job application forms, curriculum vitae, job specification, job description.
+ *Setting:* Choose a suitable time and place for the meeting. The room should be the right size and the furniture arranged appropriately, depending on the number of people involved. Consider if it is necessary to put a notice on the door to ensure you will not be interrupted, and to arrange for redirection of telephone calls.
+ *Structure:* Draw up a list of points for discussion so that you can discuss things in a logical order and make the most of the time available. Some companies have formal interview assessment forms which provide a permanent record of the interview and the applicant's suitability for the post.

During the interview:

+ Your aim should be to put the interviewee at ease and help him or her to relax by being friendly and reassuring. Beware of closed questions which need no expansion; instead use open questions which give the interviewee an opportunity to talk freely and expand on important points.
+ Give the interviewee your undivided attention. Smile, nod, use appropriate gestures to show that you have a genuine interest in what the interviewee is saying.
+ Sum up the interview by stating any action you are going to take or anything expected of the interviewee after the meeting.

The interviewee

Before the interview

Before a job interview, do some homework.

+ Try to find out as much as you can about the company – goods or services they provide, how long they have been established.
+ Be sure of the person you are to see, the address and the time of the interview.
+ Plan how you will get there and know the length of the journey. Aim to be 10 minutes early so that you can relax and gather your thoughts.

♦ Choose your clothes, shoes and accessories the previous evening. Wear something comfortable but appropriate and acceptable.

During the interview

Your aim during the interview is to give a potential employer a good idea about you as a person and your suitability for the job. There is no point in presenting a false image because this will only create problems at a later stage. Try to act naturally so that an effective exchange can take place.

How NOT to dress for an interview

♦ *Listen carefully.* You will be judged on the basis of your answers to questions, so listen to them carefully. Pick out the key details of the question and pause briefly before answering.
♦ Interviews, especially those for jobs, tend to be fairly formal occasions. *Take care to use correct expressions* and language suitable to the situation. At all costs avoid slang and expressions like 'you know', 'sort of', 'er', etc. Speak clearly and distinctly, and look directly at the interviewer(s).
♦ *Be honest.* Do not say what you think the interviewer wants or expects you to say. Putting your views and your personality across as courteously as possible is better than giving bland, non-committal responses to the interviewer's questions. Also, do not pretend you have qualifications or experience which you do not – you are bound to be caught out.
♦ *Ask questions.* A good interviewer will give you an opportunity to ask questions. This does not mean you should ask about holidays and salary! Find out about potential for the future, your responsibilities, training, and other things about the job.

Questions at interviews

1 Questions about the job and the organisation

   a) Why do you want this job?
   b) Can you work independently?
   c) What qualities do you look for in your employer?
   d) Would you work overtime if necessary?
   e) When could you start work?

2 Questions about ambitions

   a) Why did you take up this specific career?
   b) What do you hope to be doing in 5 years' time?
   c) Would you consider yourself suitable to enter management?
   e) What do you look for in your job?

3   Questions on interests and hobbies

   a) What do you do in your free time?
   b) How long have you been interested in this sport/hobby?
   c) Are you attending any part-time classes at present?
   d) Are there any courses you wish to attend?

4   Situation questions

   a) You have arranged to meet someone after work and your employer asks you to stay late. What would you do?
   b) Your employer has left for an overseas business trip and you realise he has left some important documents behind. What would you do?
   c) There is some unfortunate gossip that your employer is defrauding the company. What would you do?

LET'S CHECK

Arrange some mock interviews. Work in groups of three, with one person being the interviewee. Decide on the organisation and the job. Use the above questions and make up your own as appropriate. Allow 15 minutes for each interview. Afterwards discuss what you learnt from being the interviewee and the interviewer.

✦ The telephone

Most of us use the telephone several times a day to talk with friends or to make social arrangements. These calls are usually quite straightforward and require little planning. Using the telephone for business purposes is very different. In any organisation the person on the telephone represents the company and gives an impression of the firm to the outside world. If you are to ensure good public relations, effective telephone techniques must be mastered. You should aim to convey an impression of an efficient, friendly, progressive company eager to give good service.

Before calling

+ *Choose the right time to call.* Consider both cost, urgency and convenience. When calling overseas you must also consider the time difference.
+ *Check the number.* A great deal of money is wasted each year on dialling wrong numbers.
+ *Plan your call.* Make a list of points and questions to be raised during your call.
+ *Be prepared.* Gather together any files, papers or other information which may be needed during the call. It is unprofessional to have to say 'Hold on while I look for that.'
+ *Avoid interruptions.* Call at a time when you are unlikely to be distracted.

During the call

+ *Be courteous and establish a rapport.* Make time for suitable pleasantries like 'How are you today Jim?', 'Did you enjoy your holiday?'
+ *Put a smile in your voice.* Remember your caller cannot see you so use intonation to good effect and try to sound confident, decisive, helpful, interested.
+ *Check your notes.* Look back at your notes to ensure you have covered everything and quote figures and other data correctly.
+ *Obtain feedback.* Make sure the caller understands the message correctly, especially where deadlines and actions are involved.
+ *Be courteous.* Finish by thanking the caller for his or her time and trouble.

I don't know if I'm on hold or if they've put me on 'ignore'!

TIP

If you have to ask a caller to hold on, keep going back and assuring him/her that you will be as quick as possible.

After the call

+ *Make notes.* Let it become a habit to make notes of the call and place them in the appropriate file.

✦ *Take action.* If you need to send a letter of confirmation or inform someone in your organisation about any details of the call, do so immediately so that you do not forget important points.

Answering machines

Many businesses use answering machines to record important messages when the office is closed. A message will normally consist of a greeting, an apology that no-one can take the call in person, an assurance that the caller will be contacted as soon as possible, and an invitation to record a message after the tone.

Some people do not like leaving messages on an answering machine but it is worthwhile getting used to them as they are an important tool in business. When leaving a message, remember to include your name and telephone number, the reason for your call, and the times when you can be called back.

LET'S CHECK

You work at Aurora Holdings. Compose a message to be left on the answering machine when the office is closed.

Compose a message which a caller may leave on the answerphone.

Taking messages

Taking telephone messages requires both oral and written communication skills. A pencil and telephone message pad should always be kept by the telephone. A message pad like the one shown opposite provides headings which act as a reminder to obtain the necessary information from the caller.

When taking messages, remember that the caller cannot see you. You will need to give verbal signals to know that the message is being understood. Repeat the information given, confirm telephone numbers and spellings, to check all the details are received correctly.

A telephone message should be passed to its recipient immediately, or placed on his or her desk if the recipient is out.

W	URGENT	YES	NO

Message for _____

Time _____ Date _____

WHEN YOU WERE OUT

M _____

Of _____

Telephone _____

☐ Telephoned   ☐ Wants to see you
☐ Wants you to phone ☐ Came to see you
☐ Will phone later   ☐ Will come back later
☐ Returned your call

Message _____

_____

_____

_____

_____

_____

Taken by _____

Produced by Waterlow Business Supplies, Bletchley, MK1 1TE
Copyright © 1969, 1970, 1990 Laurel Aids Inc, VW Eimicke Associates Inc.   FORM 0A1
5/94   PRINTED IN THE UK

Reproduced courtesy of Waterlow Business Supplies

✦ Assignments

1 Explain the importance of listening in oral communication.
2 Discuss the points to be remembered when communicating with someone orally.
3 What does the expression 'non-verbal communication' mean? Give examples of some non-verbal communication signals which you might associate with:

    disagreement
    discomfort
    attentive listening
    sympathy
    boredom

4 You work at a local health centre. Compile the text of a message which you will record on the answering machine when the surgery is closed. Mention normal surgery hours and give a number for emergencies.
5 Miss Ruby Spice had arranged to meet your employer, Mr Michael Williams, at his office at 10.30 am today. At 9.45 am she telephoned (before your employer had arrived at the office) to say that trains into the city had been delayed due to a fallen tree. She has no other form of transportation so she would not be able to attend the meeting. She suggested an alternative date and time next week, and asked if your employer would confirm this. Miss Spice asked you to pass on her apologies. Write out an appropriate message for Mr Williams.
6 Discuss the errors made in the following telephone conversation and decide what should have been said instead. Then write out the telephone message as it should have been written if the call had been dealt with efficiently.

Operator	Aurora, hello.
Customer	I'd like to speak to George Freeman, Sales Manager, please.
Operator	Who's calling?
Customer	Ellie McDeal
Operator	Sorry he's not in.
Customer	Really? And when will he be back?
Operator	Actually he went out for lunch 2 hours ago and I was expecting him back ages ago.
Customer	Would you please pass on a message that I called?
Operator	Hang on, I'll find a pen. OK, fire away.
Customer	My number is 4537876 and I want to talk to him about my order number EM1423 dated 12 June.
Operator	Okey dokey. I'll pass it on. Cheers.
Customer	Goodbye!

Use of English

By the end of this unit you should be able to:

- [ ] understand why it is important to ensure the accuracy of language

- [ ] identify different parts of speech

- [ ] explain the composition of a grammatically correct sentence

- [ ] identify subjects and verbs in a variety of sentences

- [ ] state the purpose of the various punctuation marks

- [ ] punctuate sentences and passages correctly

- [ ] explain the uses of the apostrophe and use it correctly

- [ ] understand some basic rules of English grammar

- [ ] appreciate some commonly made errors in English language and identify where such errors are made.

✦ Modern business language

In any business dealing positive results can only be achieved through effective use of language. It has become universally accepted that English today should be simple, courteous, relaxed and straightforward. Good communicators go to considerable trouble to become competent in the English language. This is often achieved only gradually through a life-long learning process. However, the time, patience and hard work which go into mastering such skills do bring enormous rewards and satisfaction.

It is important to ensure that your language in all business communications is accurate for several reasons:

1 *To establish a relationship.* It is important to aim for a good relationship with people you communicate with regularly. Unsuitable and inaccurate language could be quite damaging to these relationships.
2 *To communicate your ideas precisely.* Unsuitable or incorrect expressions may mean that your meaning is not clear to the reader.
3 *To convey a good image of your organisation.* Clear, concise and accurate language will give an impression of efficiency and will fill the reader with confidence. Careless expressions which contain errors will do exactly the opposite; the reader may wonder if such carelessness will extend to other business dealings.

In this unit we will look at the fundamentals of English language and at some common errors.

✦ Parts of speech

Many people are able to speak and write perfectly well without knowing a lot about traditional rules of the English language. It has become automatic for them to apply the rules without consciously thinking about them. However, many people make language errors because they do not understand the rules properly or simply through carelessness. Such errors can lead to misunderstanding and failure in communication. It may help to understand why errors are made if you make sure you know the names of the various parts of speech and how they all work together.

- ✦ *noun* – a word used as a name of a person, thing or idea:
  The *woman* is going to *Hong Kong*. The *Principal* is giving some *money* to *charity*.
  You need to use *tact* when dealing with this *student*.
- ✦ *pronoun* – a word used in place of a noun, to avoid repeating the noun:
  we hurried, *they* are pleased, I need *it* now, *he* will go tomorrow
- ✦ *collective noun* – a word used in the singular to express many individuals:
  furniture, committee, crowd

+ *adjective* – a word that says more about a noun, qualifying or describing it: an *efficient* secretary, a *fast* typist, a *fair* manager
+ *verb* – a word around which the whole sentence revolves, which either shows what condition something is in, or which shows what is happening: my feet *ache*, I will *open* the door, *listen* to me, please *carry* this.
+ *adverb* – a word which is to a verb what an adjective is to a noun. It modifies or describes a verb, describing how/when/where/why the action (in the verb) is happening: she thinks *logically*, I walk *slowly*, I saw *clearly*.
+ *participle* – a verb form which can also be used as an adjective to qualify a noun: the *laughing* policeman, the *speaking* clock, the *hard-working* student.
+ *conjunction* – a word which links other words (or groups of words) together: *and, but, so, then*
+ *preposition* – a word used in front of a noun or pronoun to show its connection to another word: She left the book *at* work.
    Thank you for your letter *regarding* our overdue account.

LET'S CHECK

State which parts of speech are represented by each of the following words:

1	book _____	6	equipment _____
2	to _____	7	quickly _____
3	generate _____	8	concerning _____
4	genuine _____	9	innocent _____
5	machine _____	10	study _____

✦ Subject and verb agreement

The order in which we use words contributes as much meaning to a sentence as the definitions of individual words. The first rule of English language is sentence structure.

A sentence is a group of words containing a complete expression of a thought or idea. It should contain a subject and a verb. The verb is the part of the sentence which indicates what someone or something is *doing* – very often it is the word that shows *action*. Let's look at a simple sentence:

The manager wants three reports.

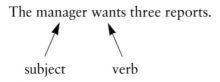

In this longer sentence you will note that the subject and verb are quite far apart:

Analysis of this month's accounts shows an increase in sales.

Very often in long sentences errors are made with subject/verb agreement. This happens when the verb ends up quite far from the subject. Look at these examples:

✗ The Chairman of the board of directors plan to announce a large profit at the meeting.

✓ The Chairman of the board of directors plans to announce a large profit at the meeting.

subject   verb

✗ The use of computers in homes have increased in recent years.

✓ The use of computers in homes has increased in recent years.

subject   verb

✗ Our sales of this exciting new product justifies an increased budget.

✓ Our sales of this exciting new product justify an increased budget.

subject   verb

✗ Communication between people in different countries are made easier with email.

✓ Communication between people in different countries is made easier with email.

subject   verb

TIP

Keep your sentences short and simple. In this way you will avoid subject/verb agreement errors and failure in communication.

LET'S CHECK

Identify the subject and choose an appropriate verb in each of these sentences.

1   This problem _____ easy to resolve.

2   The fault with our computers _____ rectified yesterday.

3   The notice in all yesterday's newspapers _____ the news.

4   A representative from all departments _____ present at the meeting.

5   A questionnaire comprising three pages _____ completed by all participants.

6   A list of items for discussion at the meeting _____ to be circulated today.

7   The minutes of the meeting _____ an important record.

8   Your report to the directors _____ discussed at yesterday's meeting.

9   The announcement to staff _____ going to be made later this afternoon.

10   Make sure that the car belonging to the new Chairman _____ cleaned carefully.

✦ Punctuation

The sole purpose of punctuation is to help the reader to understand clearly the meaning of what is written. Errors in punctuation can create confusion and lead to failure in communication. If you are using rather a lot of punctuation marks in your writing, you can be sure that errors are being made and you should begin again.

Full stop/question mark/exclamation mark

All these symbols indicate the end of a sentence.

- **.** A full stop marks the end of a sentence.
- **?** The question mark is obviously used at the end of a sentence which asks a question.
- **!** The exclamation mark is used at the end of a word, phrase or sentence which indicates strong emotion.

> **TIP**
>
> When using open punctuation full stops are no longer used to indicate abbreviations, so except for the end of a sentence there is really no need to use a full stop at all. For example:
>
>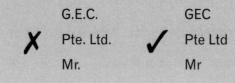
>
> | ✗ | G.E.C. | ✓ | GEC |
> |---|--------|---|------|
> | | Pte. Ltd. | | Pte Ltd |
> | | Mr. | | Mr |

Commas

Today's business writing is simple, concise and uncluttered. That means as few commas as possible. However, commas are used:

- ✦ to separate two or more nouns
  Please order some paper, envelopes and ribbons.

- ✦ to mark off two separate clauses
  I did not realise it was poor quality, otherwise I would not have bought it.

- ✦ to separate a descriptive group of words
  Teresa, the new teacher, started work today.
  The Sales Manager, Mr Colin Tan, is in a meeting.

- ✦ to separate a word or group of words from the main part of the sentence
  A word processor is, in my opinion, all I need for my work.
  A computer, on the other hand, has many more uses.

+ to mark off words like 'therefore', 'however', 'consequently', 'unfortunately' at the beginning or in the middle of sentences
  Unfortunately, I have an appointment on Friday. I can, however, see you on Thursday.

TIP

In modern writing it has become accepted to omit these commas and simply say, for example: The report has therefore been circulated.
However I would appreciate your comments.

Semi-colons

It is possible to write perfect English without any semi-colons but they can sometimes be useful.

+ Semi-colons represent a pause longer than a comma and shorter than a full stop. They are used to separate two parts of a sentence where a comma would be insufficient.
  We must buy the new book; it will be very valuable for reference purposes.

+ A semi-colon is also used to separate items in a list which already contains commas:
  Three new employees will be needed in personnel, purchasing and sales; one in marketing; two in administration and one in computing.

Colons

A colon is most commonly used to indicate that something will follow, for example a list or a quotation:

Many qualities are required: tact, diplomacy and patience.

Confucius said: 'Success can only be achieved through thorough preparation. Without such preparation there is sure to be failure.'

Dashes

A dash is used:

+ to show a change in thought in a sentence
  I never thought I would pass my exam – but I was wrong!

+ as an alternative to brackets:
  Everyone – and that includes you – must attend the staff meeting.

Hyphens

Hyphens are mainly used in compound words, where two or more words are treated as one: self-centred, user-friendly, large-scale, up-to-date.

TIP

Remember to leave one space before and one space after a dash, but no spaces are used in hyphenated words.

LET'S CHECK

Insert capital letters, full stops, commas and colons in the following passage:

The unit of the book on meetings that is Unit 13 includes the following Notice Agenda Chairman's Agenda Minutes and a series of practical assignments more practical assignments on meetings as well as many other topics are included in a separate section minutes should of course be written in third person and past tense they are an important record of what happened at a meeting.

LET'S CHECK

Insert dashes and hyphens in the following passage:

The audio transcription programme the new one by Shirley Taylor has proved an enormous success. It was introduced in this college earlier this year January to be precise. Teachers have found that it enhances the student centred learning system at the college. All students both part time and full time have found the programme very user friendly.

LET'S CHECK

Insert the necessary punctuation marks in this passage:

At the meeting today the Chairman Mr Graham Bell suggested that a training course should be held for all sales staff members agreed that a two day seminar would be most appropriate it will be held in October. It is therefore important that you and I should meet to decide on topics suggestions for speakers will also be needed of course your expertise and help in making the necessary arrangements will be very valuable please let me know when it will be convenient for us to meet any afternoon next week would be suitable for me.

Apostrophes

Apostrophes are used to indicate:

+ omission of a letter or letters
    It's important that you don't forget your textbook for all lessons.
    (It is)   (do not)

+ singular possession or ownership
    the toy belonging to the child   the child's toy
    the purse belonging to the woman   the woman's purse
    the car belonging to the director   the director's car
    the desk belonging to the manager   the manager's desk

+ plural possession or ownership
    the toys belonging to the children   the children's toys
    the purses belonging to the women   the women's purses
    the cars belonging to the directors   the directors' cars
    the desks belonging to the managers   the managers' desks

Note that sometimes the apostrophe is placed before the 's', sometimes after the 's'. A good rule of thumb is to separate the root word, as in these examples:

the child's toy   the children's toys
child = singular   children = plural

the director's car   the directors' cars
director = singular   directors = plural

Rewrite these sentences inserting the apostrophe correctly.

1. Im going to town because I havent bought my mothers birthday present yet.
2. The course is hard work but its going to be worth it in the end.
3. I wouldnt do that if I were you. Youre bound to get caught by the boss.
4. Im delighted to hear that theres a party tonight. Its going to be fun.
5. The Boards decided to introduce flexitime. The decision was theirs.
6. I hear youre moving to a new office today. Which one is yours?
7. Whose coat is this? Does it belong to the girl whos going out with Mark?
8. Its hard to persuade the Board to change policy but Im sure well succeed.
9. The dogs coat shines. Its collar says its names Rusty.
10. Is this coat yours or is it Marks? I'm sure its not Iriss.

LET'S CHECK

Rewrite the following sentences inserting the apostrophe correctly.

1. Im going to Carols house for dinner tonight; Sues coming too.
2. There are 2 cs and 2 ms in accommodation.
3. The mans shoes are very old but the womans sandals are brand new.
4. Mens shirts are on the second floor; womens dresses on the third.
5. The two girls dresses are identical but thats because theyre twins.
6. The boys attitude will have to change. Hes very rude to his teachers.
7. The teachers desk is at the front and there are 25 students desks.
8. Rosie loves Boyzone but her brothers favourite pop group is the Spice Girls.
9. The Spice Girls new single went straight to number one in this weeks charts.
10. The sales directors memo said that a regional managers meeting will be held next month.

✦ Some basic grammatical rules

Split infinitives

Avoid placing an adverb between *to* and the verb which follows:

✗ to *quickly* go   ✗ to *cautiously* enter   ✗ to *carefully* contemplate
✓ to go *quickly*   ✓ to enter *cautiously*   ✓ to contemplate *carefully*

TIP

If the construction becomes awkward, then ignore this rule,
e.g. ✓ ... to *seriously* expect ...

Participles

Phrases using participles can act as adjectives and must be attached to the correct noun or pronoun.

✗ Walking into the room, the light was bright
✓ Walking into the room, she found the light was bright.
✗ Having gone to bed, the door bell rang.
✓ Having gone to bed, the boy heard the door bell ring.

Phrases like *Hoping to hear from you soon* and *Looking forward to hearing from you* are old-fashioned as well as incomplete sentences. They should not be used. Instead say

✓ I hope to hear from you soon.
✓ I look forward to hearing from you.

Singular collective nouns

When thinking of the group as a whole, use a singular verb:

✗ A committee of eight members are to be formed.
✓ A committee of eight members *is* to be formed.

When thinking of individuals forming the group, use a plural verb:

✗ The committee was talking quietly among themselves.
✓ The committee *were* talking quietly among themselves.

Prepositions

Avoid ending a sentence with a preposition.

✗ Is there a book which I can find this information in?
✓ Is there a book *in which* I can find this information?

TIP

This rule occasionally leads to awkwardness so you can ignore this rule, e.g.:

✗ This is behaviour up with which I will not put.

✓ This is behaviour which I will not put up with.

Better still: This is behaviour which I will not *tolerate*.

Either/neither/every

All these words take singular verbs:

✗ Neither of the applicants are suitable.
✓ Neither of the applicants *is* suitable.
✗ Either one of the girls are willing to help you.
✓ Either one of the girls *is* willing to help you.

✗ Every student in the class have a computer.
✓ Every student in the class *has* a computer.

Each

When each precedes the word to which it refers it should be followed by a singular verb.

When each follows the word to which it refers it should be followed by a plural verb.

✗ Each of the students have six books.   ✗ The students each has six books.
✓ Each of the students *has* six books.   ✓ The students each *have* six books.

Shall/will

Shall/will are used in statements expressing the simple future tense:

Use shall with *I* or *we*:   ✓ I shall be pleased to visit him tomorrow
                               ✓ We shall need to go to the drug store.

Use will with *you, he, she, they, it*   ✓ They will make a decision soon.
                               ✓ She will take her exams next month.

Will is used to express determination or intention:

✓ I will pass my exams this time.
✓ We will go straight to the disco after class.

Shall is often used with I and we to express a speaker's firm intentions or instructions:

✓ We shall fight them on the beaches.
✓ Shall I tell him or not?
✓ We shall overcome this problem.

Should/would

Should and would are used as past tense equivalents of shall and will.

I/We = shall/should   You/he/she/they/it = will/would

✔ I shall see him tomorrow.   ✔ He will see me tomorrow.
✔ I said I should see him tomorrow. ✔ He said he would see him tomorrow.
✔ Shall I help her?   ✔ What will happen on national day?
✔ He asked if he should help her. ✔ He asked what would happen on national day.

The same distribution of should and would is used in main clauses linked to conditional clauses (e.g. clauses beginning with *if*).

✔ If we had not taken the train, we should not have arrived on time.
✔ If he had missed the train, he would have been late.
✔ If they had caught a train instead of the bus, they would have been early.

Use should when you mean 'ought to'.

✔ You should be able to do this.
✔ Why did they do that? They should know better.

Use would with *rather* and *sooner*.

✔ I would sooner go to the movies tonight.
✔ He would prefer a CD rather than a cassette.
✔ They would rather go to Australia for their vacation.

Do not confuse *would* and *could*. *Would* means 'if you are willing to' but *could* means 'if you are able to'.

✔ I should be grateful if you would deal with this matter urgently.
✔ I wonder if you would accompany me to the party?
(would = if you are willing to)

✔ Do you think you could clean my windows?
✔ Could you help me with my homework?
(could = if you are able to)

TIP

Check out Section 8 on Comprehension to find further help on improving your use of the English language.

✦ Some common errors

There are many books devoted to the subject of common errors in English language and I strongly recommend that you should study one of them. It is impossible in this book to cover all the commonly made errors, but here are a few of the most common ones:

alighted
The word 'alight' is used when talking about getting down from different kinds of transport.

✗ I alighted the bus.

✓ I got off the bus.
✓ The bus stopped and I alighted.
✓ I alighted at the bus stop near my home.

a lot
'a' and 'lot' are never joined.

✗ There are alot of students.

✓ There are a lot of students.

although … but
Unlike in some other languages, it is incorrect to use 'but' in a sentence beginning with 'Although'.

✗ Although I listened carefully but I did not understand.
✓ Although I listened carefully I did not understand.

between
'Between' must be followed by 'and'.

✓ There were between 200 and 300 people at the concert.
✓ The seminar will be held from 0930 to 1730.

bored/boring
The 'ed' ending describes how you are feeling.

✓ I am bored.

The 'ing' ending describes whatever gives you that feeling.

✗ I am boring.
✓ The lecture is boring.

cope

To 'cope' means 'to be able to handle something'. The preposition 'up' is not necessary.

✗ I have tried to cope up with the problem.
✓ I have tried to cope with the problem.

dated

✗ Thank you for your letter dated on 2 July.
✓ Thank you for your letter dated 2 July.
✓ Thank you for your letter of 2 July.

discuss

To discuss means 'to talk about'. So 'discuss about' is like saying 'talk about about'.

✗ I would like to discuss about the new examinations.
✓ I need to discuss the new examinations.

equipment/furniture

'Equipment' and 'furniture' are collective nouns. They cover a range of items.

✗ an equipment   ✗ all equipments   ✗ the furnitures
✗ A lot of equipments are needed.
✓ A lot of equipment is needed – copier, fax machine and printer.
✓ The new furniture arrives today – chairs, tables and drawers.

hair-cut

✗ I cut my hair yesterday.   This implies that you were the one who did the cutting, not the hairdresser.
✓ I had my hair cut yesterday.   This implies that someone else cut it for you.

having (a cold)

✗ I am having a fever.   The continuous tense 'having' is not used in this way.
✓ I have a fever.
✓ I am having a hard time.

marketing

In standard English the word 'marketing' is used to describe what companies do when they promote a new product. It is not used to describe what we do when we go to the market.

✗ My mother does her marketing in Chinatown.
✓ My mother does her shopping in Chinatown.
✓ A lot of money is spent on marketing new products.

mentioned

'Mentioned' is often used similarly to the word 'discuss'. Note the correct usage.

✗ The teacher mentioned about the homework but I have forgotten.
✓ The teacher mentioned the homework but I have forgotten.

outstation

The word 'outstation' seems to be used a lot in the Far East. It dates back to colonial times. Unfortunately, if this word is used outside the Far East, people may not understand you.

✗ Mr Tan is not in the office today. He is outstation.
✓ Mr Tan is not in the office today. He is away on business.

pass/pass up

When you pass something, you move it from one person to another.

✓ Please pass me the salt.
✗ Please pass up your homework to me for marking.
✓ Please pass your homework to me for marking.

send/take

'Take' means that you are going with the person.
'Send' means that you are not going with the person.

✗ I sent her to the airport.	This means you did not go with her.
✓ I took her to the airport.	This means you went with her.
✗ My friend will send me to work.	This means your friend will not be with you.
✓ My friend will take me to work.	This means your friend will be with you.

stay/live/staying/living

'Stay' is used to refer to short periods. 'Live' is used to refer to longer or more permanent periods of time.

✓ I am staying in Singapore.   This means I am not here all the time but I am here now.

✓ I live in Singapore.   This means Singapore is my place of residence.

✓ Where do you stay?   This is often used incorrectly when someone really wants to know where your house is.

✓ Where do you live?

✦ Assignments

1 Infinitives, participles, collective nouns and prepositions

Rewrite the following sentences correctly:

a) The team are playing very well this season.
b) Which unit can I find information about grammar in?
c) The cook asked him to slowly pour the cream into the mixing bowl.
d) The new equipment are being delivered today.
e) Walking down the street, the Christmas lights looked beautiful.
f) The furniture for the new offices are being delivered today.
g) Having declared the meeting closed, no other business could be discussed.
h) Looking forward to seeing you at the meeting.
i) My luggage are in the luggage rack above you.
j) The new cutlery for the canteen have just arrived.

2 Neither/either/every/each

Choose the correct verb to complete these sentences:

a) Neither of the students _____ ready for the examination.
b) Some of the books that the students need to buy _____ expensive.
c) Every student in the class _____ learning accurate keyboarding skills.
d) All the male students in the class _____ hoping to find jobs in big companies.
e) This student accommodation is popular because each student _____ a single room.
f) All the students each _____ their own rooms.
g) Either of the applicants _____ suitable for the position.
h) Each of the orders _____ in excess of $1000.
i) You will find that either of these dictionaries _____ very good.
j) Neither of these machines _____ in good condition.

3 Shall/will and should/would

Choose the correct word to fill in these blanks:

a) I _____ be going to the student disco next week.
b) I said I _____ be going to the student disco next week.
c) Mark said he _____ not be going to the student disco next week.
d) _____ I give you some help with your homework?
e) She asked if she _____ help her.
f) When _____ you be teaching us how to write reports?
g) The student asked when I _____ be teaching her how to write reports.
h) He _____ see his father tomorrow.
i) If you had done your homework you _____ have known the answer.
j) If I hadn't done my homework I _____ not have known the answer.

4 Correct the errors

Each of the following sentences contains at least one error of grammar or sentence construction. Rewrite the sentences correctly:

a) Neither of the girls are willing to help me.
b) Lady's clothes are on the second floor.
c) Although I didn't think it was possible, but I still passed my examination.
d) Running to catch the bus, the car hit me.
e) Each of these sentences contain one error.
f) I shall appreciate if you would look into this matter urgently.
g) If you could help me to carry my bags, I shall be very grateful.
h) Having signed the minutes, no corrections could be made.
i) A lot of new equipments are being bought this month.
j) It is easy to sometimes disregard the importance of friendship.

5 Correct the errors

The following letter contains a number of errors. Rewrite it correctly.

Thank you for your letter of complaint dated on 21 July.

I feel very disturbing that you have a problem with the television recently purchased from us. One of our representatives, Mr John Lee will call on you next Monday between 2 to 4 pm, he will endeavour to immediately rectify the fault. If he is unable to do so however, he will arrange to replace you with another television.

If this appointment is inconvenient for you please call my secretary, Joyce Smith to make alternative arrangements.

Please let me know if I could be of further assistant.

6   Correct the errors

The following letter contains a number of grammatical, punctuation and sentence construction errors. Rewrite it correctly.

You will be please to know that we are planning another seminar. This time for Executive Secretaries, it will be held at Mandarin Hotel, Orchard Road between 9.30 am to 5.30 pm. The date would be 8 October 2001.

This conference would be a practical conference, it aims to improve secretary's managerial skills and increase her productivity. A panel of professional speakers are been invited to give lectures on their specialisms, however, delegates' will be able to take part in smaller practical sessions also. Latest equipments will be demonstrated too, during breaks delegates will be able to easily operate them.

Copies of the detailed programme is enclosed. A registration form is also enclosed which you should fill up and return it to me. Don't delay – act immediately so that your registration can be attended to. Reserving a place at this seminar, your money will be spent.

Remember, first come, first serve!

SECTION

2

BUSINESS LETTERS

UNIT 4

Introducing the business letter

By the end of this unit you should be able to:

❏ state the main details found on letterheaded paper

❏ design letterheaded paper

❏ discuss the various parts of a business letter and continuation sheet

❏ discuss the basic presentation requirements in fully blocked layout with open punctuation

❏ understand the importance of consistent presentation

❏ explain how business documents should be structured

❏ describe the four-point plan for structuring business communications

❏ compose a variety of simple business letters.

Communication with people outside your organisation is vitally important. This is your means of establishing contact with the outside world. For this reason a high standard should be set and maintained in all your communications. High standards in an organisation's correspondence suggest high standards in business generally.

Despite the many modern communication methods available today, business letters are still very often the main means of establishing business relations with other organisations. Business letters are an ambassador for your company, so a good first impression is essential.

Business letters convey an impression of the company in many different ways:

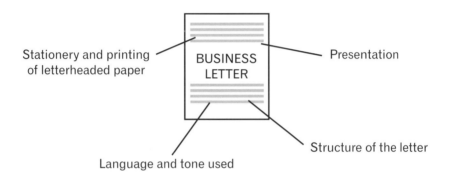

When writing a business letter (or any other business communication) your aim should be to ensure a high standard in each of these four key areas. A well-presented business letter may lead to an important business contact.

These four key areas – printed stationery, presentation, structure, language and tone – will be considered in this unit.

✦ Printed stationery

Letterheaded paper

Good quality letterheaded paper is generally used for business letters. An attractive, well-balanced letterhead enhances the prestige of an organisation. Various details are included on letterheaded paper, as shown in these examples:

**Addison
  Wesley
Longman**

Edinburgh Gate
Harlow
Essex CM20 2JE
United Kingdom

Telephone +44 (0)1279 623623
Facsimile   +44 (0)1279 431059
Website   http://www.awleurope.com

LONGMAN

ADDISON-WESLEY

A Pearson Company

Addison Wesley Longman Limited Registered Office Edinburgh Gate Harlow Essex CM20 2JE
Registered number 872828 England

Logos

A logo is a graphic symbol on the letterhead, very often the same as a trade mark used on packaging, delivery vehicles, etc. These logos are often unusual or amusing so that customers remember them easily and become familiar with them. With effective design, a company's logo can become a widely circulated medium through which a company can confirm and sustain its corporate identity.

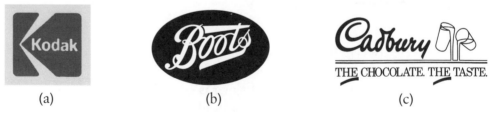

(a)   (b)   (c)

Reproduced courtesy of (a) Kodak Limited, (b) Boots the Chemists Ltd,
(c) Cadbury Ltd

✦ Presentation: fully-blocked layout

The fully-blocked layout is now the most widely used method of display for all business documents. Open punctuation is usually used with fully blocked layout. This combination is thought to have a very businesslike appearance. In this example note that it is only necessary to leave one clear line space between each section of the letter.

Logo. A special logo can help to identify a company

Letterhead. Company's name, address and telephone/fax numbers, and email address

Aurora Holdings plc
Aurora House, Temple Street, London SE1 4LL

Tel: +44(0)181 542 5555
Fax: +44(0)181 555 4444   *Email: aurora@cfb.co.uk*

Reference. Initials of writer/ typist (maybe also a filing reference)

ST/CFB

Date. UK style is day month year. Alternative styles may be preferred in other countries

2 May 2000

Inside address. Name, full postal address, town and post code

Mrs Angela Morgan
21 Chatsworth Avenue
Aston
Sheffield
S26 2ES

Salutation

Dear Angela

Heading. Give the gist of what the letter is about

FULLY BLOCKED LAYOUT

Body of letter. Separate into paragraphs with a new idea in each. Leave one clear line space between each paragraph

The fully blocked method of displaying business documents is now widely used, but do you use it correctly? The main feature of this modern display is that all lines start at the left margin - with no exceptions!

Most people combine the fully blocked layout with open punctuation. This means that no punctuation marks are used outside the body of communications. Of course we need to use commas and full stops in the main text, but no punctuation is used in the inside address, the date, the salutation, complimentary close or enclosure sections.

If you use fully blocked layout for the first page of a letter (or any communication) you must also block the second or subsequent pages. Continuation sheets which start with the page number in the middle are not fully blocked - it should be at the left margin, along with the reference, date and addressee. An example of a continuation sheet displayed in fully blocked layout is enclosed.

I know you will agree that this method of display is easy to produce and it looks good too.

Remember to use this layout in all your business documents.

Complimentary close. Make sure it matches the salutation

Yours sincerely

The writer will sign the letter here

Shirley Taylor

Sender's name (indicate females with a courtesy title in brackets)

Shirley Taylor (Miss)

Designation or department

Training Consultant

Enclosure indication if necessary (if more than one use 'Encs')

Enc

Indicate anyone receiving copies here (if more than one use alphabetical order)

Copy: Candice Graham, Personnel Manager

✦ Other parts of a business letter

Confidential/airmail/urgent

If a letter is confidential this should be indicated between the date and inside address, just as it would be shown on the envelope:

CONFIDENTIAL

Mr Martin Johnson
Managing Director
Carona Press plc
56 Walker Avenue
Leeds
LS3 5GJ

AIRMAIL

Mrs Lily Ng
54 Taman Warna
10890 Johor Bahru
West Malaysia

Attention line

Traditionally an attention line was used when the writer wanted to ensure that the letter is directed toward the desk of a specific person. The letter was addressed to the company in general and always began 'Dear Sirs'.

FOR THE ATTENTION OF MR JOHN TAYLOR, SALES MANAGER

Garden Supplies Ltd
24 Amber Street
Sheffield
S44 9DJ

Dear Sirs

In today's business communications when we usually know the name of the person to whom we are writing, it is rarely necessary to use an attention line. Simply include the recipient's name and designation in the inside address and use a personalised salutation, e.g. Dear John or Dear Mr Taylor.

Copies

When a copy of a letter is to be sent to another person (usually someone in the sender's organisation) this may be indicated by either of the following methods:

cc	Patricia McInally, Training Manager	cc stands for copy/ies circulated
Copy	Rosehannah Farrelly, Personnel Manager Patricia McInally, Training Manager Karen Murphy, Welfare Officer	Use alphabetical order when more than one person is on the circulation list

Blind copies

If the sender of the letter does not wish the recipient to know that other people are receiving copies, a blind copy may be sent. In this case the indication bcc is used on the copies only – not on the original.

bcc   Lesley Bolan, Managing Director   bcc stands for blind copy/ies circulated

Signing on someone else's behalf

You may have to sign a letter on behalf of someone else. This can be done in either of the following ways:

Yours sincerely

Sally Turner

pp   JAMES THOMPSON
Managing Director   ←————————   pp means per procurationem or on behalf of

Yours sincerely

Sally Turner

for   JAMES THOMPSON
Managing Director

✦ Open punctuation

Open punctuation is commonly used with the fully-blocked layout. Only punctuation marks which are essential to ensure grammatical sense are included within the text of correspondence. All other commas and full stops are omitted. When using open punctuation it is important to be consistent:

Dates

12 July 1999   No st, th or rd
No comma

Names

Mr & Mrs Richard Reeves   No full stops

Addresses

Mr J C Leighton   No full stops after abbreviations
Production Manager   No commas at the end of lines
JCL Engineering Ltd
245 Upper Jurong Road West
Singapore 226767

Salutation and complimentary close

Dear Mr Leighton   No commas
Yours sincerely

Abbreviations

✓	Mr	BA	MRT	✗	Mr.	B.A.	M.R.T.
	Dr	BEd	IBM		Dr.	B.Ed.	I.B.M.
	NB	RSA	SBC		N.B.	R.S.A.	S.B.C.

✦ Continuation sheets

Many organisations have printed continuation sheets which are used for second and subsequent pages of business letters. Printed continuation sheets may show simply the company's name and logo, as in these examples:

☾ *Aurora Holdings*   *Continuation*

When printed continuation sheets are not used you should use plain white paper of the same quality as the letterheaded paper.

It is important to include certain details at the top of second or subsequent pages just in case somehow the pages should become separated.

Remember that when using fully blocked style you should maintain consistency by ensuring that all the headings on continuation sheets also begin at the left margin, as in the example at the top of page 57:

When using a continuation sheet remember these guidelines:

✦ Do not include 'continued' or 'Cont' at the foot of the first page. It will be obvious that there is another page if there is no closing section or signature.
✦ Always take over at least three or four lines of text to a second or subsequent page.
✦ Try to start a new page with a new paragraph. It does not look good to leave one line of a paragraph at the foot of one page or at the top of the next.

Page number	2
Reference	ST/DA
Date	21 December 2000
Recipient's name	Miss Suzanne Sutcliffe
Leave 4/5 lines before continuing the letter	
Make the split at a suitable place, preferably not mid-sentence	Please sign and return one copy of this contract. The other copy is for you to keep.
	You will be expected to attend an induction course on your first day of work and a copy of the programme is enclosed.
	I look forward to welcoming you to Aurora Holdings.
	Yours sincerely
Some employers prefer their name to be shown in capitals	DOUG ALLEN Director (Human Resources)
	Enc
When more than one person is to receive copies, use alphabetical order	Copy: Edward Chan, Marketing Manager Sophia Nunn, Training Manager

THINK

Check out some continuation sheets which you see in your office.
Are they displayed correctly?

✦ Categories of business letter

There are many different categories of business letters. In this section we will look at some very basic letters. A sample letter is shown in each category and then you can practise writing some for yourself.

Some of the main categories of business letter are:

	Aim
Confirmation	To confirm arrangements made between sender and recipient
Acknowledgement	To acknowledge receipt of a letter, order or other item
Enquiry	To request information or prices
Reply	To respond to an enquiry
Complaint	To criticise poor service or goods

Adjustment	To respond to the complaint and hopefully make amends
Collection letters	To obtain settlement of a debt
Sales letters	To sell goods or services
Circular letters	To reach a certain group of people (customers/staff)

Letter of confirmation

The main purpose of this letter is to provide a written record of arrangements made between the sender and the recipient in person or by telephone. These letters are usually very short.

China Textiles
No 5 Dong Fang Road
Nankai District
Tianjin 300100
China

Tel: +86 23432343
Fax: +86 4878788

TWB/cfb

18 August 2000

Mr Zhao Jian Ping
Sales Manager
Zhao Fabrics Pte Ltd
Nathan Road
Kowloon
Hong Kong

Dear Mr Zhao

I am pleased to confirm our meeting at 1030 on Tuesday 12 September 2000 at our head office in Tianjin. Our Director from Beijing, Mr Ong Chee Huat, will be in Tianjin at that time and he will also join us in our meeting.

As I mentioned to you on the telephone I am very interested in seeing your new range of winter fabrics and hope you can bring some samples with you.

I look forward to seeing you again.

Yours sincerely

Tay Wee Boon
General Manager

Acknowledgement

This letter is sent to acknowledge receipt of something when a written record is appropriate. An acknowledgement may also be sent to acknowledge receipt of another letter or document which requires further attention. As such you would clearly state that you will look into the matter and reply in more detail at a later date.

✸ *Stardust Photo Studio*

Rm 9B No 3 Building
1234 Yu Yao Road
Shanghai 200040
China

Telephone +86-21-878787   Fax +86-21-878788

HMY/lk

25 May 2000

Mr Chia Lye Ann
3001 Caobao Road
Xuhui District
Shanghai 234399

Dear Mr Chia

Thank you for your letter of 22 May addressed to our General Manager, Mrs Ho Mei Ying.

Mrs Ho is overseas on business and will not be in the office again until 4 June. I shall be in contact with Mrs Ho and shall inform her about your letter, which I am sure will receive her prompt attention.

Please let me know if I can be of any help.

Yours sincerely

Lakhvinder Kaur (Miss)
PA to Ho Mei Ying
General Manager

Some organisations use printed cards for this purpose which can be completed easily.

Jonathan Ross & Partners, Solicitors, 45 Queen Street, London SW1 ERT

We acknowledge with thanks the receipt of

which will receive careful attention.

Telephone 0171 456 7890   Fax 0171 432 8765

Enquiry

Enquiries for information about goods or services are sent and received in business all the time. In your letter remember to state clearly exactly what you want – information? a catalogue? a price list? a quotation? Keep your enquiry brief and to the point.

The sender's personal address looks good balanced at the top right	34 Windsor Avenue Bolsover Chesterfield S44 2JL
When you write your own personal letters a reference is not necessary, just a date	20 January 2000
	Nautilus Cruises plc Nautilus House Temple Street London SE1 4LL
When writing to a company use the salutation 'Dear Sirs'	Dear Sirs
Introduction	My neighbour, Mr Roland Keating, has recently recommended your luxury cruises to me. He and his wife have often taken a Nautilus cruise and speak very highly about them.
Details	My wife and I are thinking of celebrating our 25th wedding anniversary in August with a special holiday.
Response required	Please send me a copy of your current brochure showing the cost of your cruises together with departure dates.
Close	I hope to hear from you soon.
Match the complimentary close with the salutation	Yours faithfully
	MARK FARRELLY

Reply to enquiry

Enquiries mean potential business so they must be acknowledged promptly. If the letter is from an established customer, say how much you appreciate it. If it is from a prospective customer, thank them for their enquiry, give all the relevant information and express the hope of good business relations.

⌇⌇ Nautilus Cruises plc

Nautilus House, Temple Street, London SE1 4LL

Tel: +44(0)181 542 5555
Fax: +44(0)181 555 4444   Email: nautilus@cfb.co.uk

TM/ST

22 January 2000

Mr Mark Farrelly
34 Windsor Avenue
Bolsover
Chesterfield
S44 2JL

Dear Mr Farrelly

Thank you for your letter of 20 January enquiring about our cruises. I am pleased that you have heard favourable comments about our luxury cruises.

I enclose our catalogue giving full details of this year's cruises. Your attention is particularly drawn to page 49 which gives departure dates for each cruise.

As there is usually a heavy demand for these cruises I suggest that you should book early, particularly as you propose to travel during the peak season.

Please do not hesitate to contact me and I shall do my best to ensure that your 25th wedding anniversary is celebrated in style.

Yours sincerely

LEE MORGAN
Sales Manager

Enc

Complaint

There are bound to be occasions in business when you have to make a complaint, or deal with one. When you have a genuine complaint you will feel angry but remember that the other party may not be to blame. They may have a perfectly good defence. Therefore, your letter should be confined to a statement of the facts followed by an enquiry about what the company will do about it or a suggestion of how you expect the matter to be dealt with. At all costs avoid rudeness or sarcasm. This will only cause ill-feeling.

THINK

Have you ever had reason to complain about goods or services?
Discuss some reasons why complaints may be necessary.

25 Finch Avenue
Marlborough
Leeds
LS20 2JT

Note that a telephone number is included with the sender's address

0113 4328432

15 June 2000

Mr Ganesh Hassan
Foster's Master Builders Ltd
21 Lodge Lane
Sheffield
S31 3ES

Dear Mr Foster

BUNGALOW AT 1 CRESCENT ROAD, MARLBOROUGH, LEEDS

Introduction and reason for writing – tone is firm but courteous

I signed the contract for the building of this property in September 1999. At that time you estimated that the work would be completed and the bungalow ready for occupation in about 8 months' time. That was 9 months ago and the work is still only half finished.

Inconvenience is emphasised

The delay is causing a great deal of inconvenience not only to me but also to the buyer of my present home. Obviously I cannot transfer until the bungalow at Crescent Road is finished.

Action expected

I hope you can proceed with this work without any further delay. Please let me know when you expect it to be finished.

Yours sincerely

RICHARD WHITLEY

Reply to complaint

Most companies will wish to hear if customers have cause to complain. It gives them an opportunity to investigate, to explain and to put things right. Good will can be preserved instead of business being taken elsewhere. Here are some general rules for dealing with complaints:

+ The customer is not always right, but it is good practice to assume that the customer may be right.
+ Acknowledge a complaint promptly. If you are unable to reply fully give an explanation and reply in full as soon as possible.
+ Be polite and try not to offend, even if the complaint is unreasonable.

- Admit blame readily if appropriate, then express regret and state how you intend to put matters right.
- Thank the customer for bringing the matter to your attention.

Foster's Master Builders Ltd
21 Lodge Lane
Sheffield
S31 3ES

Tel: 0114 2872222

GH/ST

17 June 2000

Mr Richard Whitley
25 Finch Avenue
Marlborough
Leeds
LS20 2JT

Dear Mr Whitley

BUNGALOW AT 1 CRESCENT ROAD, MARLBOROUGH, LEEDS

Acknowledge letter and express regret —— Thank you for your letter of 15 June. I am sorry that the estimated period for completion of your bungalow has already been exceeded. I realise how much inconvenience this delay must be causing you.

Circumstances are explained fully —— I would, however, ask you to remember that we have had an exceptionally severe winter. This made work on the site extremely difficult during several periods of heavy snow. Secondly there was a nationwide shortage of building materials earlier this year, from which the trade is only now recovering. Had it not been for these two unforeseen difficulties, the estimated completion period of 8 months would have been met.

Assurance that the situation will improve —— Fortunately the weather has improved a lot in recent weeks and as such work on your bungalow is now proceeding smoothly. Unless there are any other unforeseen delays I can safely guarantee that the bungalow will be ready for you by the end of August.

Courteous close —— Please do not hesitate to telephone me if you have any further questions.

Yours sincerely

GANESH HASSAN
Manager

Collection letters

Collection letters are those sent to customers who do not pay accounts promptly. In such letters tone is very important. The way you write such letters will depend on such factors as the age of the debt, whether the customer is habitually late in settling accounts and any previous reminders issued.

TANGS RETAIL PTE LTD
343 ORCHARD ROAD
#09-09 DIAMOND TOWERS
SINGAPORE 233322

TEL: 65 2343243

You may prefer to use lower case for your initials

KWM/sat

2 November 2000

Johnson & Smythe
123 Holland Crescent
Singapore 234321

Use 'Dear Sirs' when writing to the company

Dear Sirs

Appropriate heading

ACCOUNT NUMBER FT384738

State background details and amount owing

According to our records the amount shown on our statement dated 30 September 2000 has not been paid. The amount owing is $4,522.50.

The customer is given the benefit of the doubt in this case

If payment has already been made by the time you receive this letter please accept my apologies for troubling you. However if payment has been overlooked I hope you will settle this account as soon as possible.

Yours faithfully

KWOK WAI MENG
Accounts Manager

If a polite letter like this fails to produce a response, a firmer letter will be sent.

TANGS RETAIL PTE LTD
343 ORCHARD ROAD
#09-09 DIAMOND TOWERS
SINGAPORE 233322

TEL: 65 2343243

KWM/sat

20 November 2000

Johnson & Smythe
123 Holland Crescent
Singapore 234321

Dear Sirs

ACCOUNT NUMBER FT384738

Give background details again and repeat sum due — On 2 November we wrote to remind you that our September statement showed a balance of $4,522.50 outstanding and due for payment.

The tone is firmer here — Settlement of this account is now almost 2 months overdue. Therefore we must ask you either to send us your payment without delay or at least let us know the reason for this delay.

A prompt reply will be appreciated.

Yours faithfully

KWOK WAI MENG
Accounts Manager

THINK

If another polite letter does not receive any response a letter should be sent stating that legal proceedings will be begun if payment is not made within a specified period. Discuss how you think such a letter would be worded, and make a copy for your files.

✦ Other types of business letter

There are many different types of business letters. In this unit we have only looked at some of the more routine letters. Unit 5 gives more advice on the rules of good writing with some practical work for you to do. Unit 6 looks at all the letters and other documents associated with applying for a job. Unit 11 looks at more advanced letters in the form of circulars and sales letters.

Remember, there will be many occasions when you will need to write a letter which does not fall into any specific category. In these situations you must remember the general rules of good business writing and plan your letter carefully so that its objectives are met.

✦ Structure

Many business letters, like the ones we have looked at in this unit, are short and routine. They can be written without any special preparation. Other letters require more careful thought and planning. This four-point plan provides a simple framework for structuring all business communications. This diagram illustrates the four basic sections which will make up all your business communications:

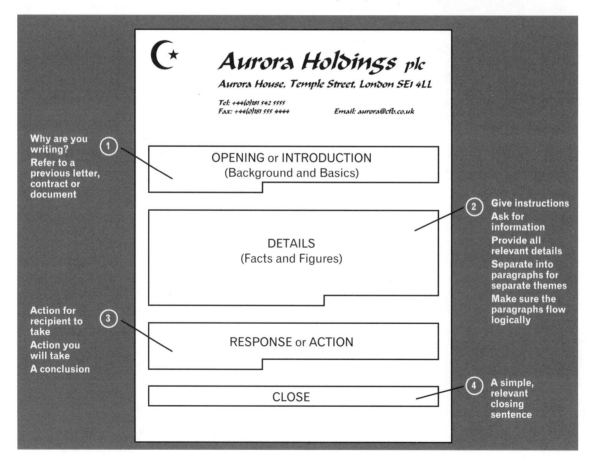

LET'S CHECK

Four-point plan

Study the following expressions and decide in which part of a business letter you might find them. Write 1, 2, 3 or 4 using the four-point plan as your guide:

1 Thank you for your letter of 4 August regarding Miss Tania Kaur's application for a post in your company. ☐

2 I hope to hear from you soon. ☐

3 Please let me know as soon as the order is ready for collection. ☐

4 I am pleased to inform you that our Crown Prince Suite is available on these dates. ☐

5 Our latest catalogue is enclosed. ☐

6 Our prices for the goods you require are as follows: ☐

7 Thank you for any assistance you are able to provide. ☐

8 Your company has been recommended to me by my colleague, Janine Chew. ☐

9 I hope to see you at the conference next month. ☐

10 Your letter of 15 July has been passed to me by Michael Green, our Customer Relations Manager. ☐

11 We are interested in holding our Annual Dinner and Dance at your hotel in November. ☐

12 Further to your letter of 29 March I am pleased to confirm reservation of our Peninsular Suite for your wedding. ☐

13 A discount of 10% will be allowed on all orders. ☐

14 These goods are in stock and can be delivered within one week of your order. ☐

15 Please do not hesitate to contact me if you require any further information. ☐

16 I can recommend Miss Harriet Tan highly and without hesitation. ☐

17 Unfortunately I am unable to accept your invitation due to a prior commitment. ☐

18 Mr Jonathan Lee has applied to us for the post of Credit Control Manager. ☐

19 I hope you will visit us at stand 26 of this exciting exhibition where we will be revealing our new range of portable computers. ☐

20 This special function will take place on Monday 26 March 2000. ☐

LET'S CHECK

Rearrange the letter

Here are cut-up parts of a business letter. Decide the correct order and rewrite the letter correctly for your files.

a   Copy: Michael Norton, Divisional Manager, Singapore

b   Yours sincerely

c   29 July 2000

d   Dear Mr Leong

e   I am pleased to say that I planned to visit Hong Kong, Malaysia and Singapore later this year, so in view of your invitation I shall schedule my Singapore visit so that I can attend your celebrations.

f   Sally Turner (Mrs)
    Sales and Marketing Director

g   Thank you for inviting me to attend your company's 20th Anniversary Celebrations at the Singapore Pagoda Hotel on Friday 15 October 2000.

h
Aurora Holdings plc
Aurora House, Temple Street, London SE1 4LL

Tel: +44(0)181 542 5555
Fax: +44(0)181 555 4444   Email: aurora@cfb.co.uk

i   I look forward to meeting you again.

j   VISIT TO SINGAPORE

k   I hope it will also be possible to meet you at your offices to discuss your proposal to become our agent in Singapore. I have asked our Divisional Manager, Michael Norton, to contact you to arrange a convenient appointment.

l   Mr John Leong
    Managing Director
    International Holdings Sdn Bhd
    12th floor Wisma Genting
    Jalan Rajah Laut
    50245 Kuala Lumpur
    West Malaysia

m   ST/bp

LET'S CHECK

Composition

1 Enquiry and reply

The letter below is an enquiry. On the following page is the reply. On the lines provided complete the missing information by matching corresponding parts of each letter.

WESSEX HOTEL GROUP

#21-10 Raffles Tower
Wessex Road
Singapore 234929

Telephone +65 2342344 Fax +64 2344244

____/LYL

21 October 2000

_____

Ward Cutlery Ltd
Richmond Street
Sheffield
United Kingdom
S20 2BJ

Dear _____.

A colleague visited England recently and passed on your catalogue to me.

We are very interested in purchasing new cutlery for our chain of hotels in South East Asia. Please send us your _____ and price list, and also let us know details of any _____ you are able to offer. Information about _____ would also be appreciated.

_____.

Yours _____

SANDRA KOH (_____)

Food and Beverage Manager

→

WARD CUTLERY LTD
Richmond Street
Sheffield _____
Telephone + 44 114 245145   Fax +44 114 2455555

____/PJ

1 November 2000

AIRMAIL

Mrs Sandra Koh

_____

Wessex Hotel Group
#21-10 Raffles Tower
Wessex Road
Singapore 234929

Dear _____

_____ 21 October asking for details of our cutlery.
I have pleasure in enclosing our current catalogue which also contains all
_____ and an order form.

On orders of £500 or more we offer a 20% discount. _____
are usually sent by air freight within 2 weeks of receipt of order.

I hope you find our _____ agreeable but if you have any
queries please _____.

_____.

Yours sincerely

WILLIAM BEAULAH
Manager

---

2   Letter of enquiry

You work for Mr Leslie Lim, Training Manager of Turner Communications, #03–03 Sapphire Building, 215 Lorong Ragu, Kuala Lumpur, Malaysia. Mr Lim has received recommendations for business and secretarial courses at Aurora Training Centre, 21 Exeter Road, #07–04 Grange Tower, Eastern Avenue, Kuala Lumpur, Malaysia. He asks you to compose a letter for him saying that he is considering upgrading some staff. Ask for details of part-time courses available at the college including the examinations which they lead to. You also need to know the dates of the next intakes. Remember to plan your letter first in accordance with the four-point plan.

3 Reply to enquiry

Compose a reply from the Principal of Aurora Training Centre giving details of the courses available at your own college. Plan it first, using a four-point plan, and make sure you include all the necessary points. Include an invitation for Mr Lim to visit your college to view the facilities and discuss their training needs further.

4 Letter of complaint

You recently received some money from an insurance policy and decided to purchase a new colour television set with remote control. Having paid cash for a modern set, the store delivered the TV to you yesterday. When you inspected the TV you were very disappointed to find several marks on the outer casing. When you telephoned the store the assistant was quite abrupt and told you that this was the last of this particular model and the new model was quite a lot more expensive. You cannot afford this. Write to Betterbuys Electrical Goods (make up a suitable address) giving full details and stating what action you expect to be taken.

LET'S CHECK

Opening and closing paragraphs

Mistakes can often be made with opening and closing paragraphs of business letters. Discuss what is wrong with the following sentences and rewrite them correctly.

Openings

1 Your letter of June 7th refers.

. . . .

2 Further to my telecon with your secretary I am writing to complain about the poor service when I visited your store today.

. . . .

3 Reference your letter regarding the above-mentioned.

. . . .

4 Thank you for your letter of complaint.

. . . .

5 I wish to inform you that goods I ordered last month have not yet been received.

. . . .

Closes

1 I look forward to your reply soonest.

. . . .

2 Thanking you in anticipation.

. . . .

3 Hoping to hear from you soon.

. . . .

4 Looking forward to meeting you again..

. . . .

5 Anything further, please contact me. . . . .

. . . .

WHAT'S WRONG?

When writing a letter of complaint it is important to get your tone and approach right. Your letter is more likely to achieve its objective if you sound hurt rather than infuriated. It is best to assume that your grievance is an oversight on the part of the company concerned rather than inefficiency.

Discuss what is wrong with this letter of complaint and then rewrite it more appropriately.

> *Dear Sir or Madam*
>
> *I am speechless at such incompetence! You obviously don't care at all about your customers otherwise you would take more care to avoid the time and trouble your inefficiency has cost me, not to mention the expense!*
>
> *In my household we pay an extra fee to have two separate entries in the local phone book – one for my wife and one for myself. As it is you have ignored my specific instructions to enter our names as we wished. The entry of E James is totally useless. Look at the book and see for yourself how many more E James there are in Sheffield! I wanted my first name including for obvious reasons of clarity, but you just ignored my request. As if that wasn't bad enough, you even printed the wrong number! For goodness sake, how much more wrong can you get?*
>
> *I demand an immediate explanation and formal apology.*
>
> *Yours faithfully*
>
> *Elton James*
>
> *Elton James*

✦ Assignments

1 You work for Mrs Zukieka Bulbilia who is General Manager of Sunshine
   Holidays Ltd, a travel agent located at Fisherman's Wharf, Bridgetown,
   Barbados. Carry out the instructions in this note from Mrs Bulbilia.

PA

Please reply to this letter.
2 options for the family —
① all inclusive package holiday — flights, hotel
and daily sight-seeing trips
② flights and accommodation only (allows
more time with friends). Sight-seeing tours
can then be booked separately.
Enclose a brochure showing the range of tours
available and also some general information
on New York. Remind her that she'll need
insurance cover.
                                          ZB

Mermaid Bungalow
Sunset Crest
Cane Garden
ST THOMAS

Mrs Zukieka Bulbulia
General Manager
Sunshine Holidays Ltd
Fisherman's Wharf
BRIDGETOWN

Dear Mrs Bulbulia

Thank you for your help in arranging our holidays last year.

Next summer my family and I wish to visit friends in New York. We are unable to stay with them, as
they live in a small flat. We would like to see as much as possible of New York when we are there
and wondered if you could provide some information on travel to the USA, accommodation in the
city and sight-seeing trips.

We would appreciate an early reply.

Yours sincerely

M D Costa

Maria Da Costa (Mrs)

(Pitman EFBC1)

2 You work for Mr Alistair Fail, Managing Director of Fail and Kato Ltd, a publishing firm in New Zealand which specialises in crime fiction. Your address is Justice House, Te Aro, Wellington, New Zealand.

PA.
Use the standard letter form to reply to this please. Book Shop Crime Club — offers inexpensive paperbacks. (Explain that some of Grace Garacho's titles included.) Purchase of a minimum of 200 a year qualifies for 10% reduction on wholesale price. Price per book after reduction is $10. Tell her also that the purchase of 75 hardback copies of 'Circles of Red' entitles her to 6 free posters and 200 leaflets for distribution. Alistair

W R Rivers Ltd
49 Geneva Lane
Palmerston North

Fail and Kato Ltd
Justice House
Te Aro
Wellington
New Zealand

Dear Sir

Book Shop Crime Club and "Circles of Red"

We would like to enquire about membership of your Book Shop Crime Club and details concerning prices and minimum purchase of books per year.

In addition we understand that Grace Garacho's new book, "Circles of Red", is to be published shortly and we would like to know about the availability of promotional material and purchase of hardback copies.

Yours faithfully

Senga Blenkiron

Senga Blenkiron (Mrs)

Promotions Manager

(Pitman EFBC1)

3 You work for Ms Anna Vinsen, General Manager of Nolan Components, an electrical and electronic parts manufacturer. Your address is 121 Lucerne Road, Auckland, New Zealand.

(Pitman EFBC1)

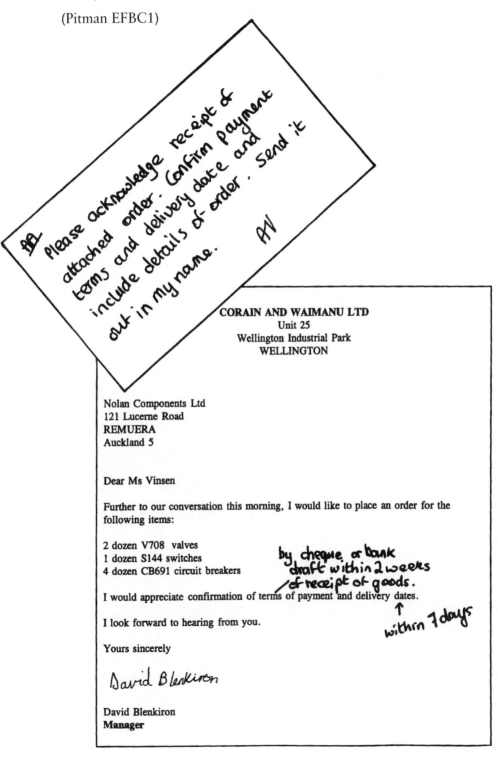

Please acknowledge receipt of attached order. Confirm payment terms and delivery date and include details of order. Send it out in my name. AV

CORAIN AND WAIMANU LTD
Unit 25
Wellington Industrial Park
WELLINGTON

Nolan Components Ltd
121 Lucerne Road
REMUERA
Auckland 5

Dear Ms Vinsen

Further to our conversation this morning, I would like to place an order for the following items:

2 dozen V708 valves
1 dozen S144 switches
4 dozen CB691 circuit breakers

by cheque or bank draft within 2 weeks of receipt of goods.

I would appreciate confirmation of terms of payment and delivery dates. ↑ within 7 days

I look forward to hearing from you.

Yours sincerely

David Blenkiron

David Blenkiron
Manager

Rules of good writing

By the end of this unit you should be able to:

❏ understand the rules of writing relating to all business documents

❏ identify and correct examples of poor business writing

❏ give examples of poor terminology used in business writing

❏ explain the general guidelines to be used in composing business letters

❏ compose a variety of business letters.

✦ Modern business communication

Business communications can be written in a
much more relaxed style than they were
decades ago. Old-fashioned, long-winded
jargon is out. You should aim to put across
your message naturally, in a friendly, informal
style. The secret of good writing is to use
plain language as if you are having a
conversation. This unit looks at two simple
rules you should follow in order to ensure
your communications are effective.

✦ Remember your ABC

If you are to be understood in business there are three things which you must
always remember. Your communications should always be: *accurate*, *brief*,
concise.

Accuracy

Your communication should be factually correct – it should tell the truth, the
whole truth and nothing but the truth. All the details should be correct. Suggest
which details should be double-checked in all your written communications:

✓ . . . .

✓ . . . .

✓ . . . .

✓ . . . .

Accuracy also means not being vague. Be specific and make sure the reader is
completely aware of all the facts. Chose better alternatives for these vague
expressions:

✗ The meeting will be postponed to a later date.   ✓ . . . .

✗ My plane arrives at 1.30.   ✓ . . . .

✗ I look forward to seeing you then.   ✓ . . . .

Brevity

Busy business people welcome letters which are direct and to the point. Save the reader's time by keeping sentences short and simple. How can these sentences be expressed more briefly?

✗ Please be informed that this order will be despatched to you on 12 July.   ✓ . . . .

✗ Please be informed that I will be unable to accept your invitation on this particular occasion.   ✓ . . . .

Brevity also means avoiding old-fashioned jargon. What can you say here?

✗ We have pleasure in enclosing herewith a copy of our latest catalogue for your reference.   ✓ . . . .

✗ I am in receipt of your letter of 8 January which we received today.   ✓ . . . .

Clarity

Use clear language which the reader will understand. Keep words plain and simple rather than using long words or elaborate phrases. What can you use instead of these words and phrases?

commence   ✓ . . . .

utilise   ✓ . . . .

terminate   ✓ . . . .

purchase   ✓ . . . .

despatch   ✓ . . . .

ascertain   ✓ . . . .

come to a decision   ✓ . . . .

in the event that   ✓ . . . .

give consideration to   ✓ . . . .

under separate cover   ✓ . . . .

despite the fact that   ✓ . . . .

in the near future   ✓ . . . .

at the present moment in time   ✓ . . . .

THINK

Can you think of any other expressions which are time-wasting and should not be used? Discuss these and make a list for your file.

✦ Use the right tone

You alter the tone of your voice to convey messages in a different way. Similarly written communications may be worded so that they sound polite, friendly, firm, bossy, sarcastic, condescending, even rude. If you use the wrong tone in a written communication you could cause real offence to your reader.

Even if you feel angry or frustrated, try not to vent your emotions in writing. Your objectives will be achieved only with carefully considered and appropriate wording.

Study the following expressions and choose an alternative way of saying the same things more tactfully.

You have deliberately failed to reply to my letter. ✗ (too emotive)

...................✓

We cannot do anything about your problem. Try calling a plumber. ✗ (too abrupt)

...................✓

Your interview will be held on Wednesday 28 August at 1400. ✗ (too bossy)

...................✓

The problem would not have happened if you had connected the wires properly in the first place. ✗ (too condescending)

...................✓

Your computer's guarantee has expired so you will have to pay for it to be repaired. ✗ (too blunt)

...................✓

It's not our fault that your curtains faded. You obviously didn't read the instructions about dry cleaning only. ✗ (too sarcastic)

...................✓

LET'S CHECK

Rewrite the following letter to keep in your files. Use simple modern business language with short, concise sentences.

Dear Mr Ramiah

I beg to acknowledge your communication of 27th ult., reference A B/J F, received by me today.

We are extremely distressed to learn that an error was made pertaining to your esteemed order. The cause of your complaint has been investigated and it actually appears that the error occurred in our packing section and it was not discerned before your order was despatched to your goodself.

I have arranged for a repeat order to be despatched to you immediately and am informed that this should leave our warehouse later today. We sincerely hope that you will have no cause for further complaint with this replacement order.

Once again I offer our humblest apologies for this unnecessary inconvenience which you have been caused in this instance.

We remain

Yours sincerely

Zachariah Creep & Partners

WHAT'S WRONG?

Read the following assignment and then study the answer given. It is not satisfactory for several reasons. Discuss the faults and then rewrite the answer correctly.

You work for Mr Michael Harrison, Sales Director of Eastwood Electrical Pte Ltd, 22 Orchard Road, #03–11 Lucky Towers, Singapore 343234. The company sells a wide range of TV and video equipment. Mr Harrison received a letter from Mr Gordon Paterson of 21 Bukit Sedap Road, Singapore 104928 complaining that a video recorder which he bought last month is not working properly. Mr Harrison talks to you about this matter. He says:

→

→

'We'd better reply to Mr Paterson's letter. It's the VCR20 Deluxe that he's complaining about. I think we'd better send one of our Technicians round to his place to check out the machine. Speak to Brian would you, and see what's the best time for him to go round some time next week. Tell Mr Paterson that I find the failure of the machine most disturbing. Something like this really shouldn't happen you know, when the products we sell are thoroughly checked out before they leave the shop. Then again, we can never be sure they've followed the instructions in the booklet correctly can we? Remember Mrs Cheong last month? It turned out that she hadn't connected the wires properly! Anyway Brian will sort it out for him when he calls and see if it's something simple which he can fix on the spot. If it really is defective, we'll give the customer a replacement immediately of course. You'd better ask him to call Brian if the appointment isn't good for him, and quote his extension number. Finish with the hope that it's resolved all right, but tell him to contact me if there's any further problem.'

WHAT'S WRONG WITH THE ANSWER?

EASTWOOD ELECTRICAL PTE LTD

22 Orchard Road
#03-11 Lucky Towers
Singapore

MH/by

Gordon Patterson
21 Bukit Sedap Road
Singapore 104928

Dear Mr Gordon

Your letter complaining about your faulty VCR20 was received by us today. We will be sending one of our technicians, Brian Lee to check out the fault next Wednesday afternoon.

The failure of the machine is very disturbing. This really shouldn't happen when our machines are checked before they leave our shop. I wonder if you've followed the instructions in the book properly?

Anyway Brian will see if it's something which can be fixed on the spot or if it's defective we'll replace you with a new VCR.

Hope it's resolved satisfactorily but if not please give me a call.

Yours faithfully

Michael Harrison (Mr)
Sales Director

✦ Guidelines for composing letters

1 Use short sentences

Short sentences will keep your meaning clear and ensure easier understanding.

2 Choose simple words

Simple words will convey your message more clearly. The use of unaffected language will help you to achieve the right tone.

3 Avoid wordiness

Choose words with care and be economical while remembering the need for courtesy.

4 Use an appropriate tone

Choose a tone to suit the reader and the subject matter. You can be firm or friendly, persuasive or conciliatory – it depends on the impression you wish to convey. Failure to adopt an appropriate tone will mean that the reader's attention is attracted more to how it is worded than to what is being said.

5 Be precise

Your letter should be long enough to serve its purpose, but no longer.

6 Ensure accuracy

Double check all figures, dates, numbers and prices, as well as spellings, punctuation, tenses, word endings, etc.

7 Check consistency

Ensure consistency of presentation (fully-blocked style with open punctuation) as well as consistency of expression (I, We, etc).

8 Use your initiative

Ensure the reader knows everything. Instead of 'next week', state a day and date. If an overseas visit is planned give the time of arrival and flight number.

LET'S CHECK

Decide whether the following statements are true or false. When a statement is false, discuss what is correct.

1 Long words should be used in letter-writing.   True/False

2 'Yours sincerely' should be used when beginning 'Dear Sir.'   True/False

3 AB/FTR is a postal code in the UK.   True/False

4 Continuation sheets should show the page number.   True/False

5 Unnecessary information should not be included in business letters.   True/False

6 Long sentences are preferable because they make things clearer.   True/False

7 A letter that begins 'Dear Mary' will end 'Yours faithfully'.   True/False

8 pp is used when you forget something and have to add it at the end of a letter.   True/False

9 Ms is used when you are writing to more than one woman.   True/False

10 cc means carbon copy.   True/False

WHAT'S WRONG?

Study the following assignment and the answer given. Discuss what is wrong with the answer shown and then rewrite it correctly.

The Personnel Officer of Design and Production Ltd, Olympia Works, Cirencester, CR2 3BW, has received a letter from the Careers Adviser, Ash Tree Upper School, Ash Lane, Gloucester GL1 2JQ requesting assistance in arranging periods of work experience for sixth form students following a course in Business Studies.

You have been asked to draft the letter which the personnel officer will send in reply to this request. Using the notes given below, draft the letter:

Regret not possible at present.

Management recognises importance of work experience; MD investigating suggestions put forward by Personnel Dept; if scheme can be worked out, it will be implemented asap.

List of schools and colleges wishing to be included being compiled –

Ash Tree Upper to be included; unlikely that everybody can be accommodated this year.

WHAT'S WRONG WITH THE ANSWER?

DESIGN AND PRODUCTION LTD
Olympia Works
Cirencester CR2 3BW

21 Sept

Careers Adviser
Ash Tree Upper School
Gloucester
GL1 2JQ

Dear Sir/Madam

ASSISTANCE IN PROVIDING PERIODS OF WORK EXPERIENCE

I regret it is not possible at the moment to acede to your request.

The management of this company recognises the importance of work experience
and the Managing Director is investigating suggestions put forward by me. If a
scheme can be worked out, we will implement it soon. Lists of schools and colleges
wishing to be included is presently being compiled - Ash Tree Upper to be included.

It is unlikely everybody can be acommodated this year though.

Please let me know if you have any queries.

Yours faithfully

MR JOE WILLIAMS
Personnel manager

✦ Assignments

1   You work for Hong Kong Hotel and Conference Centre, 73 Victory Road,
Kowloon, Hong Kong. An international company is moving its headquarters
to a site about six miles from your hotel. Write a letter to the Administration
Manager of the company describing some of the facilities you offer to
visiting business people and conferences. Some notes you have made are
shown below but you may include any other relevant details:

> *rooms – mention those specially equipped for business people*
> *restaurants, types of cuisine*
> *leisure facilities for guests*
> *rooms for conferences and equipment available*
> *transport – local and international*
> (LCCIEB EFB1 style)

2 You work for Mrs Ruth Fairless, Manager of the Bateman Hotel, Norland Road, Tenwick, Cumbria C49 8JY.

(LCCIEB EFB2 Style)

Mrs Fairless has received the following letter:

29 Yewcroft Avenue
Littleover
Derby DE7 6HU

17 April

Dear Sir or Madam

My husband and I have stayed at your hotel quite a few times in the past. We last stayed with you about four years ago. We always enjoyed staying at the Bateman Hotel which is in a lovely part of Cumbria. We would like to book a holiday at the hotel later this year but would like to ask you one or two questions.

First of all I'm sorry to say that my husband has had an accident and has hurt his leg. He cannot manage to use stairs very well. We would like to have a room on one of the upper floors of your hotel as these have lovely views of the lake - but do you have a lift?

Also we would like to bring our daughter with us and she is a vegetarian. Do you have vegetarian food on your menu? We would also prefer non-smoking rooms. Do you have these?

Yours sincerely

Mary Wilson

Mary Wilson (Mrs)

Mrs Fairless says that she remembers Mr & Mrs Wilson who are a very nice family. She asks you to write to Mrs Wilson and tell her that there is a lift but rooms with a view are very popular and need to be booked early. She asks you to mention that the lifts will not be working on 26/27 May from 0930 to 1130 and from 1430 to 1630. The hotel always has vegetarian food on its menu (it has been praised for this) and some of the newly-decorated rooms are kept for non-smoking guests but these are more expensive. Enclose our leaflet which shows full details and room rates.

Write the letter

3   You work for Mr David Fenworth, Manager of Fenworth Fashions, 117 High Street West, Hale, Cheshire WA5 7TH

(LCCIEB EFB2 style)

Mr Fenworth has received the following letter:

---

12 Elm Drive
Hale
Cheshire   WA15 8JH

Tel 061 981 2525

29 September

Mr D Fenworth
Manager
Fenworth Fashions
117 High Street West
Hale
Cheshire WA5 7TH

Dear Mr Fenworth

I am taking a course in Business Studies at college and I am now looking at how companies like Fenworth Fashions appoint new staff and also at their Human Resources policies.

I should be very grateful if I could speak to you about this. If you could spare me some time next week I could visit you at the shop. I am free on Thursday afternoon or Friday morning.

Thank you for your help.

Yours sincerely

Rachel Jones

Rachel Jones (Miss)

Mr Fenworth wrote you this note:

Please reply. Tell her that the deputy manager, Anne Gibb, deals with appointing new staff. I've spoken to Anne and she'll be happy to speak to Miss Scott. Tell her to come to the shop at 1440 on Thursday 6/10. She should come to the staff entrance at the back of the shop and bring my letter with her to show to the security guard who will let her in. Anne will look forward to meeting them. Copy the letter to AG please.

Write the letter

4   You work for Mr Rashid Hassan, Office Manager of Langland Manufacturing, Freeman Industrial Estate, Pitt Lane, Portsmouth, Hampshire PO13 7JJ. The company makes household furniture.

(LCCIEB EFB2 style)

Mr Hassan has just received this letter and has asked you to draft a reply to it.

MANTLES STORES
261 Milburn Road
Heaton
Newcastle upon Tyne
NE6 SKA

Telephone: 0191 444 7656   Fax: 0191 444 7777

KJ/PL/702   25 June 1999

Mr Rashid Hassan
Office Manager
Langland Manufacturing plc
Freeman Industrial Estate
Pitt Lane
Portsmouth
Hampshire PO13 7JJ

Dear Mr Hassan

As you may know, we are one of the largest chains of furniture stores in the North of England. We are now planning to expand and open a number of stores in the South of England, including one in the Portsmouth area.

We usually try to buy our furniture from local suppliers and I thought it would be useful for both of our companies if we could meet to consider whether you could supply us with some of our furniture, particularly dining tables, chairs and carpets.

I shall be visiting the South of England soon. I shall be in London on 19 July and shall be staying there overnight. If it is convenient I would like to come down to Portsmouth on the 20th to meet you and visit your factory.

I hope to hear from you soon.

Yours sincerely

Keith James

Keith James
Chief Buyer

Mr Hassan says to you:

Please prepare a reply to Mr James and tell him we'd be delighted to meet him and show him our factory. Please ask him how he is going to travel from London to Portsmouth on 20 July. If he's coming by train we can arrange for someone to meet him at the railway station. If he's driving here we will send him a map so that he will be able to find us. If he can arrive mid-morning he can visit the factory and see what we make. We can then talk about a deal over lunch. Let him know that we make a wide range of dining tables, chairs and cabinets and send him our latest catalogue. Say how pleased we were to hear from him.

UNIT
6

Recruitment correspondence

By the end of this unit you should be able to:

❑ state all the documents involved in the process of recruiting staff

❑ compose realistic business documents which may be used in this process.

✦ The recruitment process

Various letters and documents are involved in the process of applying for a job. In this unit we will look at the most common documents from both viewpoints – the applicant's and the employer's.

First of all reorganise this list into the most logical order using the skeleton diagram shown:

Letter to referee
Curriculum vitae
Invitation to interview
Job description
Testimonial from present company
Letter of acceptance
Contract of employment

Letter of resignation
Offer of employment
Reference
Letter of rejection to unsuitable applicants
Letter of application

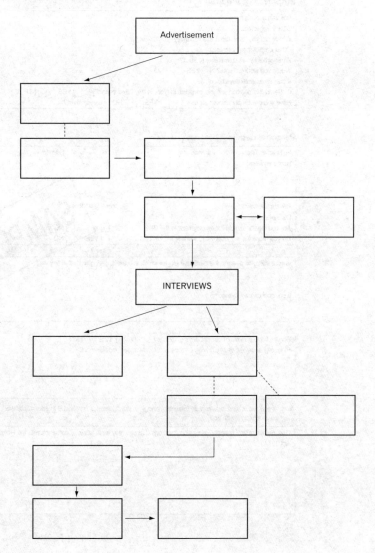

✦ Application letter

When you see an advertisement which attracts your attention, check carefully to note whether applications should be handwritten. If it is not stated, you may type your letter. Keep your application letter short and concise, with your main particulars listed in a curriculum vitae (sometimes called a resumé). This avoids your letter becoming very long and bogged down with unnecessary information.

> Things not to say on an application letter:
>
> 'Let's meet so you can ooh and aah over my experience'
>
> 'You'll want me to be Head Honcho in no time.'

APPLICATION FOR EMPLOYMENT

SHORT FORM   **PRIVATE & CONFIDENTIAL**

PLEASE PRINT CLEARLY

Employment required

Position applied for:
Salary expected: £   per
Where did you hear about this vacancy?
Other employment interests:
When would you be available to start?
Would you work full time? ☐ YES ☐ NO
If part time, state days/hours:
If offered this position will you continue to work in any other capacity? ☐ YES ☐ NO
Have you previously worked for us? ☐ YES ☐ NO   If yes, when?

Personal details

Full name: Title: Forename(s)   Surname:
Home address:
Postcode:
Private telephone: Business telephone:
Date of Birth:
Are you legally eligible for employment in the UK?   ☐ YES ☐ NO
Do you require a work permit to work in the UK?   ☐ YES ☐ NO

SAMPLE

Is your ability to perform the particular job for which you are applying limited in any way?
If so, how can we overcome this?

Do you have a relevant current driving licence?   ☐ YES ☐ NO
Please give details of any driving offences currently under endorsement:

Note: If you are invited to attend an interview, and your driving licence is relevant to your application, please bring it with you.

Give details of any unspent criminal convictions that you may have (as in accordance with the Rehabilitation of Offenders Act 1974.)

Employment

List below present and past employment, beginning with your most recent.

Name & Address of Employer	From: Month Year	To: Month Year	Starting Salary	Leaving Salary	Name of Manager
			£ per	£ per	
	Job Title:				
Telephone: Type of business:	Describe the work you did:				
	Reason for leaving:				
Name & Address of Employer	From: Month Year	To: Month Year	Starting Salary	Leaving Salary	Name of Manager
			£ per	£ per	
	Job Title:				
Telephone: Type of business:	Describe the work you did:				
	Reason for leaving:				
Name & Address of Employer	From: Month Year	To: Month Year	Starting Salary	Leaving Salary	Name of Manager
			£ per	£ per	
	Job Title:				
Telephone: Type of business:	Describe the work you did:				
	Reason for leaving:				

Education, Qualifications & Training

Beginning with the most recent events, give details of your education, qualifications and training to date. Include under 'Details' the places you attended.

Details	Dates From/To	Qualifications Gained

I declare that to the best of my knowledge and belief the information given in this application is correct:

Signature:_____   Date:_____

For Office Use Only

Application form evaluated by:	Date:
Comments:	
Offer Details:	

Reproduced courtesy of Waterlow Business Supplies

Some advertisements specify that you should write in to request an application form, in which case just send a simple letter requesting the standard form. Application forms are often preferred by larger organisations because by giving specific headings the company can be assured of obtaining the same information about each applicant.

49 Broome Avenue
Nottingham
NG2 3PJ

Tel: 0115 987654

2 June 2000

Mrs Louise Dunscombe
Human Relations Manager
Aurora Holdings plc
Aurora House
Temple Street
London
SE1 4LL

Dear Mrs Dunscombe

TELEPHONE EXECUTIVE (MARKETING)

I am interested in applying for this post as advertised in today's Nottingham Post.

I have been employed as part-time Administration Assistant in Nottingham Technical College for the last 6 months while studying there on a Business Administration course. My course finishes very soon and I am keen to join a progressive company such as Aurora Holdings.

My full particulars are shown on my enclosed Curriculum Vitae.

I shall be happy to attend an interview at any time, and look forward to hearing from you soon.

Yours sincerely

ADRIENNE LANGSTON (Miss)

Enc

✦ Curriculum vitae

Curriculum vitae is Latin, literally meaning 'the course of one's life'. A curriculum vitae (CV) sets out your personal details, education, qualifications and working experience. Make sure you organise all the information logically under headings and use columns where appropriate. All your details can then be found at a glance.

CURRICULUM VITAE

Emphasise the heading (you may prefer to use resumé)

Name
Address
Telephone
Nationality
Date of Birth
Marital Status

Appropriate personal details (you may add race, citizenship, I/C number or others)

EDUCATION

Tabulate your education in three columns (chronological order)

DATES	SCHOOL/COLLEGE	COURSE

QUALIFICATIONS

Be specific and list all your qualifications (not just '3 O levels')

DATES	EXAMINING BODY	SUBJECT

WORKING EXPERIENCE

Present job first, working backwards

DATES	EMPLOYER	POSITION/DUTIES

ADDITIONAL INFORMATION

Hobbies/sports you enjoy/special achievements/results awaited?

REFEREES

A previous employer? A teacher? Youth club leader?

1   2

Month and year only — Date

✦ Invitation to interview

A letter inviting shortlisted applicants to attend an interview should be fairly short, simply thanking the person for his/her application and giving a day/date/time for the interview.

Interview

The interview is an essential stage in the recruitment process. Unit 2 gives full guidelines on how to prepare for interviews. Perhaps you can arrange for some mock interviews to be held in your class?

Aurora Holdings plc

Aurora House, Temple Street, London SE1 4LL

Tel: +44(0)181 542 5555
Fax: +44(0)181 555 4444   Email: aurora@cfb.co.uk

LD/ST

8 June 2000

Miss Adrienne Langston
49 Broome Avenue
Nottingham
NG2 3PJ

Dear Miss Langston

TELEPHONE EXECUTIVE (MARKETING)

Thank you for your recent letter applying for the above post.

I hope you can attend an interview at 1030 on Friday 16 June.

If this appointment is inconvenient please telephone my secretary to make alternative arrangements.

Yours sincerely

Louise Dunscombe

LOUISE DUNSCOMBE (Mrs)
Human Relations Manager

Don't forget to include the courtesy title

Personalised salutation

Acknowledge the letter

State date and time for interview

Suggest how alternative arrangements can be made

✦ References

Before a candidate is offered a job the company will usually take up references. It is a good idea to take along to the interview copies of some testimonials which former employers have written about you. However, companies may still prefer to telephone or write to referees asking for comments on the character, personal qualities and work performance of the person they have singled out to be offered the job. If you have not yet started work you could give as a referee your teacher or someone who has known you for several years (not a relative).

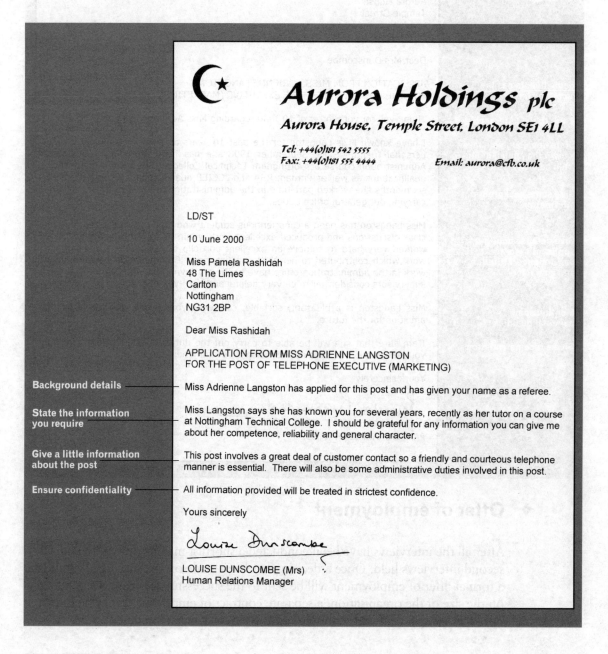

(☪ Aurora Holdings plc

Aurora House, Temple Street, London SE1 4LL

Tel: +44(0)181 542 5555
Fax: +44(0)181 555 4444

Email: aurora@cfb.co.uk

LD/ST

10 June 2000

Miss Pamela Rashidah
48 The Limes
Carlton
Nottingham
NG31 2BP

Dear Miss Rashidah

APPLICATION FROM MISS ADRIENNE LANGSTON
FOR THE POST OF TELEPHONE EXECUTIVE (MARKETING)

Background details — Miss Adrienne Langston has applied for this post and has given your name as a referee.

State the information you require — Miss Langston says she has known you for several years, recently as her tutor on a course at Nottingham Technical College. I should be grateful for any information you can give me about her competence, reliability and general character.

Give a little information about the post — This post involves a great deal of customer contact so a friendly and courteous telephone manner is essential. There will also be some administrative duties involved in this post.

Ensure confidentiality — All information provided will be treated in strictest confidence.

Yours sincerely

Louise Dunscombe

LOUISE DUNSCOMBE (Mrs)
Human Relations Manager

Some writers prefer to
centre their personal
address and telephone
number

48 The Limes
Carlton
Nottingham
NG31 2BP

Telephone: 0115 221221

11 June 2000

Use full name, title,
company name and
address as shown on
letterhead

Mrs Louise Dunscombe
Human Relations Manager
Aurora Holdings plc
Aurora House
Temple Street
London
SE1 4LL

Dear Mrs Dunscombe

Same heading as the
incoming letter

APPLICATION FROM MISS ADRIENNE LANGSTON
FOR THE POST OF TELEPHONE EXECUTIVE (MARKETING)

Refer to the letter received

Thank you for your letter of 10 June regarding Miss Adrienne Langston.

State how long you have
known the applicant and in
what capacity

Give some background
information

I have known Miss Langston for the past 10 years as she is the daughter of a
personal friend. Since September 1998 she has been attending a Business
Administration course at Nottingham Technical College. She gained many NVQ
qualifications as well as Pitman, RSA and LCCIEB qualifications. During the past
six months she worked part-time in the administration office here at the college
carrying out general office duties.

Give details about the
applicant's work
performance, attitude
and character

Miss Langston has been a conscientious student who always participated fully in
class discussions and produced excellent work within the given time frame. She
worked very hard to compile an excellent portfolio of assignments and project
work which contributed to her NVQ qualifications. Comments on her part-time
work in the administration office have been very favourable and I know that her
supervisors consider her to be very helpful and hard-working.

Mention some
personal qualities

Miss Langston is a pleasant, sociable, courteous young lady who has a lot of
ambition for the future.

Give a recommendation

I am sure that she will be able to carry out the duties involved in this post to
your satisfaction. I have no hesitation in recommending her highly.

Yours sincerely

Pamela Rashidah

PAMELA RASHIDAH (Miss)

✦ Offer of employment

After all the interviews have been conducted a shortlist may be drawn up and
second interviews held. Once a decision has been made on the successful candidate,
a formal offer of employment will be sent to the successful applicant. Depending
on the size of the organisation, a separate contract of employment may be drawn
up. Here we will deal with a simple offer letter enclosing a job description.

Aurora Holdings plc

Aurora House, Temple Street, London SE1 4LL

Tel: +44(0)181 542 5555
Fax: +44(0)181 555 4444   Email: aurora@cfb.co.uk

LD/ST

20 June 2000

Miss Adrienne Langston
49 Broome Avenue
Nottingham
NG2 3PJ

Dear Miss Langston

TELEPHONE EXECUTIVE (MARKETING)

Thank you for attending the recent interview.

[Offer the job and state commencement date] → I am pleased to offer you this post commencing on Monday 2 August 2000.

[Enclose job description and contract of employment (You may prefer to give salary in the offer letter)] → Full details of the post are shown on the attached Job Description. The terms and conditions of employment will be as laid down in our Contract of Employment which is also enclosed.

[Request written confirmation] → Please let me have written confirmation of your acceptance of this post as soon as possible.

[Give other relevant details and state instructions for first day of work] → Two other Telephone Executives will start work on the same day so the morning of 2 August will be spent on an induction training course. Please report to our reception at 0900 and ask for my Secretary, Miss Katherine Lee.

[Finish with a welcoming close] → I look forward to welcoming you to the staff of Aurora Holdings plc.

Yours sincerely

LOUISE DUNSCOMBE (Mrs)
Human Relations Manager

[Don't forget Encs and Copy if necessary]

Encs

Copy: Glen Cooper, Marketing Manager

THINK

Does your company issue a formal contract of employment?

What issues are covered in this?

✦ Job description

A job description states the title of the post and to whom the person reports, as well as giving full details of the duties and responsibilities involved.

Appropriate headings

☾ *Aurora Holdings plc*

JOB DESCRIPTION

Use headings relevant to the company and post

Job Title	Telephone Executive (Marketing)
Location	Marketing Department, Head Office
Responsible to	Marketing Manager
Main Purpose of Job	To telephone customers with the objective of identifying opportunities where business can be increased

List main duties and responsibilities

MAIN DUTIES AND RESPONSIBILITIES

Express all points consistently (To ...)

1   To achieve daily call rate targets and any target set for sales campaigns.

2   To have a good telephone manner and be courteous to customers at all times.

3   To carry out any administrative requirements generated by the telephone calls in an accurate and efficient manner. This may include sending letters, fax messages, reports, product literature, etc.

4   To undertake training courses to make good use of telephone selling techniques.

5   To undertake training on the company's products and services and to promote associated products where appropriate.

6   To carry out competitor market research by contacting their branches to gather information on pricing, product availability etc as directed by your supervisor.

7   To communicate clearly and effectively with other employees in the company as necessary.

Finish with this standard clause

8   To carry out any other tasks as requested by your supervisor.

Don't forget a reference and date

LD/ST

20 June 2000

THINK

Ask your business administration teacher to discuss the difference between a job description and a job specification.

✦ Letter of acceptance

It is usual to write a formal letter to the company accepting the post. Keep it simple.

49 Broome Avenue
Nottingham
NG2 3PJ

25 June 2000

Mrs Louise Dunscombe
Human Relations Manager
Aurora Holdings plc
Aurora House
Temple Street
London
SE1 4LL

Be consistent – display all your letters in the same style ── Dear Mrs Dunscombe

TELEPHONE EXECUTIVE (MARKETING)

Thank you for your letter of 20 June 2000.

I am pleased to confirm my acceptance of this post as detailed in the Job Description and Contract of Employment.

Finish appropriately ── I shall look forward to joining the staff of Aurora Holdings plc.

Yours sincerely

Adrienne Langston

ADRIENNE LANGSTON (Miss)

✦ Letter of resignation

When you have been in employment and wish to leave for whatever reason, it is usual to write a formal letter resigning from your post.

49 Broome Avenue
Nottingham
NG2 3PJ

25 June 2000

Mrs Helen Bradley
Administration Manager
Nottingham Technical College
123 Bridge Avenue
West Bridgford
Nottingham
NG9 7GJ

Dear Mrs Bradley

Express regret and state last day of work — Further to our discussion today I regret to inform you that I wish to give one month's notice of my resignation from the company. My last day of work will be Friday 30 July.

Explain tactfully and courteously — I have been very happy working here and found my work very varied and enjoyable. I have gained a lot of experience in many areas which I am sure I shall find useful in future employment.

Give thanks — Thank you for your help and guidance.

Yours sincerely

Adrienne Langston

ADRIENNE LANGSTON (Miss)

✦ Testimonial (letter of recommendation)

It is useful to ask previous employers for testimonials as these will be useful when applying for future posts.

NOTTINGHAM TECHNICAL COLLEGE

123 Bridge Avenue
West Bridgford
Nottingham NG9 7GJ

Telephone: 0115 876789
Fax: 0115 876889

HB/GB

28 June 2000

Use this heading in place of an inside address → **TO WHOM IT MAY CONCERN**

State position and duration of employment → Miss Adrienne Langston has been part-time Administration Assistant in our General Office from 24 May 1999 to 28 June 2000. We asked her to join us on a permanent part-time basis after she had been with us for several short periods of work experience during her Business Administration course.

Mention the duties performed → Miss Langston carried out a wide range of general office duties including opening and distributing mail, photocopying, filing, dealing with general telephone and walk-in enquiries and entering data into our computer systems.

State the employee's working attitude and how work was carried out → A conscientious, hard-working and reliable employee, Miss Langston set herself very high standards in her work. She had a pleasant telephone manner and was always courteous when dealing with her colleagues and external contacts. She was a good time-keeper and had a good attendance record.

Mention personal qualities → Miss Langston has a friendly, outgoing personality, a good sense of humour and she works well as part of a team.

Give a recommendation → I feel sure that Miss Langston will be an asset to any organisation.

No salutation and complimentary close are necessary

Helen Bradley

Helen Bradley (Mrs)
Administration Manager

TIP

To see more examples of testimonials take a look at *Gartside's Model Business Letters.* (Shirley Taylor, FT Management, 1998)

✦ Assignment

In this assignment you are going to follow the recruitment process all the way through, looking at it from the point of view of both the employer and the applicant. As you complete each stage, make sure you refer back to the specimens shown in this unit so that you display your documents correctly and consistently. Use an appropriate date on each document and keep all the documents neatly in a folder.

This advertisement will be your starting point.

☾ *Aurora Holdings plc*

Aurora Holdings is one of the busiest retailers on the high street today. We currently have a number of vacancies at our head office.

PERSONAL ASSISTANT
TO PROJECT DEVELOPMENT MANAGER

Applicants should be suitably qualified, experienced and computer literate.

ADMINISTRATION ASSISTANT
HUMAN RELATIONS DEPARTMENT

Applicants must have good communication and organisational skills and be able to work under pressure.

WORD PROCESSING OPERATORS
ADMINISTRATION DEPARTMENT

Applicants must have excellent word processing qualifications and an ability to work well as a member of a team in this busy department.

IT ASSISTANT

Applicants must have relevant experience to join the IT team which provides IT support to 150 technical and administrative staff.

Applications with full CV should be sent to:

Jake Williamson
Personnel Manager
Aurora Holdings plc
Aurora House
Temple Street
London SE1 4LL

1　Apply for one of the posts.

TIP

Remember to keep your covering letter short and concise because you will be enclosing a copy of your CV.

2   Compose your own CV to send with your application letter.

TIP

Why not ask your teacher if you can use a typewriter or word processor to prepare your CV?

3   Compose a letter from the company inviting you to attend an interview. Give a suitable date and time.

TIP

Remember to design a suitable letterheading with logo.

4   Write a letter from the company to one of the referees mentioned on your CV asking for details about your work performance, character and ability.
5   What would you like to think that your referee will say about you? Write a suitable (but believable!) reference from your referee to the company.
6   Compose a letter offering you the post at Aurora Holdings.
7   Discuss the duties which you would expect to perform in this job. Compose a suitable job description.

TIP

Perhaps you can discuss this assignment in your Business Administration lesson? Your teacher will be happy to give you some help.

8   Write a short letter accepting this post.
9   Write a letter that Aurora Holdings can send to all the unsuccessful applicants.
10   As you have accepted the post at Aurora Holdings, you must resign from your present post. Make up suitable details and compose a letter of resignation.
11   You have asked your current employer for a testimonial which you may keep. Compose a testimonial from your present company giving details of your duration of employment, the post(s) you held, your responsibilities, your work performance and any other appropriate details.

TIP

Take a look at *Gartside's Model Business Letters and Other Business Documents*. This contains lots of different references and other business documents.

SECTION

3

TELECOMMUNICATIONS

UNIT 7

Email and fax messages

By the end of this unit you should be able to:

❏ explain the principles of email messages

❏ describe the different techniques used in composing email messages

❏ explain how the Internet is changing the way we communicate and learn

❏ state the documents which may be sent via fax

❏ design fax headed paper which includes all essential components

❏ compose fax messages.

✦ Electronic mail

Businesses today operate in a highly competitive market in which high-speed communication and information transfer is essential. Most of the activities in today's offices are electronic using computer-based technology. Electronic mail, or email as it is commonly known, has evolved as an effective, low-cost and quick method of communication with friends and colleagues all over the world.

With email, messages are keyed into a computer workstation and then transmitted to the recipient. A single message may be sent simultaneously to many recipients. A lot of time and effort is saved in producing formal, printed memos, but of course you may still print out a copy of email messages if required.

Many email messages are short and may be deleted after a few days or weeks. If the messages are longer and more important they may be retained on the electronic file for a longer period of time.

The advantages of email are:

✦ high speed send/receive cycle
✦ direct input and retrieval from keyboard
✦ virtually instant despatch/retrieval
✦ simultaneous circulation to pre-selected groups
✦ other files (e.g. created on Word, Excell) can be attached to email messages for recipient to download easily
✦ instant responses can be sent.

Email is quick and easy to use, but this should not be an opportunity to forget all the basic rules of good business writing. In business use, try not to use abbreviations which you may use when emailing personal friends.

THINK

Many abbreviations like BFN (bye for now) and PCM (please call me) are used in personal email messages. Discuss other abbreviations which you have seen or used.

Netiquette

The evolution of email has brought about a special 'netiquette' as shown here (reproduced from *Model Business Letters and Other Business Documents*):

1   *Check the email address.* Correctly addressed email messages are delivered within seconds. It can take days to receive an error message letting you know that an incorrectly addressed message was not delivered.

2   *Always write a subject heading.* This will give the recipient a good idea of the contents of the message and makes for easier handling.

3   *Check the time.* It is important to keep your computer's internal clock and date settings accurate, otherwise problems may be caused in trying to sort messages chronologically.

4   *Keep caps lock off.* Capitals indicate shouting and can look threatening.

5   *Express yourself.* Emotions can be used to show mood in your email messages. Some of the more common emoticons are:

> :-)   happy
> ;-)   wink
> :-(sad
> :-I   indifference
> :-/   perplexed
> :-O shock or surprise

6   *Greetings.* Formality does not read well in email. Replace formal salutations like 'Dear David' with informal 'Hello David' or even just 'David'. Similarly 'Yours sincerely' is not appropriate in emails. Use just 'Best wishes' or 'All the best'.

7   *Check your syntax.* It is easy to allow sentences to become very long and verbose. Make an effort to keep sentences short and simple, and check your syntax. The more pride you take in your message composition, the more successful you will be in being understood and achieving the desired results.

8   *Keep copies.* Just as you would keep copies of letters, it is good practice to take a printout of email messages sent and received.

9   *Check your message.* As soon as you hit the 'send' symbol, your message may be received in seconds. There is no calling it back for second thoughts, so check it carefully and get it right first time.

When an email message is sent from one terminal it is stored at a communications postal station until the recipient gives a signal to his or her system to receive messages. This often happens automatically when a user 'logs on' to the service provider. Transmission takes only seconds, and messages will be shown on your screen with a simple 'click' of a mouse.

	To Ian.Little@awl.co.uk
Key email addresses accurately	From Shirley.Taylor@cfb.co.uk
	Date Mon 21 September 1999
The time is inserted automatically by your computer	Time 12:23:45 +0000
Use an appropriate subject heading	Subject Communication for Business 3rd edition
Keep your salutation informal and friendly	Hi Ian

Thanks for your email today. I'm glad you enjoyed your holiday in Canada.

Email messages are much less formal than other business documents, sometimes more chatty

I'm happy to report that I've been able to progress very well with the new edition of Communication for Business. I've received help from some friends and colleagues which has been very valuable. I've also been in touch with lots of big companies who have very kindly given permission for me to use some of their documents in my book.

I should be able to wrap everything up by the end of this month. Would you like to come up and collect the work next week? Shall we say Wednesday 30 September at our usual table in the Red Lion Hotel in Todwick?

Please let me know if this is OK with you.

Finish off informally too — See you soon.

Shirley

TIP

Once your message is sent, it may be read by the recipient within seconds. You cannot call it back for second thoughts. Proofread it carefully before you click 'send'.

✦ The Internet

Email is just one way of communicating using the powers of modems, computers and telephone lines, but the Internet is opening up so many more possibilities. The Internet is a rich source of information, a link to the world, an educational tool, an entertainment medium. The Internet is rewriting the way in which we communicate and learn.

Businesses, individuals and schools have gone on-line to experience this fascinating medium. With its ready acceptance come some issues which may cause concern. This should not be allowed to discourage us from making the most of this valuable resource pool. This leaflet from the Singapore Broadcasting Authority gives some tips to help you make the most of the Net – in 'Netspeak', Happy surfing!

Why should I get on the Internet when I have books and newspapers to read and TV to watch?

The Internet can give you far more information, more current news and entertainment now than what's available in other traditional means. And you don't need to go far to search for it.

There are also materials on-line that are not available elsewhere. For example, the Tampines Webtown (http://www.tampines.org.sg/) is a community web page designed to keep residents and others informed what's happening in their area.

Alternatively, personal interests can be greatly enhanced with additional information on the Internet. For example, durian lovers can buy durians (http://www.gs.com.sg/717trading/) or even get a recipe for a durian dessert (http://www. ecst.csuchico.edu/~durian/rec/ice.html). Something the whole family can enjoy!

You can find websites maintained by many companies with lots of useful information that you can use in your work. You can even apply for a job with some companies through their website! There are also websites dedicated to helping you search for a job in any field (http://www.careerasia.com/)

But the Internet isn't just about passively gaining information. One of its chief features is interactivity and connectivity. With electronic mail (e-mail), you can communicate with friends, relatives or colleagues or meet new people via the Internet for a fraction of the cost of other means. You can also post messages on Bulletin Boards or participate in chat groups on your favourite topics. Examples can be found at:

(http://www.pacific.net.sg/talk/)

(http://chat.singnet.com.sg/)

(http://www.cyberway.com.sg/chat.html)

What if I don't have what is needed to surf the Internet?

If you don't have a personal computer, a modem, a phone line and an account with an Internet Service Provider, you can also get cyber access at Cyber Cafes, various branches of the National Library, even some community centres. Many students go on-line at school as well.

I have friends who set up their own home pages. Are there any rules on what they put in there?

Remember that setting up a personal home page is like publishing a magazine or newspaper. Your home page is available to all who read it. Hence, you are responsible for what you place there. Your home page is still subject to existing laws of the land with regard to defamation, fraud, copyright, gambling etc.

I also heard that there are all sorts of weird people on the Internet.

There are dos and don'ts of Internet surfing. For example, be wary when cyber-chatting with others on the Internet. The Internet is a public forum with the added dimension of anonymity.

While you are surfing, exercise the same caution you would in ordinary life. When you talk to strangers, you shouldn't reveal too much about yourself.

What should I do if I encounter something offensive on the Internet?

We at the Singapore Broadcasting Authority encourage you to let us know of sites you find unsuitable or concerns you may have. You can write in, call us or e-mail to us through our home page at http://www.sba.gov.sg.

How do I protect my kids?

Here are some tips you may find helpful.

- Inculcate proper netiquette.
- Never disclose any personal information.
- Tell your kids to report any suspicious activities to you.
- Spend time with your children by surfing with them and guiding them through what they find on the Internet.
- Don't allow your kids to meet strangers face to face or other computer users without your permission.
- Never respond to offensive messages.
- Encourage your kids to share with you their online experiences.
- Use filter programmes which are commercially available.
- Time management is important when surfing the Internet.
- Do some initial surfing on your own and find educational sites for your kids. Bookmark them for easy reference in the future.

Look up the SBA website for further tips for parents. (http://www.sba.gov.sg/tips.htm)

Many have heard of it but few really know about it. A rich source of information, a link to the world, an educational tool, an entertainment medium. The Internet is rewriting the way we communicate and learn.

Many have jumped on the Internet bandwagon; businesses, individuals, and even schools have gone on-line to experience this fascinating medium. With its ready acceptance comes issues that may be of concern to you. Undesirable elements like scams, con men and pornography are found lurking in the dark corners of the Internet. But we should not let this discourage us from exploiting this valuable resource pool. We've listed some tips to help you get the most out of the Net. Happy surfing!

Anything else I should know?

There is an informal code of behaviour on the Internet called Netiquette. Here are some tips you may wish to bear in mind while surfing:

- You should always remember that there is a human being at the receiving end of your message, not a computer. Courtesy in cyberspace goes a long way too!
- Adhere to the same standards of behaviour on-line as you would in real life. For example, you should obey rules and laws such as those against cheating and defamation.
- Just as it is not acceptable to pry into others' private affairs in real life, so we should respect others' privacy in cyberspace.
- Sometimes, you may find "loud" shouting on the Net, where people write in capital letters. These are called flame wars. You can help keep these under control by refraining from such "shouting".
- It is annoying to send unsolicited junk mail to people you don't know.
- When you join a discussion group, take a look at the FAQ (Frequently Asked Questions) section first. These are put up so participants don't have to keep explaining the discussion happening on-line every time a new person joins.

If you would like to know more about user guidelines, you can visit http://www.albion.com/netiquette/index.html or http://www.fau.edu/rinaldi/netiquette.html.

SINGAPORE BROADCASTING AUTHORITY

Produced by
Singapore Broadcasting Authority   Tel: 270 8191 Fax: 276 2238
1 Maritime Square #09-59 World Trade Centre Singapore 099253
Website: http://www.sba.gov.sg

Figure 7.5   Reproduced courtesy of Singapore Broadcasting Authority

✦ Fax messages

A fax machine is a relatively inexpensive – and most would agree essential – item of equipment for any business. Fax transmits and receives any kind of message – handwritten, printed, word-processed; maps, messages, diagrams, photographs. Transmission of a fax message takes only seconds, depending on the length of the document.

Sending messages by fax is a popular choice today due to its versatility and speed. Fax is often used between divisions or branches of the same company instead of telephone or memos. Business letters are frequently either sent by fax or replaced by fax messages.

Most companies use a special fax letterhead for fax messages. This fax headed paper is often used with just a brief covering note explaining an accompanying document. The salutation and complimentary close are normally omitted but the message will generally be signed.

✪ Aurora

Facsimile message

To:	Classified Ads, Daily News	Fax:	3371917
From:	Tarandeep Kaur	Date:	19 August 2000
Subject:	Advertisement for Secretary	Pages:	2
Copy:	---		

☑ Urgent ☐ For Review ☐ Please Comment ☐ Please Reply ☐ Please Recycle

Further to our telephone conversation, I would like the attached advertisement to be placed in 'Secretarial Vacancies' on 29 August.

Please fax proof for approval as soon as possible.

Tarandeep

✪ Aurora Holdings plc
Aurora House, Temple Street, London SE1 4LL

Tel: +44(0)181 542 4444   Fax: +44(0)181 555 4444
Email: aurora@cfb.co.uk

THINK

Bring in some of your organisation's fax headed paper to show to your fellow students.

If you have to compile your own fax headings, the following layout is suggested:

Use letterheaded paper

☾★ *Aurora Holdings* plc

Aurora House, Temple Street, London SE1 4LL

Tel: +44(0)181 542 5555
Fax: +44(0)181 555 4444   Email: aurora@cfb.co.uk

Insert main heading 'FAX MESSAGE'

FAX MESSAGE

The details here are important so use these standard headings

Remember to include the number of pages being sent

To	Iris Tan, Regional Manager
Company	Aurora International (Asia) Ltd
Fax No	00 65 25330099
From	Michael Ng, Director - Conferences
Ref	MN/ST
Date	15 June 200-
No of Pages	2

A salutation may be included before the heading if preferred

VISIT TO SINGAPORE/MALAYSIA

Sophia Lee, Director of Asia Training Enterprises, has invited me to chair the 10th Annual Malaysian Secretaries Conference at the Mandarin International Hotel in Kuala Lumpur on 11/12 August.

Structure the body exactly as you would a business letter

I am therefore rearranging the schedule for my forthcoming trip to Singapore so that I spend a few days in Malaysia before flying down to Singapore on Monday 14 August. My flights are confirmed and a copy of my itinerary is enclosed.

I hope all the arrangements for the Regional Conference in Singapore are going smoothly. Please let me see a copy of your proposed programme soon together with a list of materials you want me to bring from London.

A complimentary close is not necessary

✦ Assignments

1   You work for Kwik-Print plc and have received instructions to print business cards for Miss Fouzia Suki, Personnel Manager at Trendsetter Training College. The artwork has been prepared but you need to obtain approval from Miss Suki. Compose a fax, leaving space for the business card to be illustrated. Include a simple form at the foot which Miss Suki may sign and fax back to you if the design is approved.

2 You work for the managing director of Stanfield Engineering who is presently visiting clients of your company in the Caribbean. During his absence you receive two important quotations for major office renovations. You know that your employer wants work to commence urgently on these renovations but he is not expected back for some time. Send him a fax message at his hotel, enclosing the quotations, and ask for his instructions.

3 You work for Mrs Zukieka Bulbulia, General Manager of Sunshine Holidays Ltd, a travel agent at Fisherman's Wharf, Bridgetown, Barbados. Carry out Mrs Bulbulia's instructions in this message which she has left for you.

MESSAGE FOR

M̶ PA
_____

WHILE YOU WERE OUT

M Zukieka Bulbulia
_____

Telephone No _____

Telephoned	✓	Please ring	
Wants to see you		Urgent	

Message: Please send an urgent fax to Mr Masu Babani, the new manager of our branch office in Jamaica (Fax No 0929 7865).

He intends to visit us to see how we publicise our holidays to passers-by. Unfortunately he has chosen the Tuesday of the week we are having the new windows fitted and therefore we will have nothing for him to see. Suggest he comes the following week when our new information on holidays to South America will be on display. Tell him ZB will arrange for him to meet William Da Silva who is in charge of our advertising so that he can talk to him about his work.

Ask him to fax agreement to the revised date and programme.

Taken by Claud

(Pitman EFBC1)

4 You work for Ms Anna Vinsen, General Manager of Nolan Components, an electrical and electronic parts manufacturer. Your office address is 121 Lucerne Road, Remuera, Auckland, New Zealand. Carry out Ms Vinsen's instructions in this note.

AA/

Draft a fax to Lyndon Davidson at Best Lighting apologising for the delay in delivery of their order. The Production Dept. form below gives you the information you need. Ask if this is acceptable - offer alternative if not.

AV

DESPATCH DELAY NOTIFICATION - INTERNAL

Order No: B423
Customer: Best Lighting
Contact: Lyndon Davidson

The above order has been delayed for the reason(s) indicated below.

☑ Parts not in stock. — awaiting delivery from our suppliers next week. Order will be made up and despatched

☐ Difficulties with our suppliers. as soon as possible. We expect to deliver in 10 days.

☐ Transport problems in our despatch department.

☐ Transport problems in our supplier's despatch department.

☐ Transport problems with national hauliers.

☑ Other Our suppliers are awaiting raw materials — due tomorrow

(Pitman EFBC1)

INTERNAL COMMUNICATION

Memoranda

By the end of this unit you should be able to:

❑   explain the purpose of memos

❑   design pre-printed memo forms which contain all essential details

❑   compose memoranda from given instructions.

✦ Why memos?

Affectionately called a 'memo' this is a written communication from one person to another (or a group of people) within the same organisation. Memos serve a variety of purposes:

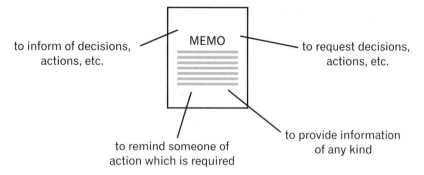

Just as letterheaded paper is used for letters, many organisations use pre-printed stationery for memos. Here are some examples:

MEMORANDUM   Aurora ☾⋆

To   Ref
From   Date

✶ **Global Enterprises**   **Kuala Lumpur**

MEMORANDUM

To _____
From _____
Date _____
Subject _____

THINK

Bring in some of your organisation's memo headed paper to discuss with your fellow students.

It is important that the memo headings show details of sender and recipient as well as reference and date. Courtesy titles (Mr/Mrs/Miss/Ms) are usually not included. If pre-printed memo forms are not used in your organisation, the following headings are suggested.

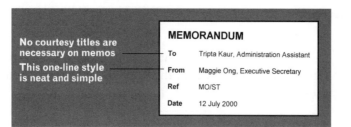

MEMORANDUM

To	Tripta Kaur, Administration Assistant
From	Maggie Ong, Executive Secretary
Ref	MO/ST
Date	12 July 2000

After these memo headings, continue in the usual fully-blocked style. When more than one topic is dealt with it is good practice to use numbered points and sub-headings. A memo will not include a salutation and complimentary close, but it will usually be signed or initialled depending on the procedure adopted within individual organisations.

MEMORANDUM

To   Tripta Kaur, Administration Assistant

From   Maggie Ong, Executive Secretary

Ref   MO/ST

Date   12 July 2000

IN-HOUSE METHODS OF DISPLAY

Congratulations on recently joining the staff in the Chief Executive's office. Here are some general guidelines on the format of correspondence preferred in this office:

1   LAYOUT OF DOCUMENTS

    All documents should be displayed in the fully blocked style with open punctuation. Some specimen documents are attached which will guide you in these requirements.

2   SIGNATURE BLOCK (LETTERS)

    On outgoing letters the Chief Executive prefers his name and title in lower case with initial capitals, ie

    Peter Nunn
    Chief Executive

    On some personal letters, no salutation or complimentary close will be required, but Mr Nunn will usually give instructions about this.

3   NUMBERED ITEMS

    When items need to be numbered they should be typed alone with no full stop or bracket. Subsequent enumeration should be decimal, eg 3.1, 3.2, etc.

I hope that these guidelines will be useful but if you have any questions please speak to me.

Maggie Ong

Encs

✦ Structure

The four-point plan for structuring all business documents should also be applied to memos.

Subject heading

Give a brief indication of the topic.

✗ Confirmation of meeting

✓ Departmental meeting, 20 June

✗ Letter of complaint

✓ Viva camera model X345

Main body of memo

Introduction	Background information: + briefly give the reason for writing + refer to previous communication + who? what? where? when?
Details	Facts and figures: + logical sequence + separate into paragraphs – each one dealing with a separate aspect of the main theme
Response	An action statement: + action you want the reader to take + action you will take + deadline?
Close	A relevant one-liner

✦ Tone

As you most likely know your recipients fairly well, memos are usually written in an informal style. You should aim to put over your message as concisely as possible while still being courteous, clear, concise and correct. The major consideration in composing memos should be the status of the sender and recipient in the organisation, and of course the topic of the memo. Try to adopt a tone which reflects these factors.

TIPS

Avoid being abrupt or impolite (add 'Please ... ')

Avoid over-politeness (do not say 'I should be very grateful ... ')

Avoid unnecessary expressions (do not say 'Thank you' or 'Kind regards')

LET'S CHECK

Here are some memos. The first thing you need to do in each case is to compose a suitable heading. Then follow the instructions in your employer's note and write a suitable reply. Prepare each memo on a separate sheet of paper.

MEMORANDUM

To   Frank Gates, Branch Manager, Leeds

From   Derek Hall, Managing Director

Ref   DH/LPO

Date   20 March 2000

Choose an appropriate heading

I will be taking Mr James Hudson, our new Sales Director, to visit all our Northern branches during week commencing 27 April.

Our visit to your branch will be on Monday 27 April and we expect to arrive at 1000.

Please arrange for a brief tour to be conducted in the morning followed by a meeting with you. After lunch Mr Hudson would like to meet all the Sales staff.

Please confirm the above arrangements as soon as possible.

Derek

Please reply –
everything's OK
for their visit
– I'll look forward
to mtg JH
FG

→

M E M O R A N D U M

To   Ian Henley, Financial Director

From   Michelle Long, Credit Manageress

Ref   ML/SP

Date   14 July 2000

Choose an appropriate heading ——————

Carter & Co have an overdue account with us in the sum of £25,430 despite 3 reminder letters over the past few weeks.

At this stage I would normally suggest that the matter should be put into the hands of our solicitor. However I know you are a personal friend of Carter's Managing Director and I wondered if you wish to write to him as a final attempt to obtain payment of this debt.

Full details are enclosed for your reference.

Please let me know your decision as soon as possible.

Michelle Long

Enc

> Reply - say I've written
> to Carter's MD today
> - enc. a copy of my
> letter. Tell Michelle
> I'll keep her informed
> of the outcome.
>
> IH

MEMORANDUM

To   All Teachers

From   Pauline Choo, Principal   *Sally Turner* ✓

Ref   PC/BOL

Date   2 November 2000

Choose an appropriate heading

I enclose a draft of a new Lecturer's Record Book which I wish to introduce from the new term in January.

This has been designed to allow space for the following records:

1   SECTION A - CLASSWORK

     Pages are provided for teachers to keep a record of the work covered in each lesson throughout the course.

2   SECTION B - ATTENDANCE

     A register of attendance is provided for individual teachers to keep attendance records for their own subjects. Use of the present class register can be discontinued.

Please let me have your comments on this record book together with any suggestions for amendments or further information pages.

The printer will be coming to finalise the proof on Thursday 15 November so your early reply will be appreciated.

P. Choo.

Enc

> *Excellent idea – shd be*
> *v. beneficial.*
> *2 additional suggestions:*
> *• In Section A, include small column down r-h side to note Homework issued.*
> *• Suggest extra pages to keep record of marks for class tests, HW, etc.*
> *ST*

WHAT'S WRONG? (1)

Study the reply to the following memo composed from the note shown.
Rewrite the memo more appropriately.

MEMORANDUM

To   Regional Sales Managers

From   K R Green, Sales Director

Ref   KRG/JKL

Date   4 June 2000

John Bird ✓
(Southern Region)

Choose an appropriate heading

There will be a meeting of all Regional Sales Managers in the Training Office at Bedford on Tuesday 26 June 2000 from 1000 to 1500.

The main subjects for discussion will be sales planning for the next half year and new promotion campaigns.

Please confirm your attendance and let me know if you have any further items which you would like to be included on the agenda.

Ken Green.

Co. cars for new reps

Please confirm that i'll be able to attend, + mention

WHAT'S WRONG WITH THE ANSWER?

MEMORANDUM

To Mr KR Green

From Regional Sales Manager

Ref KRG/CF

Date 10 June 2000

I confirm that I can attend the meeting.

I should be grateful if you would include on the agenda discussion of company cars for new reps.

Looking forward to meeting you.

WHAT'S WRONG? (2)

After reading the following assignment carefully, study the answer given. Discuss the errors in the answer shown and then rewrite the memo more appropriately.

You work with Mr Patrick Wayne, Managing Director of Wayne Machinery Pte Ltd, a large manufacturing company. Talking to you today, Mr Wayne says

'We need to send a memo to all Departmental Managers about the new car parking arrangements – they'll be in effect in two weeks' time. Tell them that unauthorised parking will create havoc – there are so many large lorries delivering raw materials and collecting goods from our factory. Make a special point to stress this. Attach a copy of the plan to the memo and say all staff must park in the areas indicated on the plan for staff parking. Managers should also pin a copy of the plan on their department's noticeboard.

All departmental managers will be issued with red permits within the next couple of days. They should be given to staff in their departments with cars. Staff should be instructed to display these permits on their cars at all times. Explain the procedure for visitors too – they should report to the security gate on arrival – they'll get green permits from security, and they'll direct them to the visitors' car park. Departmental managers should inform their staff to tell the gatehouse in advance when visitors are expected.'

Compose a suitable memo.

WHAT'S WRONG WITH THE ANSWER?

MEMORANDUM

To   Departmental Managers

From   Patrick Wayne

Date   24 June

TO INFORM ABOUT NEW CAR PARK

The new car parking arrangements will come into effect in 2 weeks' time. Your co-operation will be much appreciated in ensuring there is no unauthorised parking, as this will cause inconvenience.

A plan is attached for your information. I would be grateful if you would pin this on your notice board. Please inform all your staff that they should park in the areas indicates on the plan. Red permits will be issued to staff soon for display on their cars.

As for visitors, they will be given a permit when they report to the security gate.

Your co-operation is requested in ensuring that these new arrangements are a success.

Thank you and regards

✦ Assignments

1 You work for Ms Anna Vinsen, General Manager of Nolan Components, an electrical and electronic parts manufacturer based in Auckland, New Zealand. Carry out the instructions in this note from Ms Vinsen.

AA

There have been a couple of emergencies recently when we've had to contact employees' families. We don't have an up-to-date list of names and phone numbers (work and home). Please send round a memo to all staff in my name. Ask people to let the Personnel Department have emergency contact names and numbers in writing by next Wednesday. Stress information will be confidential. AV

(Pitman EFBC1)

2   You work for Mrs Ruth Fairless, Manager of the Bateman Hotel, Norland Road, Tenwick, Cumbria C49 8JY.

    (LCCIEB EFB2 style)

In two weeks' time (on 26/27 May) the hotel's electricity will be cut off from 0930 to 1130 and from 1430 to 1630 while repairs are made to the electrical wiring of the building. The staff in the hotel kitchen have been told about this and Mrs Fairless now wishes to tell Mr William Graham, the head of cleaning services. She gives you the following instructions:

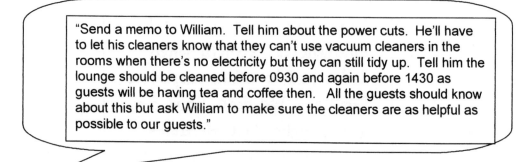

"Send a memo to William. Tell him about the power cuts. He'll have to let his cleaners know that they can't use vacuum cleaners in the rooms when there's no electricity but they can still tidy up. Tell him the lounge should be cleaned before 0930 and again before 1430 as guests will be having tea and coffee then. All the guests should know about this but ask William to make sure the cleaners are as helpful as possible to our guests."

Write the memo

3   You work for Mr David Fenworth, Manager of Fenworth Fashions.

    (LCCIEB EFB2 style)

One evening you receive a telephone call from Mr Fenworth. He is in Paris and he will have to stay there for another day. He asks you to leave a memo for the deputy manager, Miss Anne Gibb. Miss Gibb has gone home for the evening but will need to do some of the jobs which Mr Fenworth had planned to do the next day.

Your notes of Mr Fenworth's instructions are:

Tell Anne that Mr F. has to stay in Paris for another day.
0930 - she should see Mrs Moat, a customer - complaint about four expensive dresses (her letter is in Mr F's file)
1130 - make a presentation to Frank Clark who is retiring - make a speech - say how good he has been - worked for us 25 years
1400 - interview for sales assistant in hat dept. Anne will have to do this with Mrs Robson, hat dept. mgr.
Mr F. flying back tomorrow evening - will meet AG at 0900 next day.

Write the memo

4   You work for Mr Rashid Hassan, Office Manager of Langland
    Manufacturing plc, a company which makes household furniture.

    (LCCIEB EFB2 style)

One night you are watching a television programme about dangerous items in the home and you are interested in a feature about a type of chair called the 'Westmorland Settee' which seems to be made of material that could catch fire very easily. When you arrive at work the next day you find that Mr Hassan has also seen the programme. There is a problem because a chair the company sells - the 'Northumberland Settee' - has a similar name to the dangerous one and looks very much like it.

Mr Hassan asks you to send a memo to all sales staff. You made the following notes:

> *Customers could be confused. All sales staff must speak to any customer who is seen looking at chairs - tell them that all furniture we sell has passed all its safety checks and is not dangerous in any way. If anyone mentions the chair that was on television, tell them that the shop does not sell this type of chair. It is important that all customers are told that all the furniture sold by Langland Manufacturing is very safe.*

Write the memo.

Reports

By the end of this unit you should be able to:

- explain the purpose of reports

- describe some routine reports which may be written in business

- explain the differences between formal and informal reports

- describe the different formats for presenting reports

- discuss the writing skills needed for compiling reports

- identify and correct inappropriate language used in reports

- compose a suitable covering memo for a free-standing report

- compose reports according to given instructions.

✦ Types of report

Many reports are written in business. They are a very important method of gaining and giving information. Although many reports are presented orally, for example at a meeting, reports are usually presented in writing.

Examples of some reports submitted in business are:

Routine reports

- ✦ representatives' reports on sales visits
- ✦ managers' reports on the work of their departments
- ✦ equipment and maintenance report
- ✦ progress report
- ✦ safety report
- ✦ accident report.

Special reports

- ✦ reports written in response to requests for specific information
- ✦ reports made on a special topic after research and investigation
- ✦ report regarding a change of policy
- ✦ market research report.

The ultimate purpose of any report is to provide the foundation for decisions to be made and action taken.

Some reports consist of no more than a simple statement recording an event, a visit or some circumstances with a note of action taken. Other reports include detailed explanations of facts, conclusions, and perhaps recommendations for future action.

More detailed reports demand research which may involve interviews, visits, questionnaires, investigations. The information may be presented in tabular or graphic form and the writer would need to produce clear conclusions and recommendations.

TIP

Take a look at Unit 18 which discusses the techniques for designing questionnaires which may be used for gathering information for the purpose of compiling a report.

Whatever their purpose and length, all reports require the following special writing skills:

+ the ability to record facts clearly and objectively
+ the ability to interpret information and make conclusions
+ the ability to present suggestions on ways in which a situation may be improved.

THINK

What reports are submitted regularly in your organisation?

Is a standard form used for the reports? Perhaps you can bring in some copies for your colleagues to look at.

✦ Formal reports

Formal reports are usually written by a committee or group of people after fairly detailed investigation or research. They are often presented under the following prescribed series of headings:

Headings

There should be two headings to a report: the name of the company; the report heading (Report on ...)

Terms of reference

This section should state exactly why the report is being written. Why are you writing the report? What was requested? Who requested it? When were you asked to do it? A useful pattern for this section is:

To report on ... (subject) ... as requested by ... (name and title) on ... (date) ...

Procedure

Give a brief description of the methods used to collect the information. Perhaps interviews were held, visits made, questionnaires issued? Use numbered points if appropriate.

Findings

This will be the longest section of the report. Go through the procedure point by point and use numbers and sub-headings for this section. Under each heading state what information was gathered at each stage.

Conclusions

No new facts must be introduced in this section. You must look at the findings and state the logical implications of them. What can you infer or conclude from the findings?

Recommendations (if requested)

Again no new facts must be introduced here. On the basis of information presented in Findings and Conclusions, make some suggestions for action. Remember that the writer of a report cannot make decisions – he or she can only suggest what action should be taken.

Closing section

A report should be signed and there should be a name and title shown at the foot, plus the date the report was written.

Example of a formal report

AURORA HOLDINGS

**REPORT ON COMPLAINTS ABOUT POOR SERVICE
AND FOOD PROVIDED IN THE STAFF RESTAURANT**

TERMS OF REFERENCE

To investigate complaints about poor service and food provided in the staff restaurant and
to make recommendations, as requested by Mr Michael Lee, Administration Director, on
14 April 2000.

PROCEDURE

1   An interview was held with Mrs Alice Newton, Restaurant Manageress, on 15 April.

2   Interviews were held with a cross-section of staff (48) who used the restaurant
     between 15 and 20 April.

FINDINGS

1   INTERVIEW WITH RESTAURANT MANAGERESS

     1.1   STAFFING

            Mrs Newton has 3 full-time assistants. The youngest, Miss Lily Ng, attends
            day-release classes at Southpoint College on Monday, Wednesday and Friday
            each week. She works 1400–1700 on those days.

     1.2   EQUIPMENT

            A schedule of current equipment and their year of purchase is attached.
            No problems were reported. However Mrs Newton said that additional
            equipment would be useful:

            1 microwave oven
            1 slow cooker
            1 rice cooker

2   INTERVIEWS WITH STAFF

     20 staff from the 1200–1300 lunch sitting were interviewed, and 28 from the 1300–1400
     sitting.

     2.1   CHOICE

            The food available is shown on the attached schedule. 60% of the staff
            interviewed said they would prefer some cold meals to be provided. They said
            they may make alternative lunch arrangements if the variety did not improve.

Include the page number at the top left margin

2.2   QUEUEING

70% of staff took lunch from 1200 to 1300 hours as opposed to 30% from 1300 to 1400. This resulted in large queues forming at the first lunch sitting.

What are the logical implications from the 'Findings'?

CONCLUSIONS

1   There are insufficient assistants to cope with the preparation of food in the morning and with the popular first lunch sitting.

2   The present equipment is insufficient.

3   The selection of meals is not wide enough to cater for staff requirements.

4   The ratio of staff to each sitting is not balanced.

What action do you suggest should be taken, based on Findings and Conclusions?

RECOMMENDATIONS

1   A new assistant should be recruited to work 0900-1400 hours on Monday, Wednesday and Friday.

2   Mrs Newton should be asked to devise some new dishes which also include cold choices.

3   Mrs Newton should be asked to look into prices and availability of the new equipment required.

4   The number of staff attending each sitting should be reviewed so that a more even balance can be achieved.

Leave a space for the writer to sign

Name and title of writer

TAN LAY HONG (Miss)
Business Administration Officer

ML/tlh

Reference and date

24 April 2000

TIP

Reports should be objective, impersonal and factual. Write in full sentences using third person and reported speech. Do not use I/We/You.

Other formats for formal reports

It is sometimes felt that the format discussed above is suitable only for lengthy reports which stretch to many pages. Many writers are often uncomfortable with writing reports using this five-part structured format. The decision on how to present a report very often depends on the purpose of the report and the nature of the information it contains, also the preference of the writer. Look at these examples:

1 You are asked to discuss the arguments for and against a certain matter and make some recommendations:

- Introduction
- Advantages
- Disadvantages
- Conclusions
- Recommendations

2 You are asked to analyse some comment forms received from clients at a large hotel and make some recommendations

- Introduction
- Standard of service
- Facilities
- Eating places
- Conclusions
- Recommendations

The system of using a different structure and composing your own headings specific to the subject matter is illustrated here:

Company's name
Report title
Introduction (who? what? why?)
List steps taken to gather information

Findings
- use sub-headings to classify the information logically
- use enumeration consistently
- remember to use reported/ impersonal speech

Conclusions
- state the logical implication of the findings

Recommendations
- if requested, recommend action

name/title/reference/date

✦ Covering memo

Whenever a free-standing report is issued, don't just issue the report on its own or leave it on someone's desk. It is courteous to attach a brief covering memo which explains it. Here is an example of a short covering memo.

MEMORANDUM

To   Michael Lee, Administration Director

From   Tan Lay Hong, Business Administration Officer

Ref   ML/TLH

Date   24 April 2000

**REPORT ON COMPLAINTS ABOUT POOR SERVICE
AND FOOD PROVIDED IN THE STAFF RESTAURANT**

Further to your recent instructions I have completed my investigations into this matter. My report is attached.

If you have any queries please let me know.

Tan Lay Hong

Enc

✦ Informal reports

An informal report may be presented in the previously discussed format (with your own composed headings) or as a memorandum. Here is a short memorandum report.

Names/titles of sender/recipient

Date report was written

Heading – specific and clear

Introduction
- **In a memo first person can be used here**
- **Mention date report was requested**
- **State steps taken to gather the information**

Findings
- **Use sub-headings and numbered points for clarity**
- **State results of your investigations**
- **Use past tense, reported speech**

Conclusions
- **State the logical implications of the findings**

Recommendations
- **If requested, suggest action**

Final paragraph goes back to first person with suitable close

MEMORANDUM

To   John McIver, Office Manager

From   Ian Fisher, Administrative Assistant

Ref   JM/IF

Date   5 August 2000

REPORT ON POOR TIME-KEEPING OF GENERAL OFFICE STAFF

Further to our meeting on 20 June I have investigated the complaints about time-keeping of staff in the general office. An interview was held with each of the 12 employees concerned. Their times of arrival over a 2-week period were noted.

1   PRIVATE TRANSPORT

Four members of staff travel to work by car. These employees were usually punctual and no problems were noted.

2   PUBLIC TRANSPORT

2.1   Eight members of staff travel to work on public transport, using the A25 bus from the town centre. These staff were often up to 15 minutes late, arriving at work around 0915.

2.2   The A25 bus should stop outside the office at 0855 but it was quite erratic in this respect. Its arrival varied from 0900 to 0910. The previous A25 bus from town arrived outside the office between 0830 and 0840.

3   CONCLUSIONS

The staff relying on public transport cannot be blamed for the late arrival of the A25 bus from town. They also cannot be expected to arrive 30 minutes early each day to avoid being a few minutes late for work. However changes in the office routine could help the problem.

4   RECOMMENDATIONS

The staff who use public transport should be given the option of starting work at 0845 and finishing 15 minutes earlier than usual.

I hope you find this report satisfactory. If you have any questions please let me know.

Ian Fisher

TIP

Again note that the central section of the report uses reported speech and third person. The first and final paragraph use 'I' and 'My' as this is appropriate in a memo report.

Wording in reports

These expressions are not suitable for including in a report. The language may be inappropriate, details may be missing or they may be vague. Express the statements in appropriate, businesslike report language. The first one has been done for you:

1 Rachel Jones is the best person for the job.

   Rachel Jones is considered the most suitable applicant for the post of beauty salon manager.

2 Most staff are negative about the proposal but some would like to try it for a while.

   _____
   _____
   _____

3 The planning department said we should have no problem in getting permission for this new project.

   _____
   _____
   _____

4 Bob saw no reason why we shouldn't use some of the club funds to purchase new equipment.

   _____
   _____
   _____

5 We could take advantage of Aurora's special offer on office furniture.

   _____
   _____

Checklist for compiling reports

1 *State the facts*
Reports set forward a series of facts obtained through study or investigation. Someone may be required to make a decision based on the information provided. Reports should be complete with nothing of relevance omitted and nothing irrelevant included.

2 *Be objective*
Keep your own opinions and preferences out of the report, unless they have been requested. Instead, you must act like a camera, impartially recording only what it sees.

3 *Be logical*
Classify the findings under headings and sub-headings, using numbered points. How you classify the material will depend on your brief and the subject matter.

4 *Be consistent*
   Make sure all sentences in a series consistently follow the same grammatical pattern. Similarly, make sure that you use the same spacing throughout the report and that the headings and sub-headings are presented consistently. Attention to these points will make your report clear and will give a good impression.

5 *Be concise*
   Avoid long explanations and keep to the point. Check that all the information is accurate and all the reasoning valid.

6 *Be clear*
   Use a simple, easy to read style and presentation which will help the reader to understand the content easily.

TIP

Remember that a report should be understandable, without the need to ask further questions, by someone with no specialised knowledge of the subject.

LET'S CHECK

Rearrange a report
Here are the terms of reference and procedure for a report, together with cut-up sections of the rest of the report. Rewrite the report correctly for your files. You will need to compose appropriate headings, sub-headings and numbering. Sign the report as if you have written it, and decide on a suitable title. Don't forget to include an appropriate reference and date at the foot.

Terms of reference
To report on the unrest amongst factory workers and make recommendations, as requested by Mr Richard Fish, Works Manager, on 21 April 200-.

Procedure
1 The three supervisors were interviewed.
2 A meeting was held with all (25) factory workers to gather details of grievances.
3 10 factory workers, selected at random, were interviewed personally.

a) The human resource manager should hold a meeting of all factory staff and explain the findings of this report.

b) Safety regulations were being ignored by some members of staff. Protective guards had been removed from many machines.

c) A table showing rates of pay at this company and at other companies is attached.

→

d) Rules laid down in the company handbook were being contravened, with some workers leaving machines dirty after use.

e) The company's rates of pay compare favourably with those paid to apprentices at other companies in this area. Grievances might stop if our staff were made aware of this.

f) Supervisors reported that many staff were generally uncooperative and not working to their usual standards.

g) Supervisors should be reminded of the importance of ensuring that all staff comply with the company's rules and safety regulations.

h) A widespread unrest and resentment was noted in view of what is considered to be low rates of pay.

i) Removal of safety guards from machines is an offence against the Factories Act.

j) A training scheme should be compiled which will ensure balanced experience in all areas of the factory as well as adequate supervision.

k Supervisors are not enforcing compliance with rules laid down in the company handbook.

WHAT'S WRONG? (1)

Read the following assignment and then study the answer given. Decide what is wrong with it before reading the comments provided.

You work at the head office of a large group which has several branches in your area. Eighty per cent of employees from head office and branches are members of the group's sports and social club. Various social activities are arranged, including fortnightly get-togethers for younger employees which have proved very popular. Your chairman has asked you to look into whether it would be viable to buy a hi-fi system so that discos could be organised. Prepare your report, making suitable recommendations.

WHAT'S WRONG WITH THE ANSWER?

MEMORANDUM

To   Chairman   From   Sharon Tan

Referring to our conversation last week. I can now give details about the question of purchasing a music system for the sports and social club.

1   Questionaire issued to members.
All questionaires returned said it would be a good idea to have regular discos.Rock and contemporary music was preferred rather than any other music types.

2   Interviewed treasurer re financial situation.
He saw no reason why some money shouldn't be spent on new equipment.

3   I visited several department stores re cost of equipments.

The best equipment was Supersound. The most suitable being:

Sony – $3, 000
Technics – $2, 750

4   Although it would prove very popular to hold regular discos, but members felt they should be alternated – one fortnight a disco, the next fortnight a quiz night or other event.

5   I recommend the following:

a) The Sony music system should be purchased, and with Supersound's special sale now it's obviously the best deal. The Technics system referred to above does not have a CD, whereas the Sony systemon special offer comprises CD as well as record deck, not to mention cassette deck, radio andspeakers.

b) We could also take advantage of Supersound's special offer where we could buy 10 cassettes and 50 singles at half price.

c) Howard Chew, a long standing member, should be offered the job of DJ, as he has previous experience and has expressed an interest.

If you need any more information please let me know.

WHAT'S WRONG? (2)

Discuss the faults in the answer to the following question, and then rewrite the report correctly.

> You are a member of Aurora Music Society, a large amateur group which gives several public concerts each year usually in a local church hall or school. The Music Society used to enjoy strong support from local people but during the last 2 years the attendance figures for its six concerts have been:
>
> 400 (full house)   340   280   180   150
>
> It has been suggested that there could be several reasons why attendance figures are declining: the type of music performed may not appeal to popular taste; the quality of the music may have fallen; there may be insufficient rehearsal time; the arrangement whereby each member of the Music Society tries to sell tickets may not be working well; publicity could be at fault; seat prices may be too high.
>
> The Chairman of the Society, Mr Andrew Webber-Floyd, has asked you to look into the problem carefully. Prepare a formal report with your recommendations for action. You may invent any other minor details as required.

WHAT'S WRONG WITH THE ANSWER?

MEMORANDUM

To   Mr Andrew Webber-Floyd

From   Timothy Reece

Subject   PUBLIC CONCERTS

Further to your request for me to look into the above-captioned. I have investigated the declining attendance figures by issuing a questionaire to all people attending church last Sunday. Personal calls were also made by me to private houses in the area. The band members were also interviewed.

1   QUESTIONAIRES

        Concerts have been held on unpopular evenings, and the majority of people felt the timing was not suitable.

        The public did not really like the music performed.

        Everyone complained about seat prices.

        No-one had seen any advertising of our concerts. Alot of people were not aware that we held concerts and would have liked to attend.

2   DISCUSSIONS WITH BAND

        Most members were not fond of the type of music they were playing.

        Some members cannot attend rehearsals on the designated evening, as they are members of a local sports club which they attend on the same evening.

        Members don't have enough spare time to visit private houses personally to sell tickets.

3   CONCLUSIONS

        The day and time of the concerts are not suitable.
        The music performed is not popular.
        Seat prices are too high and publicity is no good.
        The rehearsal nights need changing.

4   RECOMMENDATIONS

        4.1   All future concerts will be held on Saturday nights, which the public prefer. They will start at 8.00 pm instead of at 7 pm as at present.

        4.2   Posters will be placed in music shop windows to advertise the concerts.

        4.3   Rehearsals should be held on a different night.

        4.4   Popular music should be incorporated in future concerts to satisfy both the public and the band.

✦ Assignments

1   You work for Aurora Holdings plc, a large manufacturing company. In a recent board meeting it was decided to review the company's staff benefits. At present they include only a company pension scheme and a subsidised canteen.

The human resource director asks you to research the additional benefits which could be introduced. You should also recommend three benefits which you consider would be most welcomed by all members of staff.

You have made notes about some possible benefits:

Private life assurance scheme – private hospital and medical insurance – loans at low interest rate – sports and social facilities – luncheon vouchers for local shops – arrangements for discounts at local shops – payment of fees to attend courses.

Compile your report.

2   You work for Mrs Ruth Fairless, Manager of the Bateman Hotel, Norland Road, Tenwick, Cumbria C49 8JY.

(LCCIEB EFB2 style)

When guests 'sign out' before they leave they are able to make any comments on their feelings about the hotel and the service they have received. You have to write a report each month for Mrs Fairless on the points raised. These are the comments made by guests last month:

"The service in the restaurant was not very good. We often had to wait half an hour between courses."
"EVERYTHING WAS LOVELY - IT IS A WELL RUN HOTEL."
"There aren't enough satellite channels on the TV -•no movie channels."
"Very helpful staff - very polite."
"We had a splendid holiday - but the service in the restaurant could be quicker."
"The best hotel in Cumbria. Very good value."
"It was three days before the broken light in my room was repaired."
"Lovely food - but poor service at meal times. Very slow."
"The gardens are beautiful."
"We will definitely come back. The staff are very friendly."

Write the report

3   You work for Mr David Fenworth, Fenworth Fashions, 117 High Street West, Hale, Cheshire WA5 7TH.

(LCCIEB EFB2 style)

Mr Fenworth tells you that he is thinking of allowing the staff in the shop to wear their own clothing instead of the staff uniform that everyone has to wear. Before he makes any decisions he wants to hear the opinions of staff and he has asked you to speak to them and write a report for him.

These are the notes you made when you spoke to the staff:

Why staff like the uniform

everyone looks the same - no-one seems to be better than anyone else - cheaper - the shop supplies the uniform - staff don't have to buy clothes - customers can easily recognise staff in the shop

Why staff don't like the uniform

not very fashionable - makes you look old
the same for all seasons - too hot in summer
wearing a uniform is like being at school
doesn't suit everyone - better to choose our own clothes

NB: More people against uniform than in favour of it.

Write the report

4   You work at for Mr Rashid Hassan, Office Manager of Langland
    Manufacturing plc, Freeman Industrial Estate, Pitt Lane, Portsmouth,
    Hampshire PO13 7JJ. The company makes household furniture.

    (LCCIEB EFB2 style)

The management of Langland Manufacturing know that a number of its staff are keen
footballers. Some of these have recently been to see the directors to ask if the company
would support them if they formed a football team to play in the local league on Sundays.
The directors have asked Mr Hassan to investigate this and he has asked you to produce a
report with recommendations which the directors can consider. You have spoken to some of
the staff and made these notes:

*Lots of support for football team - they are asking us to buy the football strips for the team - they
would have our name on the shirts and our company logo - good advertising.*

*Need not cost very much - one set of strips each season - we could probably get a better rate from a
supplier.*

*The company would not have to run the team - committee would select the team and organise the
games - good publicity if team is successful.*

Some problems - what if other sports teams want support?
*Can we support them all? Football team is men only - unfair to women - what happens if staff
are injured and can't come to work?*
*Good idea to try it for one season - suggest we should support one team for one year and review it
after a year.*

Write the report with your recommendations

UNIT 10

Meetings documentation

By the end of this unit you should be able to:

❏ explain the purpose of meetings

❏ describe the different types of meetings which take place in business

❏ state the documents which are used in the meetings process

❏ discuss the basic presentation requirements of each document

❏ compose agenda, chairman's agenda and minutes.

✦ Meetings in business

Many meetings take place in business and an effective meeting is an efficient tool in the communication process. Meetings enable face-to-face contact of a number of people at the same time. They provide a useful opportunity for sharing information, making suggestions and proposals, taking decisions and obtaining instant feedback. Active participation of all members of the meeting is usually encouraged.

Meetings are used for a variety of purposes:

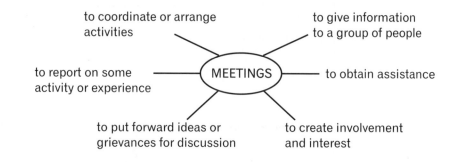

THINK

What meetings are held in your organisation? Who attends these meetings? Discuss the purpose of these meetings.

✦ Types of meeting

Formal meetings

The rules of conduct of formal meetings are laid down in a company's Articles of Association and/or Constitution or Standing Orders. With such meetings a quorum must be present, i.e. the minimum number of people who should be present in order to validate the meeting. A formal record of these meetings must be kept, usually by the company secretary.

Annual General Meeting (AGM)

AGMs are held once a year to assess the trading of the organisation over the year. All shareholders are invited to attend the AGM but they must be given 21 days' notice.

```
GLOBAL ENGINEERING PLC

ANNUAL GENERAL MEETING

NOTICE IS HEREBY GIVEN that the Tenth Annual General
Meeting of the Company will be held in the Hillview
Hall, Hillview Place, Bedford, on Wednesday 25 August 19--
at 1100 hours


A G E N D A

1  To receive and consider the Directors' Report, Accounts
   and Balance Sheet for the year ended 31 July 19--.

2  To confirm the Preference Dividend paid in May 19--
   and the Ordinary Interim Dividend paid in June 19--.

3  To declare an Ordinary Final Dividend.

4  To propose that the name of Mr D Williams be added to
   the list of authorised signatories to be attached to
   the Bank Mandates for City Bank plc, Grange Road,
   London.

5  To transact any other business that may be brought
   before an Ordinary General Meeting.




G Hope

G HOPE
Secretary

4 July 19--

JR/GH
```

Statutory meetings

Statutory meetings are called so that the directors and shareholders can communicate and consider special reports. Companies are required by law to hold these statutory meetings.

Board meetings

Board meetings are held as often as individual organisations require. They are attended by all directors and chaired by the chairman of the board.

Informal meetings

Informal meetings are not restricted by the same rules and regulations as formal meetings. Such meetings may take the form of brainstorming or discussion sessions where strict agendas may not be necessary and minutes may not be kept. However, it is usually considered good business practice for an agenda to be issued to all members prior to the meeting so that they can prepare adequately in order to make a valuable contribution.

Management meetings

These meetings are attended by a group of managers who may need to discuss a specific matter, report on progress or receive progress reports. For example the marketing manager, sales manager, production manager and research and development manager may meet to discuss the launch of a new product being launched soon.

Departmental meetings

These meetings are called by the head of department or manager of a certain section. All staff will be invited to attend so that information can be passed on or reports received from some members of staff regarding a specific project.

Working parties

Working parties may be set up to work together on a specific project or problem. At meetings, progress reports will be given and decisions for further action taken.

THINK

Discuss different situations which may require working parties to be set up. Who would attend such meetings? What matters may be discussed?

✦ Notice and agenda

The success of a meeting depends on a variety of essential preparations. An important one is to ensure that all the documentation is dealt with efficiently. The notice and agenda are usually combined in one document. The portion at the top is known as the notice. This gives details of the type, place, day, date and time of the meeting.

The agenda is the middle portion of the document. This is the list of topics to be discussed at the meeting. On the example shown here note that the first three and final two items are known as *ordinary business*. These are items which will be included on every meeting agenda. After the opening items of ordinary business there will be a list of *special business* – these are special matters to be discussed at this meeting only.

Company name and committee name	**AURORA HOLDINGS plc** **SOCIAL CLUB**
Notice states place, day, date and time of meeting	A meeting of the Sports and Social Club will be held in the Conference Suite A on Friday 14 May 2000 at 1800
Use the heading AGENDA	A G E N D A
These three items of ordinary business are included on every agenda (some committees will also include 'Correspondence')	1 Apologies for absence 2 Minutes of last meeting 3 Matters arising
	4 Chairman's Report
Special business is listed separately (any official reports come first)	5 Football Results and Matches (Frank Jones) 6 New Keep-Fit Classes (Carol Chen) 7 Purchase of Tennis Equipment (Aileen Forster) 8 Annual Dinner and Dance
Finish all agendas with these final two items of ordinary business	9 Any other business 10 Date of next meeting
Don't forget reference and date	CE/ST 7 May 2000

LET'S CHECK

1   You work with Jackie Macey, Personnel Manager of Aurora Holdings plc. Mrs Macey also acts as Secretary of the company's Social Committee. Deal with the following note which you found in your in-tray this morning:

> I need to arrange a mtg of the Social Committee – Thursday after next. The conference rm shd be free by 7pm.
>
> Mark Jones wants to talk about the Trivial Pursuits Quiz held recently & Jeremy Price wants to discuss a sponsored swim. We'd better also see how the monthly Musical Evenings are going – I'll deal with that.
>
> Please prepare the notice & agenda.
>
> Thanks
>
> *Jackie*
>
> PS   Just saw the Chairman – he has a report to make this time too.

2   You work with Joe Leighton, Safety Director of Aurora Holdings plc. Mr Leighton is also Chairman of the Safety Committee which meets monthly. Deal with the following note and attached memos which you found in your in-tray this morning:

MEMORANDUM

To   Candice

From   JL

Date   24 June

Please prepare the notice &
agenda for the next mtg of
the Safety Committee. Include
the usual items plus there
are the items mentioned in
the attached docs.

Date? Some time towards the
end of next wk – late afternoon –

       Thanks

         JL

MEMORANDUM

To   Joe Leighton, Safety Director

From   Christopher Lim, Company Secretary

Ref   CL/mlw

Date   12 June 2000

SAFETY

It is well over 6 months since our last fire drill was held.

In line with Company policy please arrange for this issue to be discussed at the next meeting of the Safety Committee so that arrangements can be made.

Chris.

```
MEMORANDUM

To       Joe Leighton, Safety Director

From     Terry Aspel, Production Director

Ref      TA/FR

Date     20 June 2000


ADAM WARD'S INDUSTRIAL INJURY - 7 MAY

The delay in reporting this accident has been the cause of a large claim for compensation
against the Company.

It is important that measures are taken to improve our present safety procedures within the
Company.

Please arrange for this item to be discussed at the next Safety Committee meeting.

                Terry
```

WHAT'S WRONG?

Study the agenda written as a result of the following scenario. Rewrite the agenda correctly.

As secretary of the Students' Union Group you have been asked by the Chairman to prepare the agenda for the next meeting. In conversation with the Chairman, she said

'The meeting is next Friday – usual time and place. This time we need to have a discussion on lunch-time queues in the refectory – they're becoming very frustrating. There's also the matter of student lockers to be resolved. The provision is quite inadequate, so we need some more urgently. John should be able to give us his report on the recent disco held for charity. Wasn't it a great night? The Students' Common Room is desperately in need of decorating so we must discuss what should be done and nominate someone to take charge. Apart from the usual other items that's about all.'

Student's Action Committee

Meeting to be held Friday 24 August, 11.30 am, Common Room.

1   Apologise

2   Minutes

3   Discussion on lunch-time queues - refectory

4   Student lockers

5   Report on recent disco held for charity

6   Student's common room

7   A.O.B.

Secretary

✦ Chairman's agenda

The Chairman has an important responsibility to manage the meeting once it is in progress. He or she must allow everyone equal opportunity to participate in discussions and control the discussion in an orderly way. In order for the Chairman to lead the meeting effectively, he or she may have a special Chairman's agenda which contains extra notes for the Chairman to use when introducing each item.

The Chairman's agenda follows the same basic format as the notice and agenda but the right-hand side is left blank. This is where the Chairman will make notes of important points discussed during the meeting. These notes should assist the Chairman when preparing the minutes.

Same main headings as the Agenda

Leave right side blank and use the heading **NOTES** Chairman will write notes in this section during the meeting

Mention any details which will help the **Chairman** to conduct the meeting

Reference and date

AURORA HOLDINGS plc

SOCIAL CLUB

A meeting of the Sports and Social Club will be held in the Conference Suite A on Friday 14 May 2000 at 1800

AGENDA ——————————————— NOTES

1   APOLOGIES FOR ABSENCE   1

    None received

2   MINUTES OF LAST MEETING   2

    Circulated on 16 May. Point out error
    in 4.1 - £1,200 should read £12,000

3   MATTERS ARISING   3

4   CHAIRMAN'S REPORT   4

    Separate notes attached

5   FOOTBALL RESULTS AND MATCHES   5

    Frank Jones to report on 3 matches held
    during April. Also future match schedule.

6   NEW KEEP-FIT CLASSES   6

    Carol Chen to propose the introduction of
    Keep Fit classes for staff.

7   PURCHASE OF TENNIS EQUIPMENT   7

    Aileen Forster to report on new tennis
    equipment needed for July tournament.

8   ANNUAL DINNER AND DANCE   8

    Discuss date and venue, ideas for
    programme and appoint person in charge.

9   ANY OTHER BUSINESS   9

10 DATE OF NEXT MEETING   10

    Suggest 24 June 2000

CE/ST
12 May 2000

LET'S CHECK

1   Prepare the Chairman's agenda for the meetings of the social committee and safety committee for which you prepared the notice and agenda earlier in this unit. Make up any necessary details.

2   You work with the managing director of a medium-sized sports equipment manufacturing company. Your employer will shortly be going overseas on a business trip, returning on 14 October. He asks you to make all the preparations for a board meeting to be held on 16 October. The main items for discussion will be next year's budget, salary increases for regional managers and sponsorship.

  a)   Write the memo you would send to the board members, giving them the necessary details and asking them to submit to you any additional items which they wish to be included on the agenda.

  b)   Prepare the agenda and Chairman's agenda for the meeting.

WHAT'S WRONG?

Study the Chairman's agenda written as a result of this assignment. Then rewrite it correctly.

You are secretary to Douglas Michaels, Managing Director of Seagrave Manufacturing Co Ltd. Mr Michaels chairs the management committee meetings which are held during the first week of each month. In a meeting with you this morning he said to you:

'There's a management committee meeting next Thursday so we need to prepare the documents. I must remember the error in item 6 – the figure for microwave ovens should be 42% not 24% as typed. What else is there? Oh yes, Mrs Wright spoke to me yesterday. She's had a request from the Head of Secretarial Studies at Southern Point Technical College asking if we can provide help with work experience placements for their students. John also mentioned that he wants to outline some problems that he's experiencing with the training schemes, so you'd better add that on the agenda too. There are also the problems in Sales to be discussed – Ken will have to announce the Northern Sales Manager's resignation effective at the end of next month – then we must discuss a replacement and decide whether to promote internally or advertise the post. I think that's all. Oh, I almost forgot ... Mike Smith (Production Manager) retires next month after 20 years. We must arrange a presentation for him. That's all. Thanks.'

WHAT'S WRONG WITH THE ANSWER?

MANAGEMENT COMMITTEE

CHAIRMANS AGENDA

NOTES

1 Apologise for absence	1.
2 Minutes of last meeting	2.
3 Matters arising	
Correct error in item 6 - microwave ovens should be 42%.	3.
4 Southern Point Technical College To discuss providing help with work experience placements.	4.
5 Problems with training schemes. John to outline problems.	5.
6 Sales Manager's resignation Announcement of Ken's resignation at end of next month. To discuss recruitment of replacement	6.
7 Mike Smith retires 20 years in company To arrange presentation	7.
8 ANY OTHER BUSINESS	8.
9 DATE OF NEXT MEETING	9.

....

....

✦ Minutes of meeting

An accurate written record of meetings is essential not only for all those who attended the meeting but also for those who were unable to attend.

Verbatim minutes

These are used primarily in court reporting where everything needs to be recorded word for word.

Minutes of resolution

Only the main conclusions which are reached at the meeting are recorded, not a note of the discussions which took place. These are usually used for minutes of AGMs and other statutory meetings. It is important to note the exact wording of any resolutions passed:

---

4   PURCHASE OF PHOTOCOPIER

The Company Secretary submitted a report from the Administration Manager containing full details of the trial of the AEZ Photocopier.

IT WAS RESOLVED THAT the AEZ Photocopier be purchased at a cost of £8,000.

Minutes of narration

These minutes will be a concise summary of all the discussions which took place, reports received, actions to be taken and decisions made.

---

4   PURCHASE OF PHOTOCOPIER

The Company Secretary submitted a report from the Administration Manager containing full details of the trial of the AEZ Photocopier. This machine had been used for a period of 4 weeks in the Printing Room. The machine's many benefits were pointed out, including reduction/enlarging facilities and collating. After discussion it was agreed that such a machine would be extremely valuable to the Company.

The Company Secretary was asked to make the necessary arrangements for the photocopier to be purchased at the quoted price of £8,000.

Layout and wording of minutes

Minutes may be displayed in a variety of formats depending on the preference of your employer and organisation. The layout shown in the example is a popular method.

As they are a record of what has taken place, minutes should be written in past tense using third person and reported speech. These minutes have been prepared from the previously shown agenda and Chairman's agenda.

THINK

Go through these minutes and study the wording carefully. Highlight the wording which is written in past tense, reported speech, e.g. '... were received' and 'The Chairman asked ...'.

AURORA HOLDINGS plc

**MINUTES OF A MEETING OF THE SPORTS & SOCIAL CLUB
HELD IN CONFERENCE SUITE A ON FRIDAY 14 MAY 2000 AT 1800**

PRESENT	Mr Chris Evans (Chairman)	Mr Frank Jones
	Miss Carol Chen	Miss Maxine Street
	Miss Aileen Forster	Mrs Wendy Williams

ACTION

1   APOLOGIES FOR ABSENCE

No apologies were received.

2   MINUTES OF LAST MEETING

The Chairman asked members to correct an error in item 3.1 where the figure £1,200 should read £12,000. After this correction the minutes were approved and signed by the Chairman as a correct record.

3   MATTERS ARISING

There were no matters arising.

4   CHAIRMAN'S REPORT

The Chairman pointed out that membership had fallen by 20% over the last 6 months. It was felt that this was due largely to lack of publicity during the present year, and also because new employees were not sure how to join. Various decisions were reached:

4.1   CIRCULAR TO STAFF

A letter would be sent to all employees who were not members of the Club outlining its aims and activities. A tear-off slip would be included for interested employees to indicate their areas of interest.   CE

4.2   SOCIAL EVENING

A social evening with refreshments would be organised specifically for non-members. Carol Chen agreed to make arrangements.   CC

5   FOOTBALL RESULTS AND MATCHES

5.1   Frank Jones reported on the results of the 3 football matches during April:

Team A v Victory Enterprises	12 April	Won 4-3
Team B v Pentagon Supplies	19 April	Lost 3-2
Team A v Ward Hi-Tech	26 April	Won 5-2

5.2 Future matches were scheduled to be:

| Team A v Team B | 18 May | 1500 | Home |
| Team A v Connolly Industries | 25 May | 1500 | Away |

6 NEW KEEP FIT CLASSES

Carol Chen proposed that Keep Fit classes should be held.
Sharon Warner from the Fun N Fitness Gym had agreed to conduct
such classes on the Company's premises every Wednesday evening
1800-1900.

A discussion was held on a suitable room for the classes, and it
was agreed that the Training Office would be suitable. Carol would
circulate a notice to all staff announcing the first Keep Fit class on
Wednesday 22 May.   CC

7 PURCHASE OF TENNIS EQUIPMENT

Aileen Forster reported that the in-house tennis tournament would
start on Monday 4 July. New nets and balls were needed and the
tennis courts needed repairing. It was agreed that Aileen should
make the necessary arrangements as soon as possible.   AF

8 ANNUAL DINNER AND DANCE

It was agreed that the Annual Dinner and Dance would be held on
Saturday 14 September. Wendy Williams agreed to take charge of
all the arrangements. She was asked to contact Aston Hall to make
preliminary enquiries about their facilities and to report back to the   WW
next meeting. Members were asked to consider ideas for the
programme for discussion at the next meeting.   Members

9 ANY OTHER BUSINESS

There was no other business.

10 DATE OF NEXT MEETING

It was agreed that the next meeting would be held in
Conference Suite A on Thursday 24 June 2000 at 1800.

Leave a space for Chairman to sign and date at the next meeting

.... (Chairman)

.... (Date)

CE/ST

16 May 2000

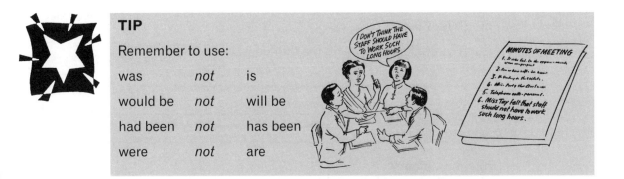

LET'S CHECK

1 When composing minutes past tense and reported speech must be used consistently. Here are some expressions which are often used in minutes. Can you add to this list with some suggestions of your own as to what could be used instead of '... said ...'?

asked   ....

reported   ....

proposed   ....

agreed   ....

2 The following are verbatim records of what was actually said at a meeting. Rewrite these as the record would show in the (narrative) minutes:

a) (The Chairman)

'Miss Jones, will you please arrange for quotations on the recarpeting of the sales office and report back next time.'

_____

_____

_____

b) (Mr Norton)

'I'd like to recommend the purchase of a photocopier for the Personnel Department.'

_____

_____

_____

→

c) (Miss Clark)

'The drinks machine on the third level is out of order.'

_____

_____

_____

d) (Mr Morgan)

'It's been brought to my attention that empty boxes are being left on the stairs next to reception. This is causing a safety hazard.'

_____

_____

_____

e) (Mrs Newman)

'All arrangements for Quiz Time next Saturday afternoon at 3 o'clock have been made. Four teams have been organised and the questions are being devised by Julie Lee.'

_____

_____

_____

f) (Chairman)

'Arrangements for Saturday morning lecturers are the responsibility of our committee, and I'd like to invite suggestions for speakers.'

_____

_____

_____

g) (Miss Graham)

'As you can see from these press cuttings, we've received a lot of publicity for our Open House in March.'

_____

_____

_____

WHAT'S WRONG?

Study the minutes written as a result of the notes made on this agenda by the Chairman, Mr Alan Hill. Discuss the errors and rewrite the minutes correctly:

AURORA HOLDINGS plc

A meeting of the Sports Club Committee will be held in Room 208 on
Monday 29 June 2000 at 1800

AGENDA

*Present — PAllen (Treasurer)
Green, Armitage, Parker
Mrs Reeves, Leighton*

1   Apologies for absence   *— James, Johnson*

2   Minutes of last meeting   *✓ OK*

3   Matters arising   *— None*

4   Treasurer's report   *— PA pleased w. bal in hand £395
— this will be chewed up by exp. bbq soon*

5   Hospital visiting (Derek Armitage)   *— took flowers recently
— letter of thanks rec'd (Northern General Hosp)*

6   Barbecue (Steven Green)   *— 9 Aug 8–11 pm — sub-committee appointed:
(Green, Johnson, Reeves, Parker) to work
out details + report back next time*

7   Squash tournament (Gary Parker)   *— final last Mon. Geoff Jones (Sales) won.
v. successful — sports highlight of yr.*

8   Any other business   *— Proposal for amendment to constitution
to be put on agenda next time*

9   Date of next meeting   *3 wks — same time — same place!*

AH/ST

16 June 2000

MINUTES OF MEETING

Sports Club Committee Meeting - Monday 29 June

Present

Mr Armitage
Mr Parker
Mr Hill
Mr Allen
Mr Green
Mrs Reeves

1   Minutes of last meeting

     The minutes were signed as a correct record.

2   Matters arising

     None

3   Treasurers Report (Mr Allen)

     The Treasure is pleased with the balance in hand. This will be chewed up by the
     expensive bbq which is coming up soon.

4   Hospital visiting

     Mr Armitage took flowers recently and a letter of thanks were received.

4   Barbecue

     The bbq will be held on 9 August at 8 to 11 pm. A sub-committee was appointed to
     report back to the next meeting. Sub-committee are Green, Johnson, Reeves, Parker.

6   Squash

     The final was held last Monday with Geoff Jones the winner. It was very successful,
     and Mr Parker said it was the sports highlight of the year.

7   AOB

     A proposal for amendment of the constitution was put. This had been placed on the
     agenda for the next meeting.

8   Date of next meeting

     The next meeting will be held in 3 weeks time in room 208.

Alan Hill (Mr)

✦ Assignments

1   You work with Mr Robert Branson, Director of Administration. Mr Branson chairs the Human Resource Policy Committee which is held at 1000 on the last Monday of each month in the Board Room. Other members of the committee are Michael Kramer, Marketing Manager, Masrita Hadi, Office Services Manager, Sharon Leng, Human Resource Manager and Mohammed Alaradi, Research and Development Manager.

Mr Branson asks you to draw up for him an Agenda as well as a Chairman's agenda for next month's meeting. During a discussion with Mr Branson you make the following notes:

Minutes of previous meeting – correct error in 2.1 – name should read Marsha Gold not Sharon Yap.

Two special items – Proposal for new promotion policy and Job Enrichment Schemes.

Present promotion policy = advertise on notice boards and in Aurora News, promote internally. Could be obstacle to progress.

Proposed new policy = advertise in local/national press (and Co. magazine) – need new people, new ideas, wider experience.

Job enrichment schemes – need to increase job satisfaction – ask for suggestions.

Prepare the Agenda for circulation to members and also the Chairman's agenda for Mr Branson to use at the meeting.

2   You work with Martin Lewis, Company Secretary of Aurora Holdings plc who is also Secretary of the company's Social Club. Mr Lewis has made some notes on the agenda of a recent meeting. Compile appropriate minutes.

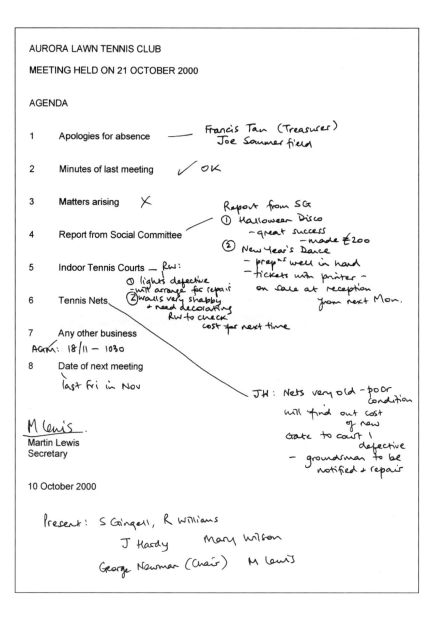

AURORA LAWN TENNIS CLUB

MEETING HELD ON 21 OCTOBER 2000

AGENDA

1   Apologies for absence   — *Francis Tan (Treasurer)*
                                 Joe Summerfield

2   Minutes of last meeting   ✓ *OK*

3   Matters arising   ✗

4   Report from Social Committee   *Report from SC*
                                      ① Halloween Disco
                                      — great success
                                      — made £200
                                      ② New Year's Dance
                                      — prep^ns well in hand
                                      — tickets with printer —

5   Indoor Tennis Courts — *RW:*   *on sale at reception*
     ① lights defective   *from next Mon.*
     — will arrange for repair
6   Tennis Nets   *② walls very shabby*
                    + need decorating
                    RW to check
                    cost for next time
7   Any other business
     AGM: 18/11 — 1030
8   Date of next meeting
     last Fri in Nov

                                      JH: Nets very old — poor
                                                condition
                                      will find out cost
                                                of new
                                      Gate to court 1
                                                defective
                                      — groundsman to be
                                                notified + repair

M Lewis.
Martin Lewis
Secretary

10 October 2000

Present: S Gingell, R Williams
          J Hardy   Mary Wilson
     George Newman (Chair)   M Lewis

---

3   The following dialogue is taken from a meeting of the Welfare Committee of Aurora Holdings plc which was held at 4 pm on Tuesday 21 October 2000 in the Chairman's office. Choosing speakers from your class, act out this meeting. Then use narrative style to prepare the minutes.

Mrs Taylor (Chairman): Well it's 4 o'clock and we all appear to be here so shall we get started? Anthony Long won't be joining us as he's attending a business conference this week. Do you all have the last meeting's minutes?

(agreement)

Are there any amendments or can I sign them as a correct record?

(Chairman signs)

Good, matters arising? Anything to report?

Mr Thomas: Yes, Georgia and I visited Reneé in hospital on the 16th to deliver our Committee's basket of flowers and our good wishes for a speedy recovery. She hopes to be back at work a week on Monday so she'll be with us again when we next meet.

Chairman: That's marvellous news. Right then, let's move on to item 4. John, you were going to talk about the restaurant I believe. Did you bring along the accounts for the half year ending 31 July?

Mr Cage: Yes, I have copies for everyone (distributes copies). As you will see, the accounts show that we made a profit of £1,300 over the first 6 months of the year. I'd like to suggest that we utilise some of this by buying a new coffee machine. The present one is rather old and frequently breaks down.

Chairman: I think we'd better obtain some estimates first before a decision can be made. Could you ask around please and we'll talk about it more next time?

(Mr Cage agrees)

Chairman: Right, we'll move on to Washroom Facilities now. I've received several complaints about the female toilets on the second floor. I've been to see what all the fuss is about and I agree that they do need upgrading.

Miss McBain: Yes, these are near my office. Apart from several locks being faulty there are chipped tiles, and the state of decoration is very poor.

Chairman: I'd like a volunteer to arrange for some local workmen to look at the washroom and give us an estimate on the cost of the repairs.

Miss McBain: I'll gladly do that. Something needs to be done quickly.

Chairman: Right, that's something else to continue with next time. Richard, you're next, I believe?

Mr Fish: Thank you. Well, as you know, as Training Officer I have a lot of contact with our young trainees. Many of them are attending Cliff College on evening courses which the Company sponsors. Examinations are coming up in December and these people don't have much time to study. I'd like to suggest that they be given two weeks' study leave prior to their exams.

Miss McBain: That's a valid point, Richard. Lesley in my department, bless her, she works very hard for us and I know she goes to college three evenings a week. It would kill me!

Chairman: I can sympathise, but I really don't think it's within our power as a committee to make such a decision. Can I suggest that you write a formal memo to the Board? They have a Board Meeting early in November I believe, so you should ask them to include this item on the agenda. By the time we meet again, we should have an answer from them.

Mr Fish: Yes, I think that will be best. I'll get a memo out tomorrow.

Chairman: Now, the final item. Christmas dinner and dance. Miss Sheppard, did you get some specimen menus from hotels?

Miss Sheppard: Yes, I have some samples for us to look at.

(distributes copies)

Mr Fish: This one looks brilliant – the Marina Hotel – quite reasonably priced too.

Mr Thomas: I agree, it seems far superior to the others.

Miss Sheppard: That's what I thought too. I suggest we should confirm with the Marina, if everyone agrees?

(agreement)

Chairman: Has a date been agreed yet?

Miss Sheppard: No, I suggest the last Saturday before Christmas, the 21st, if that's OK?

(agreement)

Chairman: Right then, Miss Sheppard, can we leave it to you to make all the necessary arrangements?

Miss Sheppard: Oh sure, I'll get in touch with the Marina to confirm with them, and I'll also put up a notice on the staff bulletin board. I hope it will be as successful as last year's.

Chairman: With everything left to you, Miss Sheppard, I'm sure it can't fail to be successful.

Right, moving on, is there anything else anyone wants to discuss? No? Right, then let's decide on a date for the next meeting ... 4 weeks' time as usual? Can I suggest the 20th November then? Same time? Good, OK then, thank you all for attending.

SECTION

5

PERSUASIVE COMMUNICATION

Many communications in business call for a persuasive approach. Circulars, sales letters, press releases, house magazines, advertisements, notices, leaflets and invitations – they all attempt to influence the reader in some way.

All these documents meet important needs within an organisation's communication system. They are generally easy to produce, effective methods of conveying information to different people.

Composition of persuasive documents is a demanding skill. It depends as much on marketing and sales skills as on language ability. In this section we will look at the specific writing requirements relating to each one of these persuasive communications.

Circulars and sales letters

By the end of this unit you should be able to:

❑ explain why circulars and sales letters may be used

❑ understand the techniques involved in writing such letters

❑ explain why tear-off slips are used

❑ design tear-off slips

❑ identify poor business writing and make appropriate corrections

❑ compose circulars and sales letters.

✦ Circular letters

A circular letter is one which is sent out to many people at the same time. The letter may be prepared once only and then duplicated. With modern technology, however, it is more likely that each letter could be personalised to look like an original. Circular letters may be sent for many reasons:

announce opening of a new office/branch

introduce new product lines

advertise special offers

inform staff of new policy matters

announce restructuring

When writing a circular letter remember these important guidelines:

- ✦ keep it brief, otherwise it may not be read
- ✦ ensure the letter is informative and direct
- ✦ use individual terms, e.g. 'you', not 'all of you'.

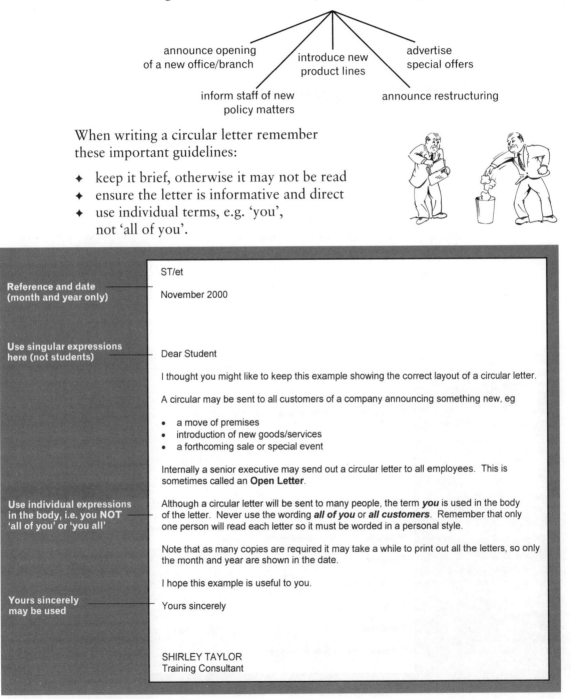

Reference and date (month and year only)

ST/et

November 2000

Use singular expressions here (not students)

Dear Student

I thought you might like to keep this example showing the correct layout of a circular letter.

A circular may be sent to all customers of a company announcing something new, eg

- a move of premises
- introduction of new goods/services
- a forthcoming sale or special event

Internally a senior executive may send out a circular letter to all employees. This is sometimes called an **Open Letter**.

Use individual expressions in the body, i.e. you NOT 'all of you' or 'you all'

Although a circular letter will be sent to many people, the term *you* is used in the body of the letter. Never use the wording *all of you* or *all customers*. Remember that only one person will read each letter so it must be worded in a personal style.

Note that as many copies are required it may take a while to print out all the letters, so only the month and year are shown in the date.

I hope this example is useful to you.

Yours sincerely may be used

Yours sincerely

SHIRLEY TAYLOR
Training Consultant

✦ Circular with tear-off slip

Sometimes when sending out a circular letter a reply is needed. To ensure that you receive the required reply from everyone, a tear-off slip may be included, which may be completed and returned to you. Remember the following points when designing a tear-off slip:

- ✦ use a continuous line of dots or hyphens for 'tearing'
- ✦ include a return date and address
- ✦ use double-spacing where details have to be completed
- ✦ leave sufficient space for completion of relevant information.

Line of hyphens and scissors symbol separate main text from tear-off portion	✂ ---
Include date for return and name/address details	Please return by 28 November 2000 to Mr Samuel Chan Sales Manager Aurora Holdings (Asia) Pte Ltd Suite 2002 Peak Towers 210 Peak Road Kowloon Hong Kong
Heading will probably be the same as the main document	OPENING OF NEW SHOWROOM - WEDNESDAY 18 DECEMBER 2000
Keep it simple and precise	I shall/shall not* be able to attend the Cocktail Evening to mark the opening of your new showroom at 1930 on Wednesday 18 December.
	Signature .... Date ....
Use double spacing for the section to be completed	Name (in capitals) ....
	Company ....
	Telephone .... Fax ....
Use this footnote when appropriate	* Please delete where appropriate

✦ Reply-paid cards

Sometimes a company will enclose a special reply-paid card for you to complete and return. The postage on these cards is pre-paid by the company. A charge will be made by the post office only for the actual cards which are returned.

BUSINESS REPLY SERVICE
LICENCE NO NG1211

2

Aurora Holdings plc
Aurora House
Temple Street
London
SE1 4LL

LET'S CHECK

You work for a charity organisation which has shops in many major cities around the UK. Your committee wants to help people suffering from the effects of a recent earthquake in China. Write a letter to be printed in a national newspaper appealing for help. Describe the disaster and its effects, the condition of the people and their needs. Ask for urgent help in the form of money which can be donated by returning a tear-off slip (cheques or credit card payments only) or clothes which can be taken to any of your shops.

✦ Sales letters

Sales letters are a very selective form of advertising. They aim to sell a company's goods or services, or they persuade readers to take up special offers. All sales letters must:

- ✦ arouse interest
- ✦ sound convincing
- ✦ create a desire
- ✦ encourage action.

In this sales letter Aurora Mobile enclose a newsletter and make everything sound so appealing and attractive.

Aurora Mobile

It's important
to stay
in touch

Dear Valued Customer

With the introduction of our new **Connect Card**, Aurora Mobile has brought a new era of convenience in mobile communications. With the **Connect Card** you can enjoy all the benefits of Aurora Mobile's leading-edge network without worrying about monthly bills. Find out how in this month's issue of **In Touch**.

In Touch also introduces you to our vastly expanded international roaming services - **Roam-a-round** - which allows you to roam to all corners of the globe. Inside **In Touch** you will find out why no-one covers the world better than Aurora Mobile.

Many more features can be found inside **In Touch** ...

- generous savings when you call another Aurora Mobile customer
- what's new at our website
- see and read about our performance at a recent Communications Exhibition

Inside **In Touch** we have also included an exciting contest for you to win fabulous prizes such as a free subscription to our value-added services, a free **Connect Card** worth £20 and restaurant privileges in leading restaurants.

With your continued support we have become the UK's leading network service provider. Thank you for staying with us.

Yours sincerely

Lesley Bolan

Lesley Bolan (Ms)
Senior Director
Marketing, Sales and Customer Service

Aurora Mobile, Aurora House, Temple Street, London SE1 4LL
Tel: +44(0)181 542 4444   Fax: +44(0)181 555 4444   Email: auroramobile@cfb.co.uk

Remember these important principles when writing sales letters:

1 Try to get on the same wavelength as your reader in the opening paragraph.
2 Present the advantages of the product or service showing relevance to the reader.
3 Write in a positive, convincing style without being aggressive.
4 Encourage the reader to respond by placing an order, completing a reply form or card, requesting further details.
5 Use singulars rather than plurals, e.g.

    ✓ Dear Customer   *not*   Dear Customers   ✗
     ✓ I know you will appreciate   *not*   I know everyone will appreciate   ✗
       this unique product   this unique product.

WHAT'S WRONG?

Study the letter written in answer to this assignment. Discuss what is wrong with the answer and then rewrite the letter correctly.

Aurora Travel arranges package holidays. On 4 February the company was informed that the Paradise Hotel at Montego Bay, which was to be used during the forthcoming season, had been badly damaged by a hurricane and would not therefore be available to accommodate their clients.

Prepare a circular letter from the sales manager to be sent to clients who have already reserved holidays at this hotel. Explain that a limited number of vacancies are available at other hotels, that the holiday price is unchanged and that the same amenities and standards apply. Some hotels are away from the beach – 5 kms from Montego Bay – but they have swimming pools and free transport provided from hotel to coast during the holiday. Twenty per cent discount given if holiday is booked immediately, or money refunded and deposits returned.

WHAT'S WRONG WITH THE ANSWER?

AURORA TRAVEL
2 Windsor Place
Sheffield
S31 0ES

Telephone 0114 2877777

21 April 2000

Dear Clients

HURRICANE SPOILS HOLIDAY

We are writing to all clients who booked holidays at the Paradise Hotel in Montego Bay with our firm.

This hotel had been badly damaged by a hurricane and we would no longer be able to accommodate our clients at this hotel.

A limited number of vacancies are available at other hotels. The holiday price is unchanged and the hotels will have same amenities and standards, etc. In addition some hotels are away from the beach, 5 miles from Montego Bay, but they do have swimming pools, etc. Free transport will be provided from hotel to coast during your holiday.

A 20% discount will be given if the above-mentioned holidays are booked immediately. However money can be refund to clients who are not satisfied with this new arrangements. Deposits will, of course, be returned.

Hope to hear from you soon.

Yours sincerely

CHLOE BRADLEY
Secretary to Sales Manager

✦ Assignments

1   You work for Aurora Enterprises Inc. The company produces a range of magazines and is shortly to introduce a new magazine called '*Sports Monthly*'. This will cover all major sports and will include reports, interviews, tactics, famous moments from the past and a range of competitions. The cost will be £3. The Marketing Director, Mr Richard Cliff, asks you to prepare a circular letter to be included in all the other magazines published by Aurora Enterprises. He leaves you this note:

Describe the new mag and give some details of the first issue. This will be sold at a special price of £2 and will include details of a special annual subscription (£30 for 12 issues).

Write the letter.

(LCCIEB EFB1 style)

2   You work for *Healthy Life*, a magazine which is published monthly. Write a circular letter which may be sent to all subscribers of the magazine informing that their subscription is due to expire. State the last issue they will receive. These readers can renew their subscription for the special annual subscription price for six bi-monthly issues of only £15.

If they renew now they will receive an exclusive discount card which entitles them to 10% off selected health farms and supplements available from Healthy Life Health Stores; 15% discount at all Green Cuisine cafés; 20% off allergy testing at Scanhealth Ltd (further details about this in next month's issue).

Design a circular which includes a tear-off portion for readers to send back to you with their subscription. Compose any details which you feel are needed.

(LCCIEB EFB2 style)

3   You work for Mr Frank Lim, Marketing Manager of Best International plc, a large retail group in the UK. The company will shortly be expanding its operations by opening a chain of furniture superstores throughout the UK. The first one will be open at Bedford in July 2000. Opening times 0900–2000, Monday to Saturday, 0900–1700 Sunday.

Use these notes from Mr Lim and prepare a letter for his signature:

Store will be of particular interest to the DIY enthusiast.
Special discounts for the first 50 customers. Visitors will be able to see on display a variety of kitchens, bathrooms, dining rooms, bedrooms and lounges. A planning service is available.
Store holds everything which may be needed – paints, wall coverings, tiles, carpets.

Each department supervised by friendly, qualified staff.
Parking for 400 cars or bus 214 stops right outside the store.
Free delivery of orders over £100 otherwise small charge.
Credit facilities available at low interest rates.

(LCCIEB EFB2 style)

4 You work for Jeremy Bonne, Senior Executive at Aurora Publishing plc,
134–138 Leng Wah Street, 10930 Kuala Lumpur, Malaysia, telephone
343234, fax 3878787. You are organising the Executive PA Show, a free
show especially for senior secretaries, to be held in 2 months' time. It is
being produced in association with the national newspaper *Malaysia Times*
and the magazine *Executive PA*. The show will offer a comprehensive
seminar programme, practical careers advice and IT clinics. There will also
be a Networking Café. The show will include everything from business
travel to office technology, conferences to recruitment. Mr Bonne says to
you today:

Please draft a circular letter to be included in the next issue of
Executive PA magazine announcing the Executive PA Show. I'm
quite excited about it and feel sure that it's guaranteed to boost the
PA's career. Include a tear-off section for readers to send off for a
free ticket to the show. Make sure we get all their details so we can
write, call, fax or email them in the future.

(LCCIEB EFB2 style)

Publicity material

By the end of this unit you should be able to:

- ❏ explain the function of the public relations department

- ❏ explain the purpose of a press release

- ❏ discuss the special writing skills needed for compiling a press release

- ❏ identify and correct inappropriate style in press releases

- ❏ explain an appropriate format for presenting press releases

- ❏ compose press releases according to given instructions.

✦ Public relations

The public relations (PR) function in any organisation is usually carried out by staff who have specialised in this sector. Public relations, as the name suggests, is all about the relationship between the organisation and the general public. One of the aims of PR is to influence the general public through the mass media, e.g. newspapers, television, radio, information services, exhibitions, sponsorship. The job of the PR person in any organisation is to be constantly on the lookout for newsworthy events, products, developments and human interest stories and then turn them into any of the following:

- a press release
- a press conference
- a photo opportunity for newspaper coverage
- corporate material for direct mailing
- briefing packs for potential customers
- briefing packs for special groups of visitors
- free educational packs for schools and colleges.

If you are responsible for helping to produce public relations material, here are some guidelines to follow. Effective PR material will:

- be factual, newsworthy and impartial
- appeal to human interest
- contain up-to-date information
- be appropriately distributed
- be produced professionally.

Here is a section of the corporate brochure produced by Sheffield Wednesday Football Club Ltd. Excellent design, effective layout with headings and bullet points, careful wording and specially selected artwork give this material a very professional, polished finish.

Sponsorship Opportunities
with Sheffield Wednesday Football Club

SWFC
Est. 1867

matchday *sponsorship*

For any company realising the value of self promotion there can be no greater opportunity than to share centre stage with Sheffield Wednesday Football Club - as the Official Matchday Sponsor.

The ultimate single matchday attraction, combining business and pleasure. So while advertising your company, let us entertain you and twenty VIP guests to a superb day out at the Club.

Guests will be greeted by a champagne reception and then sumptuously wined and dined. And, for those who enjoy the comfort and privacy of an individual box, but prefer to encounter the electrifying crowd atmosphere at first hand, the new Match Sponsors Super Box will provide the ideal setting.

Advertising
- Front cover and full page advertisement in the Match Day Programme
- Advertising board on the half-way line in full view of the T.V. cameras
- Acknowledgement over the public address system and electronic scoreboard

Hospitality
- Twenty guests have exclusive use of the Sponsors Super Box Suite
- Champagne reception
- Welcome gift pack including complimentary match programmes
- Behind the scenes tour
- VIP group commemorative photograph
- Three course lunch including wines and liqueurs
- Free complimentary hospitality bar
- Exterior box gallery, with luxurious upholstered armchair style seated viewing area
- Matchday prizes and post match presentations
- Choose your own SWFC man of the match
- Presentation of the actual matchball to the match officials
- Private car parking
- Matchday mascot

Experience the thrill of a behind the scenes matchday tour...and a chance to meet your chosen man of the match.

match ball *sponsorship*

Match Ball Sponsorship is an exclusive package created for a party of six special guests. This exciting sponsorship is an ideal means of cementing business relationships, or giving a special gift to a family member or friend.

It also takes advantage of the advertising opportunities in the Match Day Programme, P.A. announcements and the electronic scoreboard.

- Complimentary Match Day Programme
- Three course meal
- Pre and post match pay bar facilities
- Six Main South Stand Executive Seats
- VIP Photocall with commemorative photographs
- Autographed matchball presented by one of the players
- Scoreboard and P.A. announcement
- Pre-match tour
- Pre-match gift presentation
- Company name in Match Day Programme
- Car parking facilities

kit *sponsorship*

Adopt a Sheffield Wednesday Player.

SWFC Kit Sponsorship is one of the most popular sponsorship activities because of its unique combination of advertising in the programme and contact with the players themselves. What better way to support your favourite player.

- You keep forever your sponsored player's team shirt, shorts and socks at an end of season presentation
- Picture and framed photograph of you and your chosen player
- Company or individual name complete with picture of your chosen player to be printed in the Match Day Programme throughout the season
- Two complimentary matchday tickets

vip *day*

The VIP Day is an exclusive package created for two special guests. If you cannot think of a very special birthday/anniversary present for that very special person, this exciting package is for you - the VIP Day includes the same hospitality facets as the Match Ball Sponsorship package, but with the extra features of a pre-match gift presentation - autographed match ball and flowers for the lady.

programme *sponsorship*

Similar to Match Ball Sponsorship, Programme Sponsorship offers a unique combination of entertainment and advertising. You will be given a unique tour behind the scenes and then you will be introduced to one of the clubs first team players. You will also be photographed and presented with a special signed momento to commemorate the day.

For further details contact:

Sean O'Toole, Commercial Manager, Commercial Department, Sheffield Wednesday Football Club Limited, Hillsborough, Sheffield S6 1SW.

Tel: 0114 221 2333/2121   Fax: 0114 221 2122

Reproduced courtesy of Sheffield Wednesday Football Club Ltd

THINK

Does your company publish corporate material? Could you bring some in for discussion with your classmates? If you are not working, visit or write to some local companies and ask for copies of their corporate material.

✦ Press releases

A press release is an announcement which a company sends to the press and other media about anything which it considers to be newsworthy. A press release is not an advertisement but it can result in useful publicity for the company issuing the release.

In this press release Singapore MRT (Mass Rapid Transit) Ltd announce a new thematic ticket set to mark their tenth anniversary.

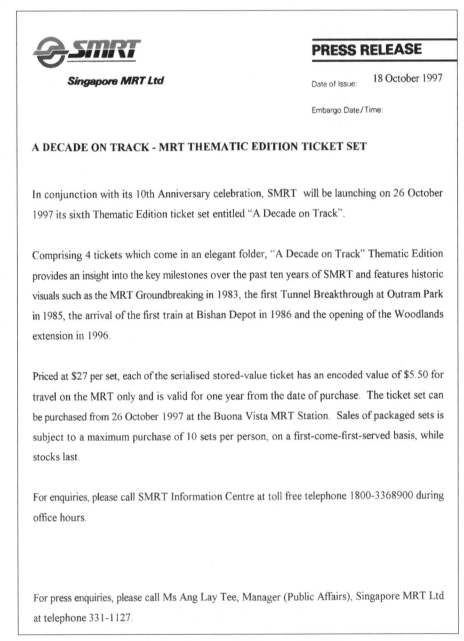

SMRT

Singapore MRT Ltd

PRESS RELEASE

Date of Issue: 18 October 1997

Embargo Date/Time:

A DECADE ON TRACK - MRT THEMATIC EDITION TICKET SET

In conjunction with its 10th Anniversary celebration, SMRT will be launching on 26 October 1997 its sixth Thematic Edition ticket set entitled "A Decade on Track".

Comprising 4 tickets which come in an elegant folder, "A Decade on Track" Thematic Edition provides an insight into the key milestones over the past ten years of SMRT and features historic visuals such as the MRT Groundbreaking in 1983, the first Tunnel Breakthrough at Outram Park in 1985, the arrival of the first train at Bishan Depot in 1986 and the opening of the Woodlands extension in 1996.

Priced at $27 per set, each of the serialised stored-value ticket has an encoded value of $5.50 for travel on the MRT only and is valid for one year from the date of purchase. The ticket set can be purchased from 26 October 1997 at the Buona Vista MRT Station. Sales of packaged sets is subject to a maximum purchase of 10 sets per person, on a first-come-first-served basis, while stocks last.

For enquiries, please call SMRT Information Centre at toll free telephone 1800-3368900 during office hours.

For press enquiries, please call Ms Ang Lay Tee, Manager (Public Affairs), Singapore MRT Ltd at telephone 331-1127.

Reproduced courtesy of Singapore MRT Ltd

Here is how this might have looked if it had appeared in a newspaper, together with some illustrations showing some of the special tickets.

SMRT – Just the ticket at 10 years old

SMRT have captured key milestones over the last 10 years in a set of 4 stored value tickets. 'A Decade on Track' will be launched on Sunday.

Visuals included in this special set include the MRT groundbreaking in 1983, the first tunnel breakthrough at Outram Park in 1985, the arrival of the first train at Bishan Depot in 1986 and the opening of the woodlands extension in 1996.

Priced at $27 per set, tickets have an encoded value of $5.50 for travel on the MRT only. Each one is valid for one year from date of purchase.

Tickets are available from Sunday onwards at Buona Vista MRT station, with a limit of 10 sets per person.

For enquiries call SMRT Information Centre during office hours on its toll free number 1800-3368900.

Reproduced courtesy of Singapore MRT Ltd

Some reasons why a company may send a press release to the media are:

+ relocation of offices
+ introduction of new products
+ purchase of new buildings
+ move to new premises
+ changes in top personnel.

THINK

Can you think of any other reasons why a company may issue a press release? Discuss this with your colleagues and make a list.

Here is another effective press release issued by Eurostar (UK) Ltd announcing improvements in its services and news of a 50% sales boost.

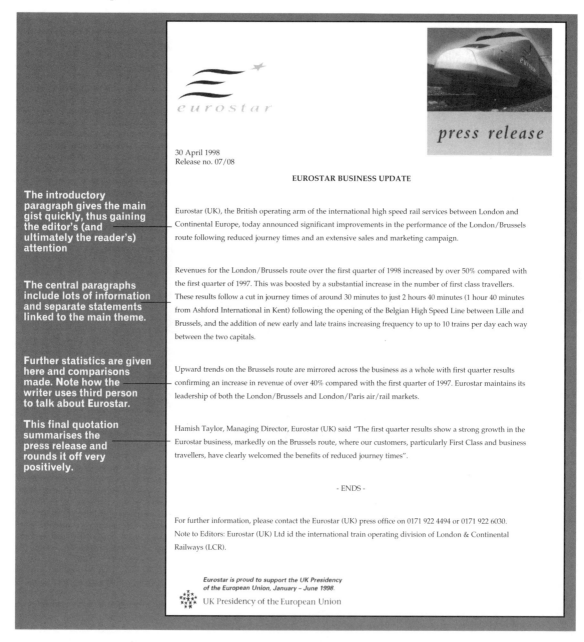

The introductory paragraph gives the main gist quickly, thus gaining the editor's (and ultimately the reader's) attention

The central paragraphs include lots of information and separate statements linked to the main theme.

Further statistics are given here and comparisons made. Note how the writer uses third person to talk about Eurostar.

This final quotation summarises the press release and rounds it off very positively.

eurostar

press release

30 April 1998
Release no. 07/08

EUROSTAR BUSINESS UPDATE

Eurostar (UK), the British operating arm of the international high speed rail services between London and Continental Europe, today announced significant improvements in the performance of the London/Brussels route following reduced journey times and an extensive sales and marketing campaign.

Revenues for the London/Brussels route over the first quarter of 1998 increased by over 50% compared with the first quarter of 1997. This was boosted by a substantial increase in the number of first class travellers. These results follow a cut in journey times of around 30 minutes to just 2 hours 40 minutes (1 hour 40 minutes from Ashford International in Kent) following the opening of the Belgian High Speed Line between Lille and Brussels, and the addition of new early and late trains increasing frequency to up to 10 trains per day each way between the two capitals.

Upward trends on the Brussels route are mirrored across the business as a whole with first quarter results confirming an increase in revenue of over 40% compared with the first quarter of 1997. Eurostar maintains its leadership of both the London/Brussels and London/Paris air/rail markets.

Hamish Taylor, Managing Director, Eurostar (UK) said "The first quarter results show a strong growth in the Eurostar business, markedly on the Brussels route, where our customers, particularly First Class and business travellers, have clearly welcomed the benefits of reduced journey times".

- ENDS -

For further information, please contact the Eurostar (UK) press office on 0171 922 4494 or 0171 922 6030. Note to Editors: Eurostar (UK) Ltd id the international train operating division of London & Continental Railways (LCR).

Eurostar is proud to support the UK Presidency of the European Union, January – June 1998.
UK Presidency of the European Union

Reproduced courtesy of Eurostar (UK) Ltd

THINK

Do you deal with press releases in your company? Do you know the person who does? Can you ask if you can see copies of some press releases and perhaps show them to the rest of your class?

Compiling a press release

Editors who receive the press release may publish an edited version, publish it as written or contact the initiator to find out further details. Unfortunately 90% of press releases are thrown in the editor's waste paper basket. Only 5–10% are actually used. To make sure your press releases are in this small percentage, special writing skills are needed:

+ *Headline* Compose an appropriate, snappy heading.
+ *Opening*   A good opening paragraph is essential to grab the editor's (and ultimately the reader's) attention. Give the main essence of the message in this opening.
+ *Middle*   Central paragraphs should be short and self-contained so that the editor can cut them out if necessary without ruining the sense or the flow.
+ *Close*   A conclusion or a summary may be appropriate at the close, or a brief repeat of the main message. It is often useful to include a quotation from a key person.

✦ Guidelines for writing press releases

+ Use third person. Write as though you are the newspaper editor, talking about your company as an outsider.
+ Do not make your press release sound like an advertisement or invitation.
+ Write in an interesting, snappy, punchy style with short sentences. Something which may seem an uninteresting event can be made into an effective story by using appropriate wording and innovative angles.
+ Try to appeal to human interests where possible.
+ Use a style which will be suitable to appear in a newspaper with as few changes as possible.
+ Your press release must answer the following questions:

What?   What is happening?
Who?   Who is involved?
Where? Where is it happening?
When?   When is it happening?
Why?   Why is it newsworthy?

TIP

Remember: a flat, vague, dull, boring, long-winded press release will end up in the editor's wastepaper bin.

Suggested layout

This press release from Singapore Airlines shows the recommended layout for you to use when composing a press release:

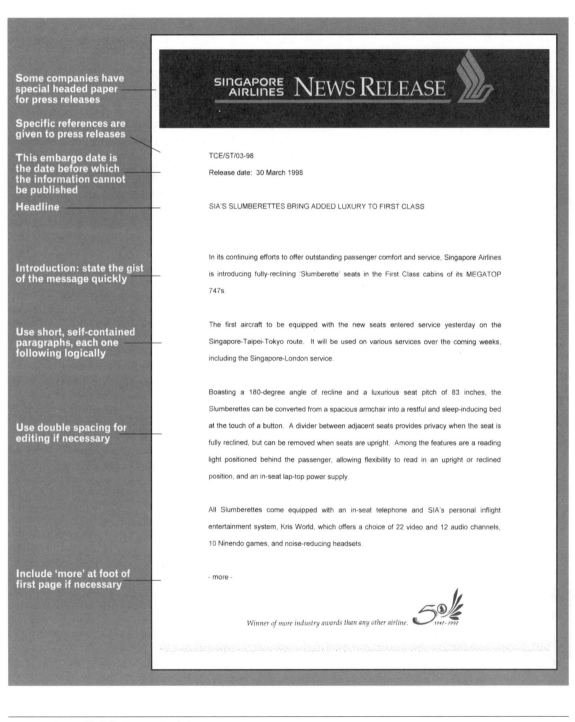

Some companies have special headed paper for press releases

Specific references are given to press releases

This embargo date is the date before which the information cannot be published

Headline

Introduction: state the gist of the message quickly

Use short, self-contained paragraphs, each one following logically

Use double spacing for editing if necessary

Include 'more' at foot of first page if necessary

SINGAPORE AIRLINES NEWS RELEASE

TCE/ST/03-98

Release date: 30 March 1998

SIA'S SLUMBERETTES BRING ADDED LUXURY TO FIRST CLASS

In its continuing efforts to offer outstanding passenger comfort and service, Singapore Airlines is introducing fully-reclining 'Slumberette' seats in the First Class cabins of its MEGATOP 747s.

The first aircraft to be equipped with the new seats entered service yesterday on the Singapore-Taipei-Tokyo route. It will be used on various services over the coming weeks, including the Singapore-London service.

Boasting a 180-degree angle of recline and a luxurious seat pitch of 83 inches, the Slumberettes can be converted from a spacious armchair into a restful and sleep-inducing bed at the touch of a button. A divider between adjacent seats provides privacy when the seat is fully reclined, but can be removed when seats are upright. Among the features are a reading light positioned behind the passenger, allowing flexibility to read in an upright or reclined position, and an in-seat lap-top power supply.

All Slumberettes come equipped with an in-seat telephone and SIA's personal inflight entertainment system, Kris World, which offers a choice of 22 video and 12 audio channels, 10 Ninendo games, and noise-reducing headsets.

- more -

Winner of more industry awards than any other airline. 50 *1947-1997*

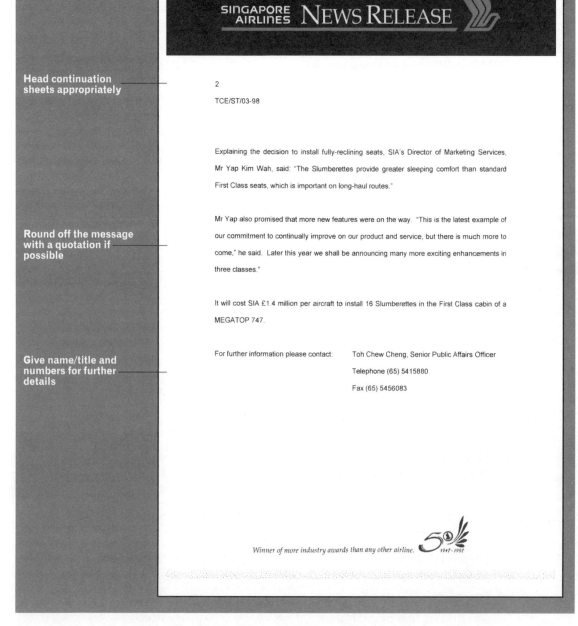

Head continuation sheets appropriately

2

TCE/ST/03-98

Explaining the decision to install fully-reclining seats, SIA's Director of Marketing Services, Mr Yap Kim Wah, said: "The Slumberettes provide greater sleeping comfort than standard First Class seats, which is important on long-haul routes."

Round off the message with a quotation if possible

Mr Yap also promised that more new features were on the way. "This is the latest example of our commitment to continually improve on our product and service, but there is much more to come," he said. Later this year we shall be announcing many more exciting enhancements in three classes."

It will cost SIA £1.4 million per aircraft to install 16 Slumberettes in the First Class cabin of a MEGATOP 747.

Give name/title and numbers for further details

For further information please contact: Toh Chew Cheng, Senior Public Affairs Officer

Telephone (65) 5415880

Fax (65) 5456083

Winner of more industry awards than any other airline.

Reproduced courtesy of Singapore Airlines Limited

LET'S CHECK

Discuss the merits of the following releases, both saying the same thing but in a different way. Which is more suitable? Why? →

Healthy Life is pleased to announce the opening of their new branch in Penang on 20 August. We promise you free gifts and special offers, as well as competitions. Radio personality, Lee Evans, will be there too, so don't miss this chance to meet him. Healthy Life opened their first store in KL earlier this year.

Radio star, Lee Evans, will open Healthy Life's new Penang store on Tuesday 20 August. This follows the the success of Healthy Life since the the first Malaysian store was opened in Kuala Lumpur in February. There will be demonstrations and talks by local experts throughout the day. Competitions, special offers and free gifts are also organised. This fun day starts at 9 am.

WHAT'S WRONG?

Study the following scenario and discuss what's wrong with the press release which follows. Rewrite the press release more appropriately.

The Principal of your college held a meeting of all staff today and had the following to say:

> 'I want to hold an Open House on Wednesday September 14th from 10 until 8. It's quite some time since our last Open House and we've made quite a few additions since then, so I'd like to invite people to look around our facilities – we could put on a demonstration of the fax machine, also the new computers. The students have some interesting wall displays so there could be a tour also – that way members of the public can learn more about what we do here. Has anyone any suggestions?'

Kathryn Yeo said 'As there are a few weeks until September 14th perhaps teachers could encourage students to prepare projects and other exhibits for display?'

Doreen Choo said: 'We could include the new library in the tour to show our up-to-date and wide range of books.'

Sharon Ho said: Perhaps we could enlist the help of some students to perform some of the demonstrations and give talks on various aspects of their course?

Angeline Lee said: 'I think it would be nice if we provided some cookies and soft drinks, free of charge of course.'

The Principal then asked for a volunteer to coordinate all arrangements. Miss Sandra Koh volunteered. It was agreed that she would draft a press release to issue to the local newspapers for insertion for a day before the Open House, encouraging visitors and describing what would happen in the school on that day.

Prepare the press release.

WHAT'S WRONG WITH THE ANSWER?

PRESS RELEASE

Super Sec Training Centre are pleased to announce their Open Day to be held at their school on 14 September to show off the latest editions to the school.

People will be invited to look around the school's facilities including a demonstration on our new computers and fax machines. A tour will be provided by teachers, showing projects prepared by students and exhibits as well as the well-stocked library. Student's help is being enlisted to give talks on various aspects of the course.

Cookies and drinks will be provided free of charge of course.

Contact: Miss Sandra Koh

✦ Assignments

1   You work for Florence Cheung, Public Relations Manager at the Pagoda Hotel in your town. She asks you to draft a press release about the new service concepts in the hotel which will gain a new perspective with the opening of the new Regency Suites wing of the hotel.

Mrs Cheung gives you the following notes which should be included:

Regency Suites wing: opens early 2001
New service concept: a wide range to be expected.

Business Centre: vital for businessmen on the move; extension of operations to 24 hours/7 days; complete range of secretarial services – fax, letters, email, internet, reference library, personal computer, private offices, conference room/lounge.

Housekeeping and laundry services: 24-hour service. Late arrivals catered for; requests for stationery, extra pillows, suits pressed.

Hotel's airport reps: greet guests on arrival, meet during departure. Two limousines plus fleet of 14 others — all times — city tours/business trips can be organised.

Professional concierge team: answer queries — provide information; from dinner reservations to theatre shows or show-makers!

Extra services — hotel positioning itself as a top deluxe hotel — perfect choice. 148 Pagoda Hotels and resorts around the world.

Prepare the press release.

2 You work in the Public Affairs Department of Aurora Bank Sdn Bhd. You have been asked to draft a press release for immediate release to announce the move of your bank to new premises. In a discussion with Neeraj Daryani, Public Affairs Manager, you made these notes:

- *Bank now occupies three floors — total built-up area of 950 sq m. Spacious banking hall = customers can conduct business transactions in comfort.*
- *Services include credit facilities, interest-free banking, many personalised services.*
- *Moved from outskirts to centre of town in Wisma Aurora, Jalan Perak.*
- *Branch Manager = Malik Jemadi. Total staff 35.*
- *New premises officially opened yesterday by Group MD, Lim Cheng Poh. He thanked all customers who have supported the bank since it opened in 1984 — even higher standards in 2000+*
- *New premises should help us reach out and serve customers better*
- *150 invited customers attended opening ceremony.*

Draft the press release.

3   You are PA to the Principal of The University College, Mrs Norma Hedges. The Senior Tutor is Karen Ashley. Respond to this request from Mrs Hedges.

PA, The Camford Times Editor phoned yesterday to remind me that in 4 weeks' time their Educational Supplement will be published, giving a guide to all courses run locally. Can you sort out a PRESS RELEASE on who we are and what we do. The Bursar, Mrs Ashley and Miss Osmond should be able to give you any help you need.
NH

PA
Notes for Press Release:

College founded 1960 - provided training for daughters of University staff. Took over large house in centre of the city. House next door bought 1970. 12 students at start - today 200 (25 overseas - Malaysia, Hong Kong, Japan, Holland).

RC
Bursar

PA
I give below a few ideas:
- Stress wide range of courses - short (12 weeks) to a full year.
- New hostel just opened - 25 students in single/double bedrooms.
- Now have special arrangement with colleges in Norway and Holland - 12 week courses.
- Former students have responsible positions in all sorts of organisations worldwide.

KA
Senior Tutor

As you asked, some information on our equipment:

Modern - latest word processors, computers. All aspects of Office Skills covered. Successful Bilingual (French/English) course. JOsmond

(Pitman EFBC2)

Newsletters

By the end of this unit you should be able to:

- ❏ explain the purpose of company newsletters for staff and customers

- ❏ give examples of information which newsletters may contain

- ❏ discuss the special writing skills needed for writing articles

- ❏ compose articles according to given instructions.

✦ Staff newsletters

One way for an organisation to keep staff informed about matters of interest is to issue a regular newsletter which is published monthly or quarterly. Other names for newsletters are in-house journals and company magazines.

Reproduced courtesy of Singapore Airlines Limited

Reproduced courtesy of Nestlé UK Limited

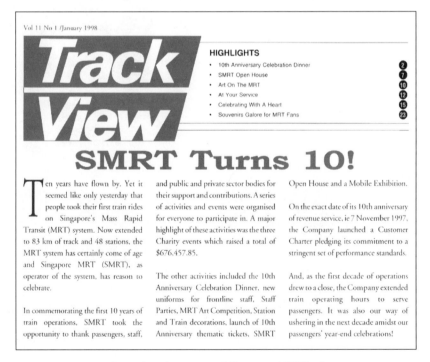

Reproduced courtesy of Singapore MRT Ltd

Reproduced courtesy of TIBS Holdings Ltd

Reproduced courtesy of Lever Brothers Limited

Many organisations find that issuing a regular newsletter is very good for improving company/staff relations. Newsletters are an effective way of reaching out to members of staff where there are many different branches of a company around the country or even internationally. These newsletters may also be sent to employees who have retired.

Company newsletters contain a variety of information such as:

+ new policies/procedures
+ updates on products/services
+ births/marriages/deaths
+ promotions
+ sports and social news
+ contributions from employees.

✦ Customer newsletters

Some companies produce newsletters especially for customers or members of a certain industry. These are a good way of keeping people informed about the latest products, news and developments within specific sectors of the industry.

Reproduced courtesy of Thistle Hotels

Reproduced courtesy of Singapore Broadcasting Authority

Reproduced courtesy of Sheffield Insulations Group plc

Reproduced courtesy of IQPS Ltd

Reproduced courtesy of Kodak Limited

THINK

If you are working, does your company issue newsletters to staff or customers? What sort of information do they contain? Are they popular? Write a memo to your teacher telling her about this, and enclose a copy of the newsletter.

Here are some extracts from company newsletters:

BA link up is celebrated

Thistle Hotels has become the first UK-only hotel group to be accepted as a recommended partner of the British Airways' Executive Club.

From 1 August 1998, members of BA's Executive Club can collect Air Miles during their stays at participating Thistle hotels. One night at a hotel at published, corporate, preferred or negotiated rates, represents 25 air miles. There is no limit on the number of nights allowed for Air Mile collection and to celebrate the link-up, Air Mile awards will be doubled to 50 per night during August and September.

Thistle is also offering a range of excellent benefits for Executive Club members. For example, for every tenth night accrued over any 12 month period, a bonus of 100 Air Miles will be awarded.

Thistle chief executive Ian Burke said: 'Executive Club members now have an unrivalled choice of hotels in key city-centre and countryside locations throughout the UK, including all BA's major gateways, in addition to a range of special benefits.'

Reproduced courtesy of Thistle Hotels

Bronze medals on silver anniversary

THE Nestlé Rowntree Athletics Club's annual 10k road race saw the club gaining bronze medals. The Rowntree trio of Ian Cain, Dave Lancaster and Peter Tuffs took third place at the event in October. This was the 25th year of the race, and it attracted a huge turnout. The field was limited to 300 participants, and latecomers had to be turned away.

Reproduced courtesy of Nestlé UK Ltd

Win tickets to the Oval

WE have three sets of four tickets to give away for the Surrey v Worcestershire match on Sunday June 28 at the Oval. Just answer this question:

Which legendary Surrey and England cricketer is also known as the master?
a) Jack Russell
b) Jack Jones
c) Jack Hobbs

Winners will be the first three correct answers drawn out of a hat. Entries should be on a postcard, for the attention of The Organiser, Cricket Competition, A1121, Nestlé UK Ltd, St George's House, Croydon, Surrey CR9 1NR, with the name and address of the entrant written in block capitals. All entries must be received by May 15. Winners will be contacted in writing by June 6. All travel costs will be the responsibility of the winners.

Reproduced courtesy of Nestlé UK Ltd

THANK YOU FOR CARING
感谢您的关怀

On behalf of the company and the Community Chest, we wish to express our appreciation to all our kind-hearted staff for your monthly contributions in support of the SHARE programme.

Your generous contributions have not only helped to provide basic necessities for some of the 178,973 needy individuals but have also enabled them to receive treatment in the form of rehabilitative activities or therapy sessions etc. Your kind generosity has meant a whole new meaning to these individuals' lives.

我们谨代表公司和公益金，向所有捐献支持分享关怀计划的善心同事表示谢意。

您的慷慨解囊不仅协助17万8973名不幸人士，提供了基本的照顾，也让他们得到所需的医药治疗例如康复计划或化疗等等。您的善心义举，经已为这不幸的一群，带来了全新的意义和光彩。

Reproduced courtesy of TIBS Holdings Ltd

Get in the swing of things

WE'VE got 10 copies of the Nestlé Jazz Workshops schools pack to give away.

The pack includes a six-track CD with accompanying sheet music and background notes on the history of jazz music from New Orleans Jazz through Big Band and Be-Bop to Jazz Fusion and beyond.

For your chance to win, just answer these three questions:

1) In which region are the Nestlé Jazz Workshops being held?
a) south east
b) north west
c) Scotland

2) In which year did the programme start?
a) 1997
c) 1996
c) 1995

3) What is the name of the group which took the workshops to schools?
a) The Duke Ellington Quartet
b) The Louis Armstrong Quartet
c) The Patrick Clahar Quartet

Easy? Now put your answers with your name and address on a postcard and send it to: Nestlé News Jazz Competition, St George's House, Croydon, Surrey CR9 1NR. Closing date Friday May 8.

Reproduced courtesy of Nestlé UK Ltd

Tibs' OWN FIRE FIGHTERS 八达的 防火英雄

Three of our staff have recently gone through a comprehensive 3-month fire safety course conducted by the Singapore Civil Defence Force. The course not only enabled them to have a better understanding of the mandatory rules and regulations of fire safety, but has also given them the foresight to pre-empt potential fire hazards and make our company a safer place to work in. They have also learnt how to conduct fire investigations. So if you've got some "heat", they've got the ways to beat it. The three "fire fighters" are: Facilities Manager, Lim Eng Tit, P&S Officer, Loh Chia Wee, and Maintenance Officer, Chua Hock Kee.

♦ Harold Lim ♦

最近，3名公司同事参加新加坡民防部队的防火课程，接受了为期3个月的训练。这项课程不但帮助他们进一步了解消防安全的法令和条例，也让他们学习到防患未然的消防知识，协助使公司变成一个更安全的地方。此外，他们也学习到如何进行火患调查工作。随着这3名同事的顺利"毕业"，公司又增添了一批训练有素的防火英雄。

♦ 林亿兴 ♦

Reproduced courtesy of TIBS Holdings Ltd

Top honour

Thistle has been voted UK Business Hotel Group of the Year for the second year running by readers of *Business Travel World* magazine. This prestigious award in the 'Best National (UK and Ireland) Suppliers' category, sponsored by Visa, recognises the service, standards and value that Thistle has provided to its corporate clients in the last year.

Tony Kimpton, Thistle Hotels' sales director, said: 'I'm delighted that our commitment to serving the travel professional and our investment in our product have been recognised.'

Reproduced courtesy of Thistle Hotels

LEADING THE WAY IN CUSTOMER SUPPORT
HIGH RATINGS IN CUSTOMER SURVEY

Fast, reliable delivery, both into stock and direct to site, is a merchant priority consistently met by Sheffield Insulations, according to a recent survey of merchant customers

Specialist technical support, impartial advice and product training are other services features pinpointed in the survey as being highly valued by merchants when sourcing insulation.

The findings reflect the difficulties merchants sales staff have in providing the extensive application knowledge demanded by customers as the insulation market becomes increasingly fragmented and complex.

Reproduced courtesy of Sheffield Insulations Group plc

✦ Writing skills

The same basic writing skills are needed to write articles for in-house magazines as are needed for writing press releases. The following guidelines should be noted:

- ✦ use reported speech, third person
- ✦ write in an interesting, readable style
- ✦ use short sentences and a crisp, snappy style
- ✦ try to appeal to human interests
- ✦ be as factual as possible
- ✦ build the article logically.

Here is a good article from *Nestlé News* showing correct writing techniques, and you can also see the finished article which appeared in the magazine:

Punchy headline ——— SAFETY FIRST

Give the main gist in the opening paragraph ——— A two day workshop on Health & Safety in Laboratories was held recently at the group and regional laboratory in York.

Short self-contained paragraphs ——— Staff from factories across the country attended the workshop which was organised by Simon Freeman and Ellie Winn of the regional laboratory and Ian Burke of the group occupational health & safety department.

Give full details and information ——— The speakers considered the legal and company requirements for safety matters, including risk assessments, accidents and their prevention, fire safety, dealing with spillages in laboratories, and the correct procedures for arranging for disposal of wastes.

Humour helps ——— In one of the practical exercises, Simon Freeman 'volunteered' to use the emergency shower, to check that it worked properly and to demonstrate that it is quite difficult to remove clothing whilst standing under a torrent of cold water!

It's a good idea to finish with a quotation ——— Says Simon: "The social side of the workshop was enlivened by joining one of the ghost tours of York during the evening, when we heard stories of York's macabre past."

ST/JKL

24 October 2000

Safety first

A TWO day workshop on Health & Safety in Laboratories was held recently at the group and regional laboratory in York. Staff from factories across the country attended the workshop organised by Simon Freeman and Ellie Winn of the regional laboratory and Ian Burke of the group occupational health & safety department.

The speakers considered the legal and company requirements for safety matters, including, risk assessments, accidents and their prevention, fire safety, dealing with spillages in laboratories, and the correct procedures for arranging for disposal of wastes. In one of the practical exercises, Simon Freeman 'volunteered' to use the emergency shower, to check that it worked properly and to demonstrate that it is quite difficult to remove clothing whilst standing under a torrent of cold water!

Says Simon: "The social side of the workshop was enlivened by joining one of the ghost tours of York during the evening, when we heard stories of York's macabre past."

Reproduced courtesy of Nestlé UK Ltd

✦ Assignments

1   One of your employees has just won a local sporting competition. Write an article for the staff magazine. Make up appropriate details – name, job, department, branch, nature of the competition, what it involved, the prize he/she won.

2   You have been given the responsibility of organising the company's annual dinner and dance. Write an article announcing details. Include details of how staff can register.

3   You work at Aurora Holdings plc. Write an memo to Tracie Stannard, Communications Manager, enclosing an article you have written. Ask her to consider this for inclusion in the next issue of the staff newsletter (give it a name). In your article tactfully criticise some aspect of the company (a policy or procedure, organisation, salary structure) and make suggestions for how it could be improved.

4   You work for David Fenworth, Manager of Fenworth Fashions, 117 High Street West, Hale, Cheshire WA5 7TJ

(LCCIEB EFB2 style)

You know that a famous film star, Saffron Sinclair, was born in Hale and lived in the town before she left to go to college to study drama. Saffron has won an award as best actress in the new film 'Silver Vision'. She is your favourite film actress and you plan to write a short article about her for the magazine of the Hale Film Society.

Mr Fenworth knows that you are very interested in Saffron and he tells you that he knew Saffron when she was a young girl. You decide to write an article about when she lived in Fenworth.

Here are our notes on what Mr Fenworth tells you:

Real name - Pauline Sinclair - changed her name to Saffron when she became an actress
Born in Hale - went to Hale Grammar School - always loved acting - was the star of school plays - played Juliet in school production of 'Romeo and Juliet' - local newspaper said she had 'star quality'.
Also a good dancer - had to give this up when she hurt her back.
Her mother is a nurse at Bowdon General Hospital - her father is retired - used to be a teacher.
Saffron worked at Fenworth Fashions shop on Saturdays when she was at school to earn pocket money.
Loves music - plays piano and guitar - sang in school choir.
Doesn't like smoking - always hated the smell.
Left Fenworth when she was 18 to go to college - still comes home when she can - sister at Hale Technical College.

Write the article

Notices and advertisements

UNIT 14

By the end of this unit you should be able to:

❏ state the purposes of notices

❏ explain the responsibilities of the person nominated to look after a notice board

❏ list guidelines for drawing up notices

❏ design attractive and effective notices from given instructions

❏ explain the reasons for advertisements

❏ understand the difference between small ads and display ads

❏ discuss the special techniques used in compiling advertisements

❏ identify effective advertisements

❏ compose advertisements according to given instructions.

✦ Notices

Notices are also around us everywhere we go – in the supermarket, on the underground, at the entrance of shoppi centres, at the railway station, the bus station, the cinema.

Most organisations have notice boards posted around the offices which are used to bring special items to the attention of all staff.

Notice boards may be sectioned according to different topics for example policy matters, health and safety, staff announcements. It is a good idea to nominate one person to be in charge of each notice board. This person should be responsible for:

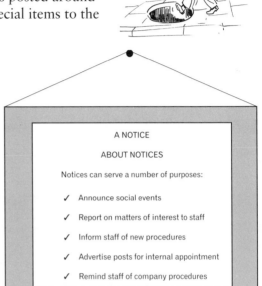

A NOTICE

ABOUT NOTICES

Notices can serve a number of purposes:

✓ Announce social events

✓ Report on matters of interest to staff

✓ Inform staff of new procedures

✓ Advertise posts for internal appointment

✓ Remind staff of company procedures

- ✦ removing obsolete notices
- ✦ sectioning notices under appropriate headings where possible
- ✦ removing 'dead' notices (but retaining them for a short while in case of queries)
- ✦ keeping the notice board tidy and clean

THINK

Look around your school or college and consider the merits of the notices which you see on the corridors.

✦ Designing notices

When designing a notice your aim must be to ensure that your notice is seen and acted upon where necessary. Long, rambling paragraphs will not achieve this aim. When designing notices bear in mind these guidelines:

- ✦ give the notice a clear heading
- ✦ use different size print for emphasis
- ✦ use sub-headings to break up the main information logically
- ✦ use asterisks/bullet points to display points on separate lines
- ✦ use the paper effectively to display the notice attractively
- ✦ include the name of the writer at the bottom as well as a reference and date.

A notice must contain the essential information displayed attractively so that it
receives attention and cooperation. Here are two examples of effective notices which
meet all these requirements. The first is a notice used within a company to point out
safety procedures, and the second is a notice which Midland Mainline display at
railway stations drawing the attention of passengers to the central door locking:

AURORA HOLDINGS

SAFETY PROCEDURES IN THE EVENT OF FIRE

FIRE DRILLS

A fire drill will be conducted every 6 months. Staff must
be aware of all fire exits, escape routes and procedures
for what to do in emergencies.

HOSE REELS

These will be tested once every 6 months at the same
time as the fire drill.

FIRE ALARMS

One fire alarm will be tested every week.

SPRINKLERS

These will be tested every week.

EXTINGUISHERS

These will be checked every week. Fire extinguishers
must not be moved from specified location.

EXITS

Exit doors must not be locked during working hours
and they must be kept clear at all times.

FIRE EXITS

Fire exit doors must never be jammed open.

FIRE DOORS

Fire check doors must never be jammed open. These
will be tested every 3 months to ensure correct
operation of the closing mechanism.

GANGWAYS

Gangways must be kept clear at all times.

FIRE CERTIFICATE

The fire certificate must be kept in a safe place in the
Safety Manager's office ready for inspection by the Fire
Brigade.

R. Wallace.

ROBERT WALLACE
Safety Manager

RW/ST
24 July 2001

MIDLAND MAINLINE

CENTRAL DOOR LOCKING
is fitted to all Midland Mainline trains

Boarding the Train

When the train has stopped at the platform, the Train Manager will release the Central Door Locks. The orange indicator next to each passenger door will then light up. You can then open the door using the handle as normal.

Leaving the Train

When the train has stopped at the platform, the Train Manager will release the Central Door Locks. The orange indicator above each passenger door will light up to read 'Door Unlocked'. The window can then be lowered and the door opened using the outside handle.

Don't Get Carried Away

You can't get on or off the train once the doors are locked. Make sure you don't miss your train by getting on a few minutes before it is due to leave. Please do not board the train unless you intend to travel.

Reproduced courtesy of Midland Mainline

✦ Advertisements

Many companies advertise in newspapers, magazines or trade journals so as to reach out to a wide, and sometimes specific, market.

- ✦ to advertise vacant posts
- ✦ to promote products or services
- ✦ to announce special events or functions
- ✦ to publicise changes in the organisation.

The classified sections of newspapers categorise advertisements according to subject so that you can find any section quickly.

✦ Types of advertisement

There are two kinds of advertisement which you may be involved in helping to design: the *small ad* or *line advertisement*, and the *display ad*.

Small ads or line ads

In these ads the information is run on from line to line, often using the same font throughout, with no special layout. Charges are made by the line and there is normally a minimum charge for three or four lines.

Lots of small ads appear in a relatively small space, so you must try to use an opening which will catch the reader's attention. Then give as much summarised information as possible in as few lines as possible. But make sure you choose the right wording when considering the words to fit in a small space.

Capitol Bata/ MRT City Hall

PREMIER SECURITY PRIVATE INVESTIGATION BRANCH THE ONE NAME FOR ALL PRIVATE INVESTIGATION NEEDS (Owned by the Singapore Police Multi-Purpose Co-Operative Society Ltd and The Singapore Government Servant's Co-Operative Thrift & Loan Society Ltd).

Call Krishna at tel: 289 0479 (DIR) Ronnie at tel: 281 4431 (DIR) Fax: 2852709

61 Other Personal Services

MR FIX-IT: We fix anything and everything (carpentry, electrical etc). Enquiries: 2540021 anytime.

72 Packing/ Storage/ Delivery/ Removal

A BUDGET PRICE REMOVAL SVS Professional household/ office removal & disposal services. Experienced uniformed workers with effective team leaders pro-

73 Office Equipment/ Supplies

USED THOMSON PABX Telephone system with capacity of 6 lines + 20 extns, model: P10-A. $800. Used Nitsuko 516 key telephone system with 5 lines + 12 key telephone set $800. Used Switching system 2 lines + 3 extns $300. Pls. call 2742754.

1ST TELEPHONE EMPORIUM in town for major brand of new & used key telephone system. Ranges from 2 lines 3 extensions to 20 lines 50 extensions. Maintenance service is available. Call Sangai Enterprises at tel: 4713988 for details

G'TEED. BRAND NEW. Canon copiers NP150 $1280 up to A3 copy size. 1 yr. g'tee. NP155: zoom/ enlargement, reduction up to A3 size $550. Key phone $680. Fax $750 Speedcoms 7483375.

NEW MINI-PABX telephone system with 2 lines + 6 extns. c/w 1 unit of loudspeaker phone & speed dial memories & 4 unit of standard set. $980. Call 2748450.

RENT OR BUY Ricoh copier with full warranty and backup service. We also sell liquid copier for photocopy centre. Delta O.A. Tel 2721266

WELL KNOWN KEY telephone available. Reasonable price to suit your budget. Call 2722371 for more information. After 5.30pm. Pg. 7012430

BRAND NEW 7 months Rank Xerox model 6002 electronic typewriter & Rank Xerox model 1012 recopier for sale. Page: 8038774.

BRAND NEW PORTABLE typewriters (electronic and manual) for sale. Economical and durable. Enquries, please call: 5332585.

AUTO NEW FAX $890. Canon enlargement/ reduction copier from $500 typewriter $265 3374968.

BRAND NEW FAX with lines sharing feature avail. at attractive price. Call: 4713988.

CANON NP270, 305, 120, PC20/ 30. Xerox 1012, Minolta EP410Z, 350Z, Toshiba 5511. 7450417

FAX $800 ONLY. Typewriter $328. Low Cost Copier, Shredder, Key Phone. Tel: 2704436.

GOOD BUY. BRAND new typewriters, copier, fax, paper shredder, chequewriter, etc. 3388855.

KEY TELEPHONE HYBRID system (8 lines x 32 ext.) for sale. Call: 256 2214 for details.

NEW KEY TELEPHONE system with 2 lines & 3 units of key telephone sets. $780.00. Call 2706383

Display adverts

Display advertisements may incorporate a variety of font styles and sizes. Artwork or colour may be included. Charges will be based on the number of column centimetres, often with a minimum size. Information can be displayed within the advertisement to attract special attention to specific points.

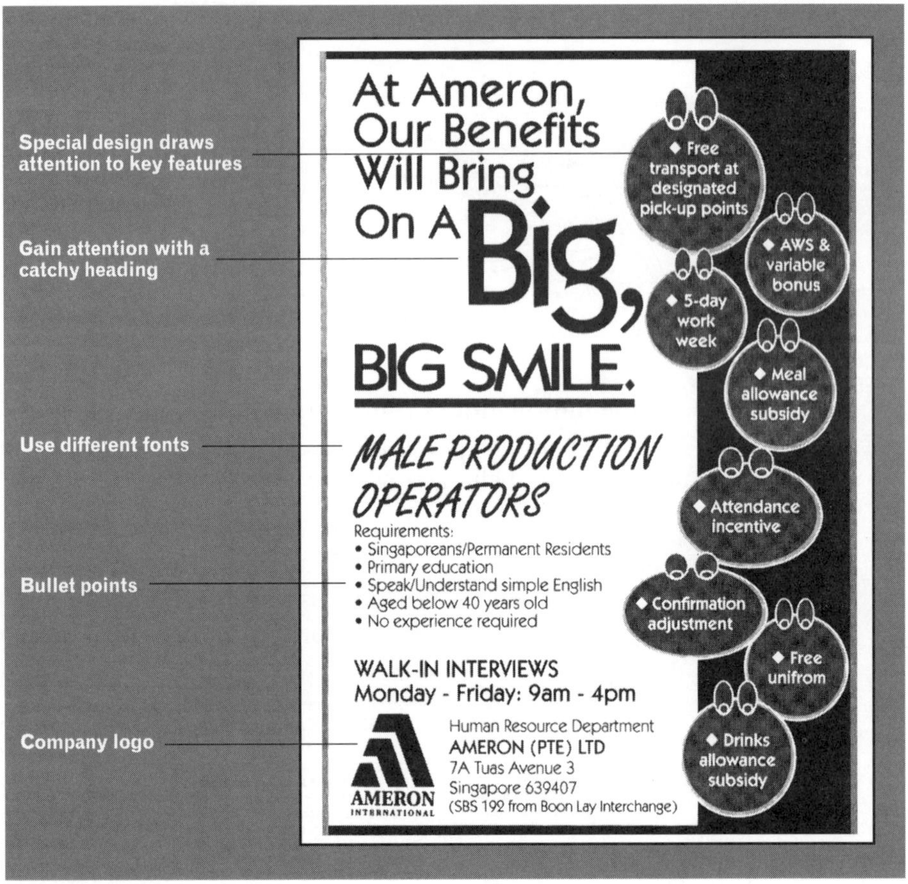
Special design draws attention to key features
Gain attention with a catchy heading
Use different fonts
Bullet points
Company logo
At Ameron, Our Benefits Will Bring On A Big, BIG SMILE.
MALE PRODUCTION OPERATORS
Requirements:
• Singaporeans/Permanent Residents
• Primary education
• Speak/Understand simple English
• Aged below 40 years old
• No experience required
WALK-IN INTERVIEWS
Monday - Friday: 9am - 4pm
AMERON INTERNATIONAL
Human Resource Department
AMERON (PTE) LTD
7A Tuas Avenue 3
Singapore 639407
(SBS 192 from Boon Lay Interchange)
◆ Free transport at designated pick-up points
◆ AWS & variable bonus
◆ 5-day work week
◆ Meal allowance subsidy
◆ Attendance incentive
◆ Confirmation adjustment
◆ Free unifrom
◆ Drinks allowance subsidy

Reproduced courtesy of AMERON (PTE) LTD

✦ Writing style

When asked to compile an advertisement you must be able to pick out the main points or features of whatever is being advertised and then put them over in an interesting, attractive way. It is essential to aim for your advertisement to be 'seen' when it stands next to lots of other advertisements. Here is 'AIDA' from the advertising department explaining the technique for meeting this objective:

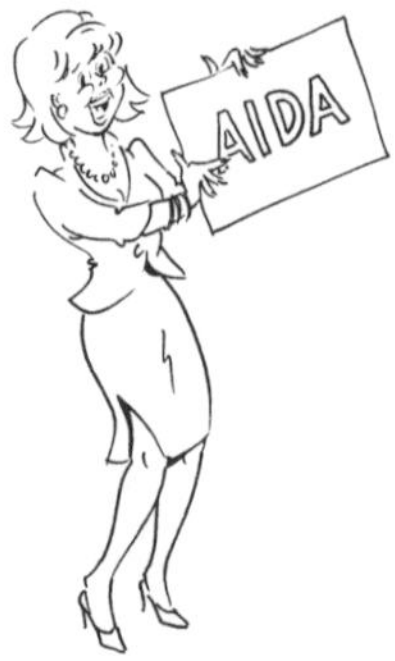
AIDA

Attention	you must attract the reader's attention
Interest	get the reader's interest by mentioning something which will appeal to them
Desire	arouse the reader's desire to buy, to attend a function to find out more or to contact the writer
Action	make the audience want to do something as a result of reading the ad.

You will achieve these AIDA objectives if you follow these guidelines:

+ use a company logo, prominently displayed
+ compose a catchy headline and display it prominently
+ use spacing to advantage, giving special items prominence
+ categorise the information using sub-headings, bullet points
+ clearly state the action you want the reader to take
+ make your advertisement eye-catching
+ aim for your advertisement to stand out from all the others around it.

Study these effective advertisements and discuss which job might appeal to you.

Reproduced courtesy of Youth Hostels Association (England and Wales)Ltd

Are you game for a challenge?

If you are looking for an exciting career and believe in service excellence, CISCO is the right place for you. Join Singapore's premier security and loss prevention organisation as:

Confidential Secretary

Duties:
- To provide secretarial and administrative support

Requirements:
- GCE A levels or 5 GCE O levels with a credit in English
- Certificate in Business Studies (Secretarial Practice) preferred
- Computer literate
- 2 years' experience in a similar capacity would be an advantage

Accounts Assistant

Duties:
- To maintain general accounting records including accounts receivables

Requirements:
- 3 GCE O or 5 GCE N levels with a credit in Maths
- LCCI Intermediate Bookkeeping Certificate
- Computer literate
- Experience would be an advantage

Walk-In Interview

Date : 5 -7 May (Tue-Thu)
Time: 9am to 11am or 2pm to 4pm

Applicants are requested to come personally with originals and photocopies of their educational certificates and other documents, or write/fax in to the address below. For more information on CISCO, visit our Website *www.cisco.com.sg.*

Director, Human Resource
CISCO Centre, 20 Jalan Afifi
Singapore 409179
Tel: 842 8748 Fax: 746 2284
Email: hrd@cisco.com.sg

CISCO

Reproduced courtesy of CISCO Centre

ENGLISH
NATIONAL
BALLET
SCHOOL

SCHOOL SECRETARY

Situated in Chelsea, the School offers Vocational training for 16-19 year old students to prepare them as professional ballet dancers.

English National Ballet School requires a School Secretary with excellent interpersonal and well proven administrative skills.

- The ideal candidate should be prepared to participate fully in all aspects of the School's activities working in conjunction with other members of staff who are an enthusiastic, energetic and friendly team.
- Previous experience of Windows 95 and Excel would be an advantage.
- Knowledge of ballet not essential.
- Salary in the region of £17,000.

Applications, with curriculum vitae and names, with contact details of two referees, by Wednesday 23rd September to:

English National Ballet School, Carlyle Building, Hortensia Road, London SW10 OQS
Tel: 0171 376 7076   Fax: 0171 376 3404   email: school@ballet.org.uk

Reproduced courtesy of English National Ballet School

THINK

Bring in to class a copy of a local newspaper, journal or magazine. Turn to the classified ads section and see if any adverts jump out at you. What makes these adverts so successful?

WHAT'S WRONG?

Study this assignment and the following advertisement. Discuss what is wrong with it and then design something more appropriate:

Aurora Holdings will soon be opening a new superstore in Kowloon and they require a supervisor for the customer services department. Human Relations Manager, Chew Mei Mei, asks you to draft an advert for her. This department will deal with requests for product information, give advice and deal with complaints. Applicants must enjoy dealing directly with the public. Therefore it is essential that the supervisor has a pleasant manner, tact, diplomacy and ability to cope under pressure. O levels are essential (English and Maths) or equivalent qualification. The ability to lead and motivate is important. This will be a busy and challenging post with good opportunities for career progression. The supervisor may occasionally have to visit customers' homes when investigating complaints, so a clean driving licence is essential. Previous experience in this type of work would be useful but not essential – training will be given. We offer an attractive salary with other benefits – staff discount on purchases, subsidised meals. Working hours 40 a week, Monday to Saturday, with 20 days annual leave plus statutory holidays. Applications to Chew Mei Mei at Aurora House, Nathan Road, Hong Kong, by the end of next month.

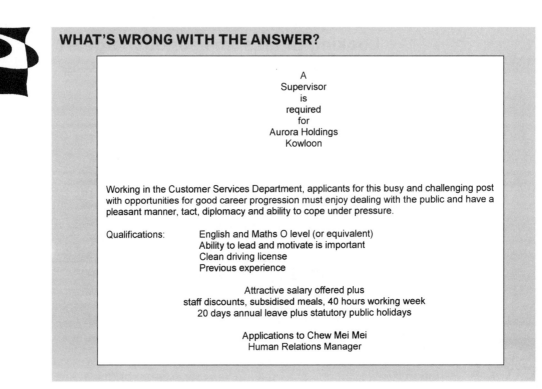

A
Supervisor
is
required
for
Aurora Holdings
Kowloon

Working in the Customer Services Department, applicants for this busy and challenging post with opportunities for good career progression must enjoy dealing with the public and have a pleasant manner, tact, diplomacy and ability to cope under pressure.

Qualifications: English and Maths O level (or equivalent)
                       Ability to lead and motivate is important
                       Clean driving license
                       Previous experience

Attractive salary offered plus
staff discounts, subsidised meals, 40 hours working week
20 days annual leave plus statutory public holidays

Applications to Chew Mei Mei
Human Relations Manager

✦ Assignments

1   Design a small line ad announcing a new Business English course starting soon at your college. Mention the duration and how many hours a week. Include a contact number.

2   You work for Aurora School of Physical Therapies in Bedford, telephone 0119 387472. You offer weekend courses in Reflexology, Aromatherapy and Massage – also various post graduate courses. Design a small line ad. Anyone who wants a prospectus can call the school.

3   Design a small line ad regarding an item of office equipment which your company wishes to sell. Make up the details.

4   You work for Mr James Tan, Human Resource Manager at Victory Enterprises Pte Ltd, 201 Nathan Road, Kowloon, Hong Kong. Mr Tan said to you today:

'Can you help me to design an ad – we need someone to help Robert in the Sales Department – he needs an assistant because he's away so often. Male or female, a couple of A levels would be good. Not too young though, 25-35-ish. We need someone with lots of common sense, able to work alone. Good telephone manner and diplomacy are essential for this job. You can't be rude to our customers or they'll be off straight away. Good old-fashioned politeness – that's all we ask. Mention that we'll offer a good salary, 4 weeks' holiday, hours 9-5,

good career prospects, medical and dental benefits – but in return we expect loyalty and hard work. Try to make it really eye-catching and they'll come flooding in!

Design a suitable advertisement.

5   You work for Aurora International Ltd, a large travel company based in modern headquarters at Aurora Court, 14-18 Holborn, London EC1N 9JE. The company offers all employees a competitive salary and many benefits including use of worldwide holiday accommodation and discounts on flights. Your fax number is 0181 333 1782. The Manager said to you today:

Please draft an advert for me. We urgently need bright, intelligent reservation agents to join our team. We provide thorough training so previous experience in the travel industry isn't essential. Applicants do need basic keyboard skills though, and a reasonable geographical knowledge. Oh, and a good telephone manner goes without saying. The next training session will start on the 30th of next month so applicants must be available for that.
Applicants need to be interested in quality customer service, a real people person.
Faxes only I think so don't give our address.

Design a suitable advertisement.

6   You work for Mrs Ruth Fairless, Manager of the Bateman Hotel, Norland Road, Tenwick, Cumbria C49 8JY.

(LCCIEB EFB2 style)

The Bateman Hotel is an old building and some of the electrical wiring is going to be replaced. While work is being carried out all the hotel's electricity will be cut off. As the hotel cannot operate without electricity for a long period of time, it has been decided that the work will be carried out over two days - 26 and 27 May. On these days there will be no electricity in the hotel between 0930 and 1130 and then again between 1430 and 1630. This should cause few problems as not many guests will be in the hotel during those times.

Mrs Fairless asks you to write a notice which can be left in all the rooms and displayed around the building. Here are her notes:

Say sorry to guests.
It's only for two days – tell them times – say why it's needed
Remind them that nothing electrical will work (lights, kettle, hairdryer etc)
No hot water – better not use bath/shower
Limited room cleaning – no vacuum cleaners
We'll supply free tea and coffee in the lounge from flasks
Lifts won't work – we'll help anyone to use stairs if necessary
Fire alarm will still work – different system

Write the notice

7   You work for Mr Rashid Hassan, Office Manager of Langland
    Manufacturing plc, Freeman Industrial Estate, Pitt Lane, Portsmouth,
    Hampshire PO13 7JJ. The company makes household furniture.

    (LCCIEB EFB2 style)

The company is concerned about a number of the costs of providing various services in the
offices. Mr Hassan is very worried about the cost of photocopying as this is rising greatly
every month. He does not want to put a limit on the number of copies each person can
make but he wants to put a notice next to each photocopying machine asking staff tactfully if
they could be careful how many copies they make. He wants to remind staff that there are
cheaper ways of making many copies than using the photocopier such as using the printing
department, and he wants staff to think about whether the copying is really necessary. It
would help everyone if they were able to cut down and if they do not do so there may have
to be a limit placed on the number of copies any person can take, or even only allow senior
staff to use the machines.

Draft the notice

8   You work for Mr David Fenworth, Manager of Fenworth Fashions,
    117 High Street, Hale, Cheshire WA5 7TJ

    (LCCIEB EFB2 style)

Mr Fenworth has just been told that some urgent repair work is being made to the staff car
park next week and the car park will be closed for three days from 8 to 10 August. During
this time staff who use their cars to come to work can use the customers' car park but there
isn't a lot of room in this. It would be helpful if staff didn't use their cars for these three days
and would use the bus or make alternative transport arrangements to get to the shop. It
would also help if staff could give each other lifts to work so there won't be so many cars
using the car park. Mr Fenworth has asked you to write a notice about the car park to be
placed on the staff notice boards.

Write the notice

Leaflets

By the end of this unit you should be able to:

❑ explain why leaflets may be produced in business

❑ describe different designs which may be used for leaflets

❑ identify effective leaflets

❑ discuss special writing skills needed in designing leaflets

❑ design leaflets according to given instructions.

✦ Types of leaflet

Most organisations produce leaflets or brochures for any number of reasons:

- ✦ to publicise goods or services
- ✦ to promote special events and promotions
- ✦ to give information of any kind.

Such leaflets may take the form of a single page, o they could be designed as a folded document – A4 size could be folded once or twice to make a four-page or six-page leaflet as shown here:

Here is an example of an effective single-sided leaflet:

Reproduced courtesy of Boots the Chemists Ltd

This leaflet is more complicated, extending to six pages. Note the effective use of sub-headings, bullet points and illustrations.

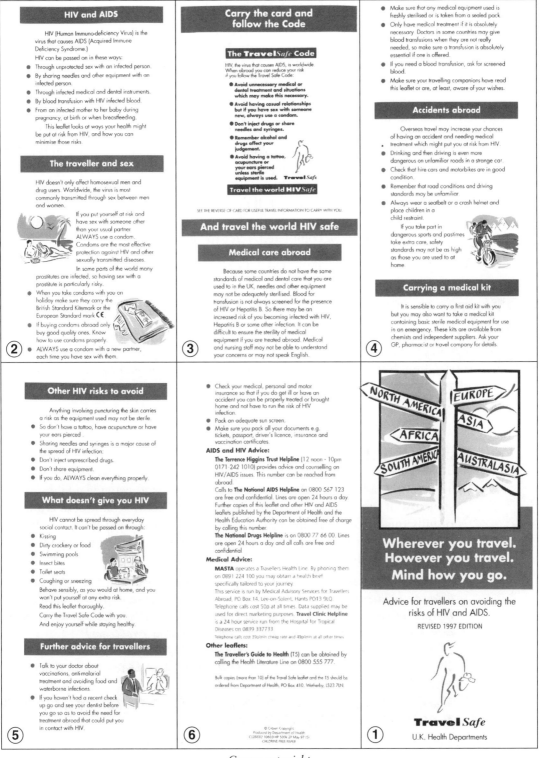

HIV and AIDS

HIV (Human Immuno-deficiency Virus) is the virus that causes AIDS (Acquired Immune Deficiency Syndrome.)

HIV can be passed on in these ways:

- Through unprotected sex with an infected person.
- By sharing needles and other equipment with an infected person.
- Through infected medical and dental instruments.
- By blood transfusion with HIV infected blood.
- From an infected mother to her baby during pregnancy, at birth or when breastfeeding.

This leaflet looks at ways your health might be put at risk from HIV, and how you can minimise those risks.

The traveller and sex

HIV doesn't only affect homosexual men and drug users. Worldwide, the virus is most commonly transmitted through sex between men and women.

If you put yourself at risk and have sex with someone other than your usual partner ALWAYS use a condom. Condoms are the most effective protection against HIV and other sexually transmitted diseases.

In some parts of the world many prostitutes are infected, so having sex with a prostitute is particularly risky.

- When you take condoms with you on holiday make sure they carry the British Standard Kitemark or the European Standard mark CE
- If buying condoms abroad only buy good quality ones. Know how to use condoms properly.
- ALWAYS use a condom with a new partner, each time you have sex with them.

②

Carry the card and follow the Code

The TravelSafe Code

HIV, the virus that causes AIDS, is worldwide. When abroad you can reduce your risk if you follow the Travel Safe Code:

- Avoid unnecessary medical or dental treatment and situations which may make this necessary.
- Avoid having casual relationships but if you have sex with someone new, always use a condom.
- Don't inject drugs or share needles and syringes.
- Remember alcohol and drugs affect your judgement.
- Avoid having a tattoo, acupuncture or your ears pierced unless sterile equipment is used. **Travel**Safe

Travel the world **HIV**Safe

SEE THE REVERSE OF CARD FOR USEFUL TRAVEL INFORMATION TO CARRY WITH YOU.

And travel the world HIV safe

Medical care abroad

Because some countries do not have the same standards of medical and dental care that you are used to in the UK, needles and other equipment may not be adequately sterilised. Blood for transfusion is not always screened for the presence of HIV or Hepatitis B. So there may be an increased risk of you becoming infected with HIV, Hepatitis B or some other infection. It can be difficult to ensure the sterility of medical equipment if you are treated abroad. Medical and nursing staff may not be able to understand your concerns or may not speak English.

③

- Make sure that any medical equipment used is freshly sterilised or is taken from a sealed pack.
- Only have medical treatment if it is absolutely necessary. Doctors in some countries may give blood transfusions when they are not really needed, so make sure a transfusion is absolutely essential if one is offered.
- If you need a blood transfusion, ask for screened blood.
- Make sure your travelling companions have read this leaflet or are, at least, aware of your wishes.

Accidents abroad

Overseas travel may increase your chances of having an accident and needing medical treatment which might put you at risk from HIV.

- Drinking and then driving is even more dangerous on unfamiliar roads in a strange car.
- Check that hire cars and motorbikes are in good condition.
- Remember that road conditions and driving standards may be unfamiliar.
- Always wear a seatbelt or a crash helmet and place children in a child restraint.

If you take part in dangerous sports and pastimes take extra care, safety standards may not be as high as those you are used to at home.

Carrying a medical kit

It is sensible to carry a first aid kit with you but you may also want to take a medical kit containing basic sterile medical equipment for use in an emergency. These kits are available from chemists and independent suppliers. Ask your GP, pharmacist or travel company for details.

④

Other HIV risks to avoid

Anything involving puncturing the skin carries a risk as the equipment used may not be sterile.

- So don't have a tattoo, have acupuncture or have your ears pierced:
- Sharing needles and syringes is a major cause of the spread of HIV infection:
- Don't inject unprescribed drugs.
- Don't share equipment.
- If you do, ALWAYS clean everything properly.

What doesn't give you HIV

HIV cannot be spread through everyday social contact. It can't be passed on through:

- Kissing
- Dirty crockery or food
- Swimming pools
- Insect bites
- Toilet seats
- Coughing or sneezing

Behave sensibly, as you would at home, and you won't put yourself at any extra risk.

Read this leaflet thoroughly.

Carry the Travel Safe Code with you.

And enjoy yourself while staying healthy.

Further advice for travellers

- Talk to your doctor about vaccinations, anti-malarial treatment and avoiding food and waterborne infections.
- If you haven't had a recent check up go and see your dentist before you go so as to avoid the need for treatment abroad that could put you in contact with HIV.

⑤

- Check your medical, personal and motor insurance so that if you do get ill or have an accident you can be properly treated or brought home and not have to run the risk of HIV infection.
- Pack an adequate sun screen.
- Make sure you pack all your documents e.g. tickets, passport, driver's licence, insurance and vaccination certificates.

AIDS and HIV Advice:

The Terrence Higgins Trust Helpline (12 noon - 10pm 0171-242 1010) provides advice and counselling on HIV/AIDS issues. This number can be reached from abroad.

Calls to **The National AIDS Helpline** on 0800 567 123 are free and confidential. Lines are open 24 hours a day. Further copies of this leaflet and other HIV and AIDS leaflets published by the Department of Health and the Health Education Authority can be obtained free of charge by calling this number.

The National Drugs Helpline is on 0800 77 66 00. Lines are open 24 hours a day and all calls are free and confidential

Medical Advice:

MASTA operates a Travellers Health Line. By phoning them on 0891 224 100 you may obtain a health brief specifically tailored to your journey.

This service is run by Medical Advisory Services for Travellers Abroad, PO Box 14, Lee-on-Solent, Hants PO13 9LQ. Telephone calls cost 50p at all times. Data supplied may be used for direct marketing purposes. **Travel Clinic Helpline** is a 24 hour service run from the Hospital for Tropical Diseases on 0839 337733.

Telephone calls cost 39p/min cheap rate and 49p/min at all other times

Other leaflets:

The Traveller's Guide to Health (T5) can be obtained by calling the Health Literature Line on 0800 555 777.

Bulk copies (more than 10) of the Travel Safe leaflet and the T5 should be ordered from Department of Health, PO Box 410, Wetherby, LS23 7LN.

© Crown Copyright
Produced by Department of Health
C128002 10603 HP 500k 2P May 97 (S)
CHLORINE FREE PAPER

⑥

Wherever you travel. However you travel. Mind how you go.

Advice for travellers on avoiding the risks of HIV and AIDS.

REVISED 1997 EDITION

TravelSafe

U.K. Health Departments

①

Crown copyright

✦ Designing leaflets

The AIDA techniques in Unit 15 can be used when writing leaflets. Other guidelines you should consider are:

1 Use a company logo, prominently displayed.
2 Use an appropriate heading which clearly states what the leaflet is about.
3 Consider carefully the information which needs to be included in the main body of the leaflet. Break it up according to different aspects of the main theme.
4 Use sub-headings and bullet points where possible.
5 Use straightforward, simple language and short sentences.
6 Be as persuasive as possible, making everything sound interesting and beneficial.
7 Use everyday language instead of technical jargon.
8 Aim for an effective and attractive display which uses space to advantage.
9 If you want a response give full details – what to do, who to contact, telephone number, etc.
10 If a portion is to be completed, refer to Unit 17 on form design.

Another example of a well designed leaflet is shown on the opposite page:

THINK

Is there a leaflet or brochure describing the college where you are studying? While you are out and about, pick up some leaflets in shops or offices and bring them into class. Have a look at the layout of the leaflets and see how they conform to the guidelines in this unit.

✦ Assignments

1 You work at a local health centre where the aim is to provide a high standard of service for all patients. To help to meet this aim there is a team of fully qualified and trained practice nurses and health visitors. You have been asked to design a leaflet to highlight the work of the nursing team. Here are your notes of what must be included:

Practice Nurses and Health Visitors = role developed to bridge the gap between medical and nursing care. They see anyone with minor illnesses (sore throats, earache, coughs/hayfever/asthma, diarrhoea and vomiting, minor traumas, sticky eyes, infant colic, feeding problems)
Doctors = more time for more serious consultations.
Nursing Team always works closely with Doctors to ensure best possible care for all.
Practice Nurses are available Mon-Fri 8.30-12.15, Mon/Wed/Fri 2.00-6.00, Tues/Thurs 4.00-6.00.

Design either a leaflet (either A4 size, or fold A4 into three to make a six-sided leaflet) to issue to patients at the health centre.

Most infections get better without antibiotics

In cases where patients will get better without antibiotics, it makes sense for your doctor not to prescribe them. Your body's defence system can often protect against infection without the need for antibiotics.

Listen to your doctor

Your doctor will be able to recognise whether you have an infection that needs antibiotics, so you should not always expect to be given a prescription. Doctors need to prescribe antibiotics with care. This is because inappropriate use of antibiotics can be dangerous for individual patients and for the whole population.

Overuse of antibiotics can also cause resistance and result in them not working in the future. This is a very worrying trend, especially for patients with serious life-threatening infections.

Harmful side-effects

Potential side-effects are another reason why doctors are cautious about prescribing antibiotics. Some antibiotic treatment can cause side-effects such as stomach upset and thrush. For women on the pill, antibiotics can reduce contraceptive protection.

Antibiotic facts

- Antibiotics have no effect on viral infections *(eg. colds, flu and most sore throats)*. Viral infections are much more common than bacterial infections.
- Inappropriate use of antibiotics can encourage the development of resistant bacteria. This could mean that the antibiotic may not work when you really need it.
- Some antibiotics have harmful side-effects such as diarrhoea and allergic reactions.
- Antibiotics do not just attack the infection they are prescribed for – they can also kill useful bacteria which normally protect you against other infections such as thrush.

- There are effective alternative remedies for managing the symptoms of many infections.

If you are prescribed antibiotics ensure you take the medication according to instructions.
- Although you may begin to feel better, you must take the full course of antibiotics to prevent your illness coming back.
- Not taking the full course of antibiotics can lead to future antibiotic resistance.

If you have an infection such as a cold, flu or sore throat
- Take paracetamol according to the instructions to help reduce fever and relieve aches and pains.
- Drink plenty of water to avoid dehydration.
- Ask your pharmacist *(chemist)* for advice. Many infections can be managed effectively with over-the-counter medications. The pharmacist will refer you to your doctor or practice nurse if they think it is necessary.

When to contact your GP

Call your GP's surgery for advice if, after taking over-the-counter medications as directed, you or your child are experiencing any of the following:
- symptoms which are severe or unusually prolonged.
- extreme shortness of breath.
- coughing up of blood or large amounts of yellow or green phlegm.

DOCTOR PATIENT PARTNERSHIP

Promoting a healthy partnership between patients and health professionals

BMA House Tavistock Square London WC1H 9JP
Fax: 0171 383 6403 Internet: www.doctorpatient.org.uk

Reproduced courtesy of Doctor Patient Partnership

2   You work for Mr Rashid Hassan, Office Manager of Langland
     Manufacturing plc, Freeman Industrial Estate, Pitt Lane, Portsmouth,
     Hampshire PO13 7JJ. The company makes household furniture.
     (LCCIEB EFB2 style)

The company has built up a large amount of stock in its warehouse, and some of this was slightly damaged when rain came in through the roof one weekend. Mr Hassan has decided to sell off this furniture and other items which have been in stock for a long time. He gives you these instructions:

We need a leaflet we can send to people in the area to tell them about our sale which will be at 10.00 am on Saturday 27 September in our main warehouse. Say that we have a wide range of furniture for sale (chairs, tables, cabinets, beds, wardrobes and chests of drawers). Some of this is damaged slightly but some is perfect and it's all going to be sold at bargain prices. Everything will be at least half price. We'll open the warehouse for a couple of hours from 6 o'clock on Friday night so people can see what we have for sale. You'd better say that we can't deliver anything we sell so customers will have to be able to take away anything they buy.

Draft the leaflet.

3   You work for Mrs Ruth Fairless, Office Manager of the Bateman Hotel,
     Norland Road, Tenwick, Cumbria C49 8JY.
     (LCCIEB EFB2 style)

The hotel is well known for its Christmas lunches and often guests enjoy staying over the Christmas period. For the first time this year the hotel is planning to offer something similar on New Year's Eve and New Year's Day. Many people enjoy celebrating the New Year and Mrs Fairless has asked you to draft a leaflet to send to all the guests who have ever stayed at the hotel informing them about these New Year celebrations.

You made some notes when speaking to Mrs Fairless, as follows:

Guests staying for one night on 31 December and will be able to go to the hotel's grand dinner and dance that evening. A special five course dinner will be served and guests will be able to celebrate until 2 am.
On the following day there will be a special boat trip on the lake next to the hotel and lunch will be served on the boat. Afternoon tea will be served back at the hotel before guests leave.
Entertainment will be provided for children on 31 December and there will be a disco for older children.
All included in special price.
Children who stay in their parents' room will be free.
If guests stay on longer, regular rates will apply.

Draft the leaflet.

UNIT 16

Invitations

By the end of this unit you should be able to:

❏   state reasons why invitations are used

❏   compose formal and informal invitations

❏   reply to formal and informal invitations.

Many companies organise special functions for various reasons:

- ✦ to publicise a special event
- ✦ the launch of a new product
- ✦ the opening of a new branch office
- ✦ the retirement of a senior executive.

You may be expected to know how to prepare invitations to such functions, or how to reply to such invitations, when your employer gives you an instruction simply to accept or refuse.

✦ Formal invitations

Formal invitations are usually printed on A5 or A6 good quality paper or card. Often they are specially printed. They should include the following details

- ✦ who the invitation is from
- ✦ who is invited (usually a blank space)
- ✦ what is happening
- ✦ the date
- ✦ the time
- ✦ an address for a reply.

Use double spacing and centre each line

The recipient's name will be handwritten on this line

Include all details, dates and times

Name and address for reply

Include a reply date

> The Directors of
>
> Aurora Holdings plc
>
> request the pleasure of the company of
>
> ....
>
> at their Bi-Centenary Celebrations
>
> to be held at
>
> Celebrities Ballroom
> Beijing Friendship Hotel
> San Ma Road
> Beijing 100011
>
> on Friday 12 July 2000
>
> Cocktails at 1930
> Dinner at 2000
>
> The Directors
> Aurora Holdings plc
> No 16 Chaoyangmen Nandajie
> Chaoyang District
> Beijing 100020
> China   RSVP by 31 May 2000

When a formal invitation is accepted or refused it is usual to prepare the reply in a similar, formal style. If an invitation is refused, it is courteous to give a reason.

Use similar presentation and double spacing	*Miss Mavis Lee*
	thanks the Directors of
	Aurora Holdings plc
Use third person and formal wording	*for their kind invitation to their*
	Bi-Centenary Celebrations
	to be held at
Repeat details	*Celebrities Ballroom*
	Beijing Friendship Hotel
	San Ma Road
	Beijing 100011
	on Friday 12 July 2000
A formal acceptance	*and has much pleasure in accepting*
Sender's address	*No 4 Dong Ji Street*
	Nankai District
	Tianjin 300100
	China
Date	*15 May 2000*

Ashley Ow Yong

thanks the Directors of

Aurora Holdings plc

for their kind invitation to their

Bi-Centenary Celebrations

on Friday 12 July 2000

but is unable to attend as he will be overseas on business

6G No 127 Yu Yao Road
Shanghai 200040
China

28 May 2000

✦ Informal invitations

Invitations may also be presented in the form of a letter. Remember to reply in a similar manner.

Silver Grange
Scarborough Road
PERTH
WA 4459

Tel (618) 9454323

2 August 2000

Dear Eileen & Norman

Fifty years and we are still together! We are pleased to announce our Golden Wedding Anniversary on Saturday 4 September 2000.

We are planning to celebrate by holding a cocktail and buffet evening at our home at 1930 on that date. We have pleasure in inviting you to attend.

We sincerely hope you will be able to join us to celebrate this special occasion.

Liz & Keith

✦ Assignments

1　Your company will be opening its new branch in a nearby town next month and is arranging a cocktail reception to mark the occasion. Prepare an invitation which can be printed to send to a number of special clients.

2　Prepare a reply accepting the invitation from one of the clients.

3　Prepare a reply from Doctor Anthony Long of Orchard Medisave Pte Ltd. Unfortunately Dr Long cannot attend the cocktail reception as he will be overseas on a business trip.

4   Here is an invitation which I received. Follow my instructions and prepare a reply.

5   Your company, Aurora Holdings, of Temple House, Temple Street, London SE1 4LL, has recently appointed a new office manager – Mr John Hamilton – who will replace Mr Thomas Hunter. Write a letter to be signed by the Managing Director – Sally Thompson – to one of your customers (make up the details). Invite the customer and his partner to a reception to mark Mr Hunter's retirement and to introduce Mr Hamilton to them. It is to be held on 14 October at 7.30 pm at the Westminster Hotel, London WC1A 4WW.

VISUAL COMMUNICATION

Form design

By the end of this unit you should be able to:

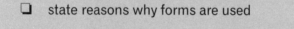

❑ state reasons why forms are used

❑ explain the techniques used to design effective forms

❑ identify poor design of forms and suggest improvements

❑ design forms for use internally and externally.

✦ The reason for forms

Form-filling is almost an everyday occurrence. In almost every aspect of our personal lives forms cannot be avoided. This is also true in the business world. Even with the impact of information technology, pre-printed forms are being used more and more for a variety of reasons:

- ✦ They are extremely valuable for collecting data in procedures which are standardised.
- ✦ They ensure that every piece of information required is completed by the form filler.
- ✦ The sequence of information is included in a priority order.
- ✦ They act as computer data input sources.
- ✦ They provide useful sources of reference.
- ✦ New forms can be designed easily to meet new policies or revised procedures.

Here are a variety of well-designed forms in everyday use in business:

Reproduced courtesy of Waterlow Business Supplies

✦ Designing forms

One reason why some people hate forms is because some designers do not allow sufficient space for the person completing the form to insert all the information.

If you have ever had a similar experience in completing a form, this should help you to ensure that your created forms are a pleasure to use. Effective form design can save many people valuable time, so study these guidelines for some useful techniques.

1   Consider these questions:

    a) Who will be completing the form?
    b) Who needs the information?
    c) Why is this information needed?
    d) How would the information be most effectively presented?

2   Make a checklist of all the information needed, for example: name, address, telephone number, fax number, age, date of birth, sex, nationality

3   Divide your checklist into appropriate sub-sections and choose titles for each section.

4   Decide on a logical structure for the form according to priority.

5   Design your form in draft, making sure that you:

    a) word your questions carefully so that they will obtain the required response
    b) use options boxes where a variety of responses could be given
    c) leave sufficient spaces and lines where the required information will fit
    d) allow sufficient space when asking open questions
    e) ensure questions and instructions are simple, clear and unambiguous.

6   Try your form out on a colleague and ask for constructive criticism. Make any amendments based on the useful information obtained from this trial.

7   Print the form properly but monitor the first few forms completed. Check that users understand requirements completely and that sufficient space for answers is provided.

8   Monitor forms regularly and ask yourself, is the form

    a) essential?
    b) straightforward and simple to complete?
    c) logical in the sequence of questions?
    d) printed on appropriate paper (colour/size/quality)?
    e) relevant?
    f) suitable for the purpose for which it is intended?

✦ Reply forms

On many occasions in business replies are required from recipients of letters. In Unit 11 we discussed tear-off slips which are often used when sending out circular letters. Sometimes when a tear-off slip is not big enough for the information required a separate reply form may be necessary.

A reply form enables the sender to specify the information required from everyone to whom the form is sent. This guarantees that the correct information will be obtained and is a much better way of obtaining information than by requesting a written reply.

Sometimes reply coupons are included in advertisements so that interested parties can reply easily.

Reproduced courtesy of Singapore Exhibition Services Pte Ltd

REPLY COUPON

CommunicAsia98 ᵗ ᵃᵗ   **MobileCommAsia98**   **NetworkAsia98**

FAX TO: (65) 339 5651

Yes! I am interested in
CommunicAsia98 / MobileCommAsia98 / NetworkAsia98.

☐ I am interested in **visiting** the event. Please send me more information closer to the event.

☐ I am interested in **exhibiting**. I would like to reserve _____ sqm (min. 9 sqm)

☐ I am interested in group participation.

☐ I am interested in *attending/presenting a paper at the Conference. Please send me more information.
delete where appropriate

Name _____

Job Title _____

Company _____

Address _____

_____

Country _____

Tel _____ Fax _____

E-mail _____
or attach your business card

Please mail/fax to:

Singapore Exhibition Services Pte Ltd
A Member of The Montgomery Network
2 Handy Road, #15-09 Cathay Building, Singapore 229233
Tel: (65) 338 4747 Fax: (65) 339 5651 E-mail: info@sesmontnet.com   TIME/CMMA98

When you design a reply form, remember that if you omit important details or word a question badly, it could result in your receiving many phone calls asking for clarification. Alternatively you could have to make hundreds of phone calls requesting extra information which you forgot to ask for on the form. Bear this in mind when you are designing forms.

I'm sorry, there was no space on the form for your address. Could you give it to me now please?

Headers and footers

Two important features of reply forms are the details shown at the head and foot. These details will differ on forms used within an organisation and forms used externally. Here are examples of header and footer details for forms used both internally and externally:

Internal forms

Date name and title only

REPLY FORM

Please return by 25 May 2000 to Mrs Mavis Tan, Training Manager

Signature .... Date ....

Name (in capitals) ....

Internal forms don't need company name/address, etc.

Designation/Department ....

Extension Number ....

External forms

REPLY FORM

Forms used externally need full name/title/ company name/address

Please return by 20 August 2000 to   Mrs Rosehannah Wethern
Marketing Manager
Timeless Traders Ltd
219 Rue de Chanson
Bridel L-85-96
Luxembourg

Always remember signature and date

Signature .... Date ....

Name (in capitals) ....

Designation/Department ....

Remember to allow sufficient space for appropriate details

Company ....

Address ....

....

.... Post code ....

Telephone Number .... Fax Number ....

TIP

When thinking of the opening and closing details for forms, just ask yourself who will be completing the form and what details you need to know!

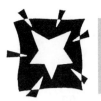

✦ Specimen form

Here is an example of a reply form sent out with a letter to clients of a training organisation. Clients were asked to specify whether or not they would like to attend a one-day management conference, when accommodation will be required, and enclose a cheque to cover the cost.

REPLY FORM

Always give a return by date and address

Please return by 15 February 2000 to Mr Sim Fook Chin
Training Manager
Professional Training Sdn Bhd
126 Buona Vista Boulevard
13006 Kuala Lumpur
Malaysia

Use same heading as on covering document

ONE-DAY MANAGEMENT CONFERENCE
SATURDAY 3 APRIL 2000

Use numbered points where appropriate

I wish/do not wish* to attend this conference.

I require accommodation on

Use options/tick boxes where relevant

❑ Friday 2 April

❑ Saturday 3 April (please tick)

Use I/my as if the person completing the form is speaking

My cheque for M$500 is attached (made payable to Professional Training Sdn Bhd)

Always include signature and date

Signature .... Date ....

Choose appropriate details here dependent upon the person completing. Use double spacing

Name (in capitals) ....

Designation/Department ....

Company ....

Address ....

....

.... Post code ....

Telephone Number .... Fax Number ....

Don't forget the footnote if applicable

* Please delete as necessary

WHAT'S WRONG?

After reading this assignment carefully, study the answer given. Discuss what is wrong with the reply form and then rewrite it correctly.

The Human Relations Manager has written to all employees informing them about the company's 25th anniversary dinner and dance to be held in three months' time. You have been asked to design a reply form for employees to return to you. Staff must let you know if they will be attending and also if they will be bringing a partner. You need a full list of names of those attending. Design a suitable form.

REPLY FORM

To be returned by 31 April to

Human Relations Manager
Aurora Holdings plc
Aurora House
Temple Street
London
SE1 4LL

I, ... (name) from ....

(department) do/do not* wish to attend the dinner and dance on 12 May.

I will/will not* be bringing my partner.

Signed ....

* Please delete

✦ Assignments

1 Your manager has written a circular letter to all customers announcing a cocktail evening to celebrate your company's 10th year of trading. Prepare a reply form which may be returned stating whether or not customers will attend.

2 Your manager has written an open letter to all employees announcing the retirement of the chairman and inviting them to attend a special presentation. This will be held at a local hotel in 2 months' time. Design a form to be sent with the letter for employees to return to you with the necessary information.

3 You are responsible for organising the company's annual dinner and dance. When you write to employees they will need to let you know whether or not they are attending. You also need to know if they are bringing a partner. Full payment must be sent with replies. Design an effective form.

4 You have written to departmental heads in all branches of your company asking them to nominate staff in their departments to attend a training workshop on effective communication. This will be a half-day course held in 2 months' time. Design a form to send with the memo for departmental heads to complete and return to you.

Questionnaires

By the end of this unit you should be able to:

- [ ] state why questionnaires may be used

- [ ] explain techniques used in designing effective questionnaires

- [ ] illustrate the different types of question used on questionnaires

- [ ] identify faults of questionnaire design and make appropriate corrections

- [ ] design effective questionnaires according to given instructions.

✦ The purpose of questionnaires

Questionnaires are a special type of form designed to record opinions or suggestions from different groups of people. They are widely used in business, for example:

+ for researching the preferences of consumers
+ for investigating public attitudes to major issues
+ for requesting the opinions of staff on issues like canteen facilities and flexihours.

A questionnaire may well form part of the research undertaken in the preparation of a formal report, as discussed in Unit 9.

All the guidelines mentioned about the design of forms apply also to the presentation of questionnaires. People who complete a questionnaire are often under no pressure to do so; therefore their design is even more important because they are dependent on the public's desire to help. To avoid putting people off, the questionnaire must be as straightforward as possible. Humour also helps, as in this extract from a feedback form used at Changi Airport, Singapore.

Please tick on the appropriate faces

	Excellent	Good	Average	Poor
Check-in Facilities & Services	☺	☺	☺	☹
Arrival Facilities & Services	☺	☺	☺	☹
Transit/Transfer Facilities & Services	☺	☺	☺	☹
Airport Cleanliness	☺	☺	☺	☹
Friendliness of Airport Staff	☺	☺	☺	☹
Shopping Facilities	☺	☺	☺	☹
Other Facilities (Please specify)	☺	☺	☺	☹

Reproduced courtesy of Civil Aviation Authority of Singapore

To achieve the objective of ensuring that people fill in your questionnaire, follow these guidelines:

- ✦ Ensure your questionnaire is clear and attractive.
- ✦ Use language which is simple and direct; it should not offend anyone.
- ✦ Use wording which will create a good relationship with the reader.
- ✦ Include only essential questions so that the form is not made unduly long.
- ✦ Begin with a polite request to the reader to complete the form and briefly mention why the information is needed.
- ✦ Include an assurance that all information will be treated in confidence.
- ✦ Thank the reader for completing the form.
- ✦ Include clear instructions about where to send the form after completion.

Here is a well-designed questionnaire used by Cold Storage in Singapore to obtain feedback from customers visiting their supermarket.

✦ Types of question

Different techniques can be used for asking questions on a questionnaire.

<u>Alternative questions</u> are used to establish facts and circumstances before asking further opinions.

Care must be taken to ensure that the alternative answers are specific.

How often do you buy cold drinks?

✗ Often/sometimes/rarely/never

✓ Several times a day/every day/twice a week/once a week/less often/never

<u>Closed questions</u> require specific answers. The most basic closed questions are those requiring yes/no answers:

Have you bought any drinks from the college vending machines during the past month?	Yes/No
Do you feel a vending machine for snacks should be provided?	Yes/No

<u>Multiple choice</u> questions are those giving a list of responses to be ticked. This type of question needs planning carefully to ensure complete coverage of possible answers:

THE FRESH FOOD PEOPLE

◀ Cold Storage

YOUR VIEWS MATTER

Dear Valued Customers,

Thank you for shopping at Cold Storage. We would be very much obliged if you could assist us to complete this questionnaire. Please base your response on your experience today. Your feedback is invaluable in helping us to provide better service.

Mr. Lester Quah
Operations Director

COLD STORAGE RETAIL
HOLLAND VILLAGE

OUTLET: _____ DATE: _____

Kindly tick responses accordingly.

SERVICE AT CHECKOUT (Counter no. ____)	AGREE	DISAGREE	NOT SURE
1. Staff greeted me with a **smile**	☐	☐	☐
2. Staff bagged **all** my items carefully	☐	☐	☐
3. Staff returned change & receipt with **both hands**	☐	☐	☐
4. Staff was courteous **at all times**	☐	☐	☐
5. **Efficiency** of transaction met my expectation	☐	☐	☐

DELICATESSEN / MEAT DEPARTMENT	AGREE	DISAGREE	NOT SURE
1. **Freshness & Quality** of product met my expectation	☐	☐	☐
2. Price tag / ticket was **clearly displayed**	☐	☐	☐

SEAFOOD DEPARTMENT	AGREE	DISAGREE	NOT SURE
1. **Freshness & Quality** of product met my expectation	☐	☐	☐
2. Price tag / ticket was **clearly displayed**	☐	☐	☐

FRUITS AND VEGETABLES DEPARTMENT	AGREE	DISAGREE	NOT SURE
1. Freshness & Quality of product met my expectation	☐	☐	☐
2. Price "chalkboard" was clearly displayed	☐	☐	☐

SUPERMARKET OVERVIEW

1. Any **new product** that you may want us to include into our product range ?_____

2. Any product that you **could not find easily** (no proper signage, obstructions)_____

3. You may wish to share your shopping experience with us :_____
_____
_____

MAY WE HAVE YOUR PARTICULARS PLEASE.

NAME: MISS/MRS/MDM/MR/DR _____

PHONE NUMBER: _____ PAGER NUMBER : _____

ADDRESS:_____
_____

Reproduced courtesy of Cold Storage Singapore (1983) Pte Ltd

Which of the following drinks have you bought recently?

Coffee	Sprite
Tea	Cola
Chocolate	Diet Cola
Milo	Orange Juice

(please tick)

Rating or preference questions ask for an opinion. Gradings are provided for ticking:

What is your opinion on the quality of the drinks from the vending machine?

	Good	Average	Fair
Coffee			
Tea			
Chocolate			
Milo			
Sprite			
Cola			
Diet Cola			
Orange			

Open questions invite comment:

Name any additional items you would like to be available from the college vending machines.

Drinks . . . .

Snacks . . . .

Here is a questionnaire inserted in boxes of The Sunshine Supplement Kira (St John's Wort) by manufacturers Lichtwer Pharma UK Ltd. They use various different questioning techniques in this leaflet to obtain feedback which will assist them in developing the product suitably.

About Kira

Is this the first time you have tried Kira?

Yes [ ]   No [ ]

How did you first hear about Kira?

Newspaper Advertisement [ ]   Radio [ ]
Newspaper Article [ ]   T.V. [ ]
Magazine Advertisement [ ]   Friend's Recommendation [ ]
Magazine Feature [ ]   Chemist's Recommendation [ ]
Saw in-store [ ]   Doctor's Recommendation [ ]

In which type of shop did you purchase Kira?

Healthfood [ ]   Chemist [ ]

Please tell us your reasons for buying Kira

Have you ever bought Hypericum products for health reasons before?

Yes [ ]   No [ ]

If yes, please specify which product and why?

How satisfied are you with Kira?

Too soon to say [ ]   Very Satisfied [ ]   Satisfied [ ]   Dissatisfied [ ]

Do you intend to buy Kira again?

Definitely Yes [ ]   Probably Yes [ ]   Probably Not [ ]
Definitely Not [ ]   Why?

How much do you spend on supplements per month?

If there are any further comments which you would like to make to us we would be delighted to receive them on a separate piece of paper enclosed with your questionnaire.

Please Tell Us About Yourself   Male [ ]   Female [ ]

Title _____ Name _____

Address _____

Age   Up to 25 [ ]   25-35 [ ]   36-50 [ ]   51-65 [ ]   Over 65 [ ]

Occupation

Administration/Clerical [ ]   Housewife [ ]
Manual [ ]   Professional/management [ ]
Retired [ ]   Student [ ]
Unemployed [ ]   Other [ ]

May we contact you again?   Yes [ ]   No [ ]

Data Protection: the information you supply will be treated in the strictest confidence and will not be linked with your name. Relevant data will be recorded on our database. It is our policy never to rent out or release our lists to other companies for their use.

Thank you for completing this questionnaire.

Please send to (no stamp required):

Lichtwer Pharma UK Limited FREEPOST SL 1171 Marlow Bucks SL7 1BT

Reproduced courtesy of Lichtwer Pharma UK Ltd

✦ Summary

If they are designed and used correctly, questionnaires can make life much easier for all concerned. They can ensure that an organisation obtains the information it needs, thus leading to an improved public image and increased customer rapport. Here is part of a feedback form used at the Marché Restaurant in Singapore which would certainly achieve these objectives:

RESTAURANT Marché MÖVENPICK

Day/Date of Visit: _____

Time: ☐ 11:30am – 2:00pm ☐ 2:00pm – 5:30pm
       ☐ 5:30pm – 8:00pm   ☐ 8:00pm – 11:00pm

No. of people in your party: _____

Area that you sat in: _____

Sex: Male ☐   Female ☐

Local ☐   Tourist ☐

Age:

Occupation:

Student ☐ Executive/Professional ☐ Homemaker ☐
Others (please specify) : _____

---

1 = Unacceptable   2 = Needs improvement   3 = Acceptable   4 = Good   5 = Excellent

A.   Food & Beverage:

Choice/Variety:	1......2......3......4......5
Freshness/Quality	1......2......3......4......5
Presentation	1......2......3......4......5

Pricing:

Pasta/Pizza	inexpensive......fair......expensive
Seafood	inexpensive......fair......expensive
Grilled Meats	inexpensive......fair......expensive
Salad	inexpensive......fair......expensive
Dessert	inexpensive......fair......expensive
Beverages	inexpensive......fair......expensive

Comments:

_____
_____
_____

B.   Staff

Presentation:	1......2......3......4......5
Friendliness	1......2......3......4......5
Efficiency	1......2......3......4......5
Attentiveness	1......2......3......4......5

Comments:

_____
_____
_____

C.   Restaurant

Cleanliness	1......2......3......4......5
Ambience	1......2......3......4......5
Decor	1......2......3......4......5
Background Music	1......2......3......4......5

Comments:

_____
_____

Reproduced courtesy of Mövenpick Marché Restaurant Singapore

LET'S CHECK

You are designing a questionnaire for use at your local health centre. What sort of question would you use to ask people:

1 Their date of birth?

2 How often they visit the doctor?

3 How long they usually have to wait before being seen by a doctor?

4 If they have ever had any of several common illnesses?

5 If they have any suggestions for improvements?

WHAT'S WRONG?

Your colleague has been asked to find out the opinions of staff on the food and service provided in the staff restaurant in your company. The results of this research will be analysed carefully to form the basis of a report. Discuss what is wrong with this questionnaire so that you can tactfully suggest to your colleague how it could be improved. When you have done this, redesign the questionnaire more appropriately.

CIRCULAR

Please complete this form and return it to Susan Gingell as soon as possible.

1 Which lunch sitting do you attend?　　　　　　　　　_____

2 How many times a week do you use
   the staff restaurant?　　　　　　　　　　　　　　_____

3 What else do you sometimes do at lunch time?　　　_____

4 Do you ever have to queue for meals?　　　　　　　_____

5 Are you satisfied with the selection of food available?　Yes/No

6 Are you satisfied with the service provided?　　　　　Yes/No

7 Are you satisfied with the food?　　　　　　　　　　Yes/No

Any other comments?

....

....

....

....

Signature .... Date ....

✦ Assignments

1 You work at Mills and Starks, a large retail store with many branches in your country. Design a small feedback form for customers to complete which will give feedback on how the company is rated in terms of customer service, selection of goods, quality of goods and value for money. If customers complete their name and address they will also be entered in a monthly lucky draw for Mills and Starks gift vouchers.

2 You work at a large hotel in your country. Design a small feedback form to be completed by visitors to any of your many coffee houses/restaurants. Use your initiative to decide which categories and statements should appear on the questionnaire so that it will be valuable to management in gauging customers' opinions.

3 You work at Rapid Repair car repair workshop with many branches in the region. You specialise in tyres, exhausts, batteries, shock absorbers and many other items. The General Manager has asked you to design a simple questionnaire which can be completed by customers so that standards can be maintained and improved. Use the following notes to help you to design the questionnaire:

> *This visit – what did they buy?*
>
> *Why us? (TV, radio, newspaper, yellow pages = think of others here)*
>
> *Questions – seat covers used? frank and honest appraisal given? informed of cost before work started? finished work examined in customer's presence? any parts removed offered to customer? depot clean/tidy?*
>
> *Overall rating?*

Include any other details you think are appropriate and design a questionnaire.

Visual presentation

By the end of this unit you should be able to:

❏ state the reasons for choosing visual presentation of information

❏ list the main forms of visual presentation and describe each one

❏ choose the best method for presenting different types of information.

✦ The appeal of visual presentation

Visual presentation of information is having an increasing impact on our lives. You only need turn on the television set or open any newspaper to appreciate the widespread use and effectiveness of such presentation. Visual presentation is beneficial for many reasons:

- ✦ Complex facts and figures can be much more easily absorbed.
- ✦ Visual presentation adds impact to the information.
- ✦ It enables quicker understanding due to its simplified format.
- ✦ It enables comparisons to be made and recognised easily.
- ✦ Audiences are more likely to be interested in a chart or diagram than a long explanation or lots of words.
- ✦ Charts or diagrams can easily be transferred onto overhead transparencies for presentation to large groups.

This illustration shows the percentage of information which is remembered when it is seen as compared to other means of communication. Compare too the illustration with the table shown alongside it. The pictorial presentation of the information is much more vivid, simpler and more effective compared to the words and figures.

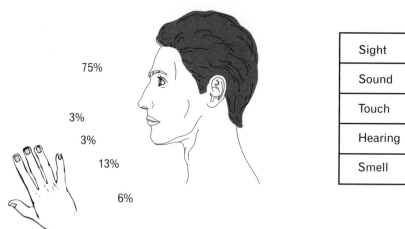

Sight	75%
Sound	3%
Touch	6%
Hearing	13%
Smell	3%

✦ Methods of presentation

To ensure the effectiveness of the presentation, it is important to select the most appropriate method. There are many ways in which information can be presented:

- tabulated data
- line graphs
- bar charts
- Gantt charts
- pie charts
- pictograms
- maps and diagrams
- cartograms
- flowcharts
- visual planning boards
- computer graphics.

✦ Tabulated data

Information is very often provided in the form of tables. Tables present data in an immediate and carefully ordered way, but they rely on the reader to interpret the data shown on them. This often means that the full significance of the data is not always immediately obvious until it has been carefully studied.

Turnover by region (%)

	1995	1996	1997	1998	1999	2000
Europe	52	50	49	46	45	40
Australasia	21	20	18	20	19	20
Africa and Middle East	11	10	14	10	14	12
USA/Canada	16	20	17	24	22	28

THINK

How could this information be presented in a different format so that the breakdowns for each year are easy to see at a glance?

Some tabular displays can be highly inventive and unusual with symbols and graphics which attract the reader to the page and which make all the information very easy to interpret at a glance, as shown in these extracts from a leaflet produced by Boots the Chemist.

Your Quick Guide to Hayfever Symptoms and Treatments

Symptoms		Minor	Moderate	Severe
Eyes		✔	✔	✔
Nose		✔	✔	✔
Throat			✔	✔
Chest				✔
Suitable Treatments	**P8**	Antihistamine tablets	Antihistamine tablets	Antihistamine tablets
	P10	Decongestant nasal spray/drops for occasional use	Preventative nasal spray/drops for season long use	Preventative nasal spray/drops for season long use
	P11	Eye drops for occasional use	Preventative eye drops for season long use	Preventative eye drops for season long use
			Throat lozenges for immediate relief	Throat lozenges for immediate relief

Reproduced courtesy of Boots the Chemists Ltd

Hayfever Calendar

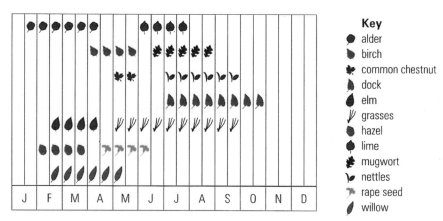

Key
- alder
- birch
- common chestnut
- dock
- elm
- grasses
- hazel
- lime
- mugwort
- nettles
- rape seed
- willow

Reproduced courtesy of Dr Jean Emberlin, National Pollen Research Unit, University College Worcester

✦ Line graphs

Line graphs are useful to show comparisons or indicate trends. Two sets of figures are used – the horizontal scale (or *x* axis) from left to right, and the vertical scale (or *y* axis) from top to bottom. Two or more items may be shown on the same graph by using contrasting lines or different colours.

A single line graph

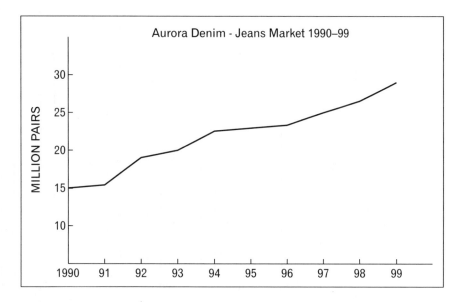

A multi-line graph

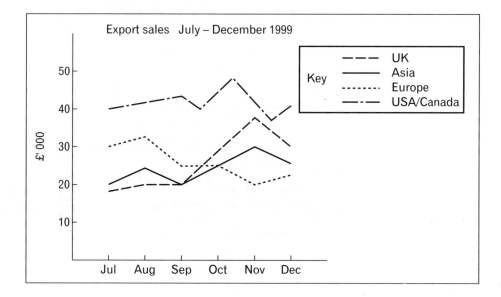

✦ Bar charts

Bar charts may be displayed vertically or horizontally and can be made up of single or multiple bars. They are useful for showing comparisons:

A vertical bar chart

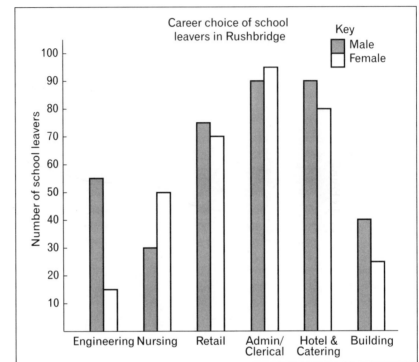

A horizontal bar chart

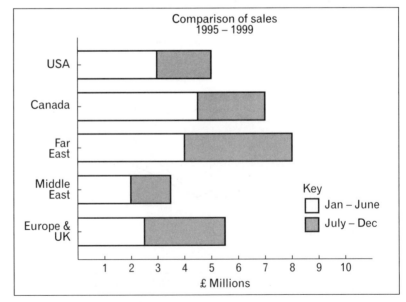

✦ Gantt charts

A Gantt chart is used to show the comparison between work which has been scheduled and work which has actually been accomplished in relation to time. In this example, scheduled work is represented by a pale line and completed work by a dark line. In practice, colour could be used to good effect in such a chart.

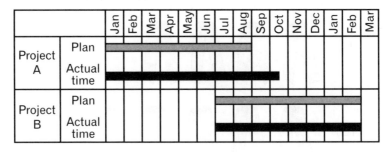

✦ Pie charts

Pie charts are often used when it is necessary to show the relationship of parts to a whole. It is preferable not to use too many segments in the pie, otherwise the impact could be lost. Shading may be used to focus special attention on a single element, or the segment may be separated from the remainder of the pie.

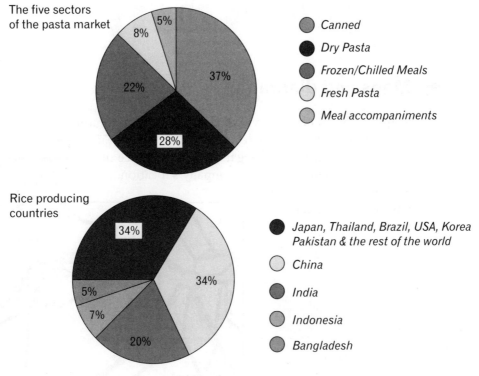

Reproduced courtesy of Van den Bergh Foods

✦ Pictograms

A pictogram shows information represented in the form of figures or symbols. The value of each figure is indicated by either the size or the number of figures shown. Pictograms are visually interesting and easily understood.

SALES OF JEANS

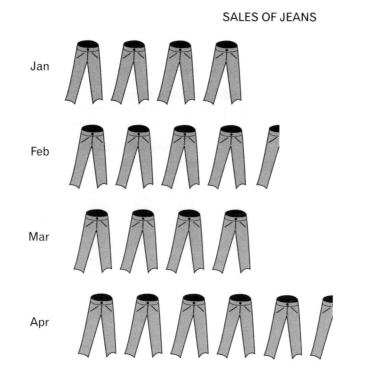

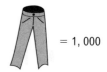 = 1, 000

✦ Maps and diagrams

Maps can be an effective visual aid (consider the weather forecast maps shown on television). Maps or diagrams may also be sent out to delegates of a conference or to customers showing a new company's location. Such maps have obvious advantages over the written word.

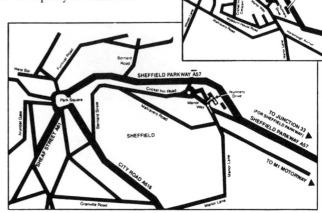

Reproduced courtesy of Sheffield Insulations Group plc

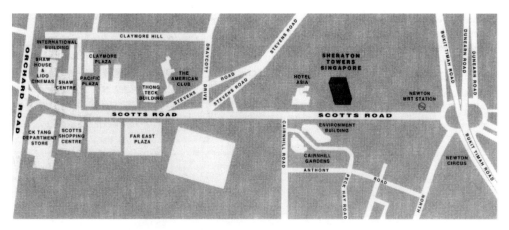

Reproduced courtesy of Michael De Kretser Consultants

✦ Cartograms

A cartogram is a special kind of map which is used to give information about the distribution of people or things within a country or region. Things which may be depicted clearly in a cartogram are, for example, the density of population in China, the number of dog owners in Britain. Here is a cartogram showing the number of Aurora Hotels in Europe, and another showing the location of Thistle Hotels in the UK.

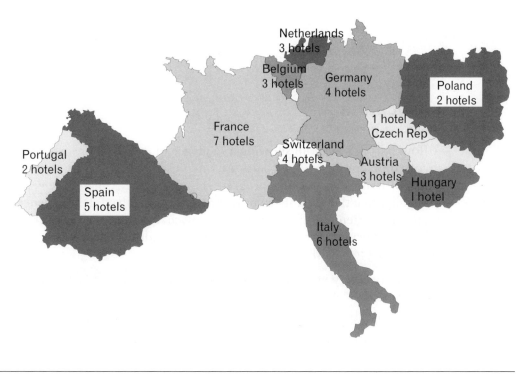

Reproduced courtesy of Thistle Hotels

✦ Flowcharts

A flowchart is a diagram showing a sequence of decisions or instructions involved in a process. Flowcharts are often used in business to work out the stages of writing a computer program. However, they can also be very valuable in highlighting the separate steps or procedures involved in a sequence of events. It is often useful to construct a flowchart when faced with the task of achieving a new objective or simplifying a procedure. This process is useful in encouraging logical thought.

Here are two very effective flowcharts included in the publicity material of Cadbury Ltd.

The first flowchart shows the sequence of events involved in the production of chocolate, from the cocoa bean to the end product.

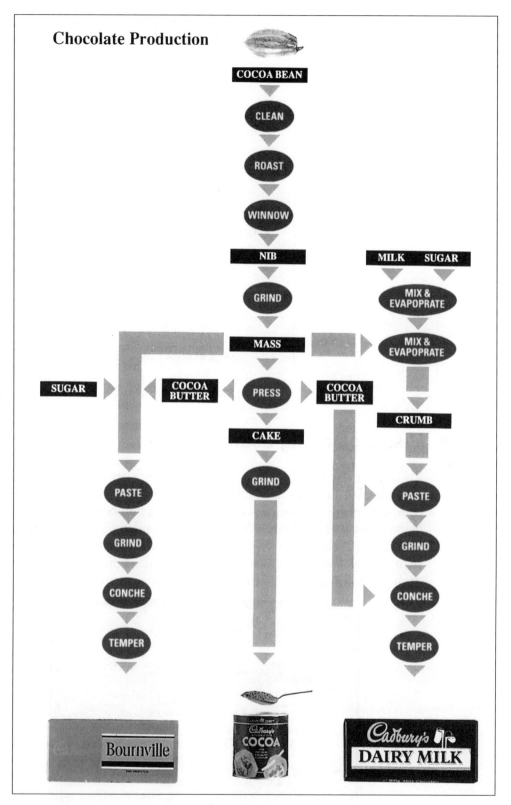

Chocolate Production

Reproduced courtesy of Cadbury Ltd

This flowchart highlights the steps involved in market research and new product development, from the initial idea through to the final launch and continuous research.

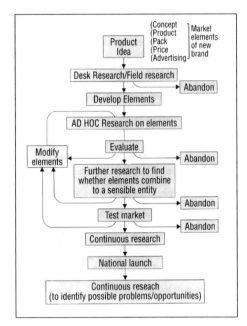

Reproduced courtesy of Cadbury Ltd

✦ Visual planning boards

Visual planning boards can be built up to show virtually any information – from a simple plan showing staff holidays to a complex plan showing activities of a company over a 12-month period, featuring a number of variables. Visual planning boards offer flexibility and ease of updating. They enable future trends to be plotted, changes to be foreseen and realistic forward planning to be made. Many visual planning boards are available, from simple paper charts to sophisticated magnetic wall boards using shapes, strips and symbols.

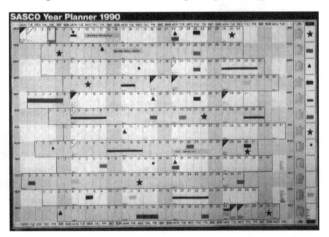

✦ Computer graphics

Most managers are very busy and they welcome information being presented to them in the form of high quality graphics – as charts, graphs, maps, coloured tables, and so on. These are visually attractive and easily interpreted.

The use of graphics application software packages has increased rapidly over recent years, enabling users to present data easily and quickly in any graphics format.

It will be advantageous for anyone working in the business world today to become familiar with the range of graphics software. This will become part of your own 'package' to offer future employers.

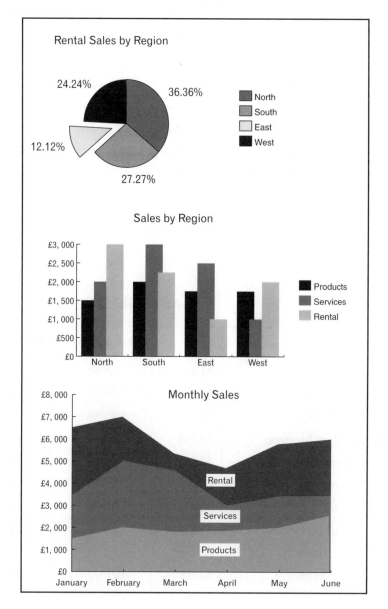

✦ Assignments

1 You work for Collectibles plc, a company which deals with anything that people collect – autographs, model cars, dolls, stamps, etc. Study these pages from your collectibles catalogue and then answer the following questions.

(LCCIEB EFB1 style)

STAMPS AND COVERS

Item	Ref	Very good	Good	Poor
Penny Black	SPB	£1000	£700	£200
Penny Black Cover	SPBC	£2000	£1000	£500
Twopenny Blue	STB	£600	£400	£100
Victoria Jubilee	SVJ	£100	£60	£25
Seahorses Set	SSHS	£450	£300	£125
Seahorses Cover	SSHC	£600	£400	N/A
George V Jubilee	SGVJ	£200	£100	£50
Edward VIII Set	SEE	£40	£20	N/A
George VI Coronation	SGC	£50	£30	£10
George VI Silver Wedding	SGSW	£300	£200	£60

AUTOGRAPHS

	Ref	Personalised	Photograph	Plain
Frank Sinatra	AFS	£500	£300	£100
Elvis Presley	AEP	£2000	£1000	£300
The Beatles	ATB	£4000	£2000	£600
Marilyn Monroe	AMM	£2000	£1800	£400
Martin Luther King	AMK	£500	£100	£50
Nelson Mandela	ANM	£750	£400	£100
Laurence Olivier	ALO	£1000	£600	£200
Laurel & Hardy	ALH	$650	£300	£100
Mike Tyson	AMT	£175	£125	£60
Harry Houdini	AHH	£2000	£1000	£250

POSTCARDS

Type	Ref	Posted	Unposted	Poor
Seaside Views	PSV	£1	£2	–
Train Crashes	PTC	£5	£2	£1
Teddy Bears	PTB	£10	£20	£2
Father Christmas	PFC	£5	£10	£3
Trams	PT	£1	£2	–
Comic	PC	£2	£3	£1
Military	PM	£3	£5	£2
Birthday Cards	PBC	£10	£5	£1
Royalty	PR	£9	£3	£1
Film Stars	PFS	£3	£5	£1

1   What is the price of item SSHC in good condition? . . . .

2   What is the reference for Mike Tyson's autograph? . . . .

3   How much would you pay for a Teddy Bear postcard in poor condition? . . . .

4   How much is a photograph/autograph of Marilyn Monroe? . . . .

5   What is the cheapest price for a George VI Silver Wedding set of stamps and coins? . . . .

6   To what does ATB refer? . . . .

7   How much is an unposted Royalty card? . . . .

8   Does the shop list more autographs than postcards? . . . .

9   To what does SEE refer? . . . .

10   How much is a plain autograph of Nelson Mandela? . . . .

11   How much is a good set of the Victoria Jubilee stamps? . . . .

12   How much would you pay for a Teddy Bear card that had been posted? . . . .

13 Is a plain Laurence Olivier autograph more
    expensive than a personalised Mike Tyson
    autograph?   . . . .

14 Which stamp would you pay £2000 for?   . . . .

15 Which postcard is the most expensive?   . . . .

16 How much is the cheapest item under
    ref SGVJ?   . . . .

17 How much would you pay for a photograph/
    autograph of Frank Sinatra?   . . . .

18 To what does PC refer?   . . . .

19 Which postcard would cost you £9?   . . . .

20 How much would you pay for a personalised
    Beatles autograph?

2   You work in the travel department of a company in Sheffield and have to
    arrange rail and air travel for managers. Using the information in the
    timetable answer the following questions. Your answers should be in the
    form of single words, times, numbers or short phrases:

    1   Is there a non-stop service from Sheffield
        to London?   . . . .

    2   Is the restaurant service available on all the
        morning trains from Monday to Friday?   . . . .

    3   If I catch the Master Cutler on Thursday,
        at what time will I arrive in London?   . . . .

    4   If I wish to book a ticket over the phone,
        how much notice should I give?   . . . .

    5   Will these times still be in force on a bank
        holiday (i.e. public holiday)?   . . . .

    6   Can I use a Saver ticket on the Robin Hood
        train to London?   . . . .

    7   On which days can I leave Sheffield at 0740? . . . .

    8   How can I find out some additional
        information which does not appear on
        the timetable?   . . . .

    9   If I book a ticket on Premier Service, on
        which trains is continental breakfast service
        included?   . . . .

    10 Do I have to pay for my own tea and coffee
        if I use Standard Class accommodation on
        the train?   . . . .

MIDLAND MAINLINE

Sheffield and Chesterfield- London

Principal train service 27 September 1998 to 29 May 1999

Mondays to Fridays

	Sheffield depart	Chesterfield depart	London St. Pancras arrive
R ✕ ▲	0517	0530	0753
R ✕ ▲	0622	0635	0850
R ✕ ▲ H	0638	0651	0909
R ✕ ▲ M	0720	0733	0926
▲	0740	0753	1027
▼	0824	0837	1045
	0924	0937	1149
	1024	1037	1245
	1124	1137	1348
	1224	1237	1449
	1324	1337	1545
	1424	1437	1649
	1524	1537	1749
	1624	1637	1855
	1724	1737	1950
	1924	1937	2157
	2030	2043	2332

Saturdays

	Sheffield depart	Chesterfield depart	London St. Pancras arrive
	0622	0635	0847
✕	0739	0753	1001
✕	0750	0803	1037
✕	0824	0837	1046
	0839	0853	1114
	0953	1007	1224
	1124	1137	1352
	1254	1307	1523
	1424	1437	1652
	1554	1607	1824
	1724	1737	1956
	1924	1937	2203

Sundays

	Sheffield depart	Chesterfield depart	London St. Pancras arrive
B	0834	0847	1211
A	0856	0909	1211
B	1044	1059	1411
E	1102	1117	1411
C	1103	1117	1411
B	1108	1123	1511
E	1132	1147	1454
C	1132	1147	1511
B	1231	1245	1617
C	1254	1309	1617
E	1300	1314	1608
E	1432	1445	1721
F	1455	1509	1718
	1624	1638	1856
	1655	1709	1922
	1822	1835	2056
	1936	1951	2219

Notes

A   Runs 27 September 1998 to 3 January 1999 and from 28 March to 23 May 1999.

B   Runs 10 January to 21 March 1999.

C   Runs 27 September 1998 to 3 January 1999.

E   Runs 28 March to 23 May 1999.

F   Runs 27 September 1998 to 21 March 1999.

✕   Inclusive full English and Continental breakfast service available to Premier Service ticket holders only. Seats for breakfast may be available on the train to First Class ticket holders, at the Train Manager's discretion.

╲   Inclusive Continental breakfast service available to Premier Service ticket holders only. Seats for breakfast may be available on the train to First Class ticket holders, at the Train Manager's discretion.

✕   Full English and Continental breakfast service available only when booked in advance. Seats for breakfast may be available on the day at the Train Manager's discretion.

R   Reservations required for Premier Service and First Saver tickets and strongly recommended for all other tickets.

H   The Robin Hood

M   The Master Cutler

▲   OUTWARD portion of SAVER, SUPERSAVER and RETURN portion of SUPERSAVER tickets are NOT valid to or from London on this service.

▼   OUTWARD and RETURN portions of SUPERSAVER tickets are NOT valid to or from London on this rail service.

Midland Mainline Trains offer:
- First Class and Standard Class accommodation
- A buffet counter or at-seat trolley service on all trains with hot and cold drinks, light refreshments and snacks
- Free tea and coffee for all customers (subject to availability)
- Free seat reservations for all customers with a valid travel ticket

For National Rail and Fares Information please call:
Telephone Enquiries **0345 48 49 50***
Telephone Sales **0345 125 678**
(Please allow 5 days for tickets to be posted to you)

If wishing to travel over Christmas or Bank Holiday periods, please check at your local station as services are subject to change.

Reproduced courtesy of Midland Mainline

3   You work for Sporting Ventures plc. Your company owns five golf clubs in the South of England. Each of the golf clubs is named after a famous golfing professional – Faldo, Woods, Player, Nicklaus and Else. This table shows the features of each of these golf clubs. Use the information in the table to answer the following questions.

(LCCIEB EFB1 style)

Club features	FALDO	WOODS	PLAYER	NICKLAUS	ELSE
Holes	18	18 + 9	18 + 18	18	18
Driving range/s	2	No	4	1	No
Tuition	£25 ph	£20 ph	£40 half day	£18 ph	None
Joining fees	£100	£150	£250	£125	£180
Car park spaces	100	200	345	80	50
Opening dates	March-October	All year	All year	February-September	April-September
Practice greens	Yes	No	Yes	No	No
Age limits	None	21+	18+	None	None
Floodlight putting	Yes	No	No	No	No
Licensed bar	Yes	Yes	Yes	No	No
Restaurant facilities	No	Yes	Yes	Yes	Small cafeteria
Changing rooms	Male	Male & female	Male & female	No	No
Buggy hire	£10 ph	£20 ph	£40 (3 hrs)	No	No
Visitor fees	£30 half day	£35 half day	£50 per day	£20 half day	No
Visitors	Weekdays only	Weekends only	Thursdays	Any time	No visitors
Insurance	£25 pa	Own scheme	Included in fee	£50 pa	£50 pa
Annual fee	£500	£500	£750	£350	£200
Professionals employed	1	1	3	2	1
Languages spoken	French Japanese	French Italian Japanese	German Japanese	German Italian	None
Shop hours	9 – 5.00	10 – 4.00	8 – 8.00	10 – 4.00	None

	QUESTION	ANSWER
1	Which club has most holes?	. . . .
2	How many clubs have more than one driving range?	. . . .
3	Which club offers the cheapest tuition for one hour?	. . . .
4	Which club does not offer any tuition?	. . . .
5	Which club is the most expensive to join?	. . . .
6	Which club is the cheapest to join?	. . . .
7	How many clubs provide more than 60 parking spaces?	. . . .
8	Which club has fewest parking spaces?	. . . .
9	How many clubs are closed on 25 February	. . . .
10	How many clubs have practice greens?	. . . .
11	How many clubs do not accept 20 year olds?	. . . .
12	Where could you practise putting at night?	. . . .
13	How many clubs do not have a licensed bar?	. . . .
14	How many clubs do not have a restaurant?	. . . .
15	How many clubs have no changing rooms for ladies?	. . . .
16	Which club charges the most for a buggy for three hours?	. . . .
17	How many shops are open at 9.30 a.m.?	. . . .
18	How many clubs do not have an age limit?	. . . .
19	How many clubs accept visitors on a Friday?	. . . .
20	Which club offers a visitor the cheapest rate for a full day?	. . . .
21	How many clubs charge a specific sum for insurance?	. . . .
22	How many clubs charge more than £400 for their annual fee?	. . . .
23	How many clubs employ fewer than three professionals?	. . . .
24	Which foreign language is most readily available?	. . . .
25	Which club(s) would be most suitable for a 17 year old German speaker?	. . . .

4 These three pie charts show the breakdown of season ticket holders for a particular football club over three years. The charts indicate the proportions of men, women, under 16s and over 65s. Study the charts and answer the questions which follow:

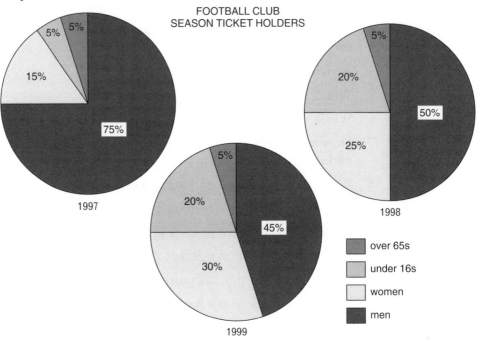

FOOTBALL CLUB
SEASON TICKET HOLDERS

1997

1998

1999

over 65s
under 16s
women
men

1 Less than _____ the total season ticket holders in 1999 were males.

2 In 1998 the relationship of male to female supporters was _____ .

3 In 1998 and 1999 there were _____ numbers of under 16s and over 65 season ticket holders.

4 From 1997 to 1999 the percentage of women season ticket holders _____ .

5 The number of male season ticket holders has _____ every year.

6 The number of women season ticket holders has _____ every year.

7 The number of over 65 season ticket holders has _____ every year.

8 The number of under 16 season ticket holders has _____ since 1997.

9 If this trend continues, in the year 2000 there may be almost an _____ number of male and female supporters.

10 Draw a graph to show the changing patterns in season ticket holders.

11 Prepare a series of bar charts to show the same information.

12 Which form of presentation, if any, do you consider is more effective in this case?

REFORMULATING AND SUMMARISING

By the end of this section you should be able to:

❏ complete 'look and write' production tasks involving labelling a diagram, form or flow chart

❏ complete 'reformulation' tasks involving expanding, reducing or selectively rewriting a passage of English for a specific purpose

❏ use summarising skills effectively

❏ produce a business summary from a given passage of English.

✦ What is a summary?

To make a summary means to convey all or most of a section of text using a reduced number of words. We use summarising skills all the time in response to questions like 'What did you do last night?' or 'So how was your holiday?' This is usually done orally instead of in writing.

The written summary will not be new to you. It is something most of us have done throughout our school days. However, it is very rare in business to be asked to do a straightforward continuous prose summary. Summaries in business may be written in the form of an advertisement or notice, an article for the staff newsletter, a handout for issue to trainees. These are all exercises in summarising, picking out relevant and important information and then presenting it in an appropriate manner.

It is to this type of more realistic exercise which many examiners are now turning in order to provide realistic tasks which an employee may very well be asked to perform in the business world. This type of 'business summary' will be discussed in more detail later.

✦ Using synonyms

When summarising or reformulating you may be expected to use your own words as far as possible, instead of quoting huge chunks of the original passage. This exercise is designed to give you practice in choosing synonyms for words.

Provide synonyms for each of the following words (remember that very often more than one word could be used):

1	huge	_____	11	certain	_____
2	afraid	_____	12	vital	_____
3	regularly	_____	13	price	_____
4	retain	_____	14	desire	_____
5	impression	_____	15	apparent	_____
6	accurate	_____	16	inquisition	_____
7	honesty	_____	17	objective	_____
8	specimen	_____	18	reluctant	_____
9	common	_____	19	inadequate	_____
10	immune	_____	20	terminate	_____

✦ Reducing phrases

There are many expressions in the English language which are long-winded and could be expressed in a simpler or shorter way. This exercise will help you be aware of such expressions and spot them, and others like them, when summarising.

Reduce the expressions shown without changing the meanings. Use the number of words shown in brackets:

1   in the near future (1)   _____

2   it appears that (1)   _____

3   put up with (1)   _____

4   the same amount of (1)   _____

5   in modern times (1)   _____

6   as a result (1)   _____

7   because of this (1)   _____

8   always bear in mind (1)   _____

9   a lot of (1)   _____

10 at all times (1)   _____

11 at the beginning of each day (2)   _____

12 owned by private individuals (2)   _____

13 equipment should be checked (2)   _____

14 make a record of all appointments (3)   _____

15 on the day of the interview (3)   _____

✦ One word for many

Summarising means saying the same thing but in not so many words. In these sentences replace the section in italics by providing just one word.

1   When the meeting is over, you must produce the *accurate transcript of the main discussions which took place and the decisions made.*   _____

2   She's not interested in work – only in *tennis, swimming, hockey, golf – anything requiring physical activity.*   _____

3   The next meeting of the Board is coming up
    soon. I must prepare the *list of items to be
    discussed at the meeting*.   _____

4   The *person who greets visitors to an organisation*
    must portray a good impression.   _____

5   When goods have been purchased, it is usual to
    send out an *itemised statement informing the
    buyer of the quantity, description and price of
    the goods which were bought*.   _____

6   We must send out a *document to all the
    customers on our mailing list*.   _____

7   This is a *list of all the duties which the employee
    may be required to perform*. (2 words)   _____

8   Some job advertisements require applicants to
    send a *separate schedule showing their education,
    qualifications, employment history and other
    personal details* when applying for jobs. (2 words) _____

✦ Retain or remove?

Summarising anything requires the ability to find and remove unimportant
details or, more to the point, choose which details should be retained. A lot of
information which can be removed from summarising exercises can be
categorised, e.g. examples, definitions, additions and rephrasing. 'Clues' are
often given in such cases, as shown below.

	Categories	*Clues*
1	Examples	'For example … '
		' …, e.g. … '
2	Definitions	'This is … '
		'This means … '
3	Rephrasing	'In other words … '
		'That is … '
		' …, i.e. … '
4	Additions	' …, especially … '
		' …, particularly … '

Example: (the information to be removed has been underlined)
It has been argued, (1) especially in recent years, that an examination summary
is not a realistic exercise, (2) i.e. not the type of summary one is required to do
in the business world.

Number 1: Why should it be removed? (addition)
          What was the clue given? (especially)

Number 2: Why should it be removed? (rephrasing)
          What was the clue given? (i.e.)

The sentences below all contain some information which should be removed from a summary – examples, definitions, rephrasing or additions. Highlight the details which should be *retained*, and state the reason why the rest should be *removed*, together with the *clue* which was given.

1   An essential part of any documentary evidence, for example letters, invoices, orders, is that it should have the names and the addresses of both parties to the correspondence.

    Reason? _____
    Clue?   _____

2   References often include departments and file numbers, especially in correspondence with government departments.

    Reason? _____
    Clue?   _____

3   All business documents should be grammatically correct, i.e. they should contain no errors in grammar, spelling or punctuation.

    Reason? _____
    Clue?   _____

4   It is becoming popular for larger organisations to use a 'house style' for their correspondence. This means all typists and secretaries present correspondence in the same, standardised formats.

    Reason? _____
    Clue?   _____

5   Business letters should be free of slang and other colloquialisms, i.e. expressions used only in conversation.

    Reason? _____
    Clue?   _____

6   Some circular letters are unsolicited. This means the recipients have no particular interest in the message.

    Reason? _____
    Clue?   _____

7   It is important to retain grammatical precision when writing business documents. In other words, all sentences in a series should consistently follow the same grammatical pattern.

    Reason? _____
    Clue?   _____

8 Many companies, particularly the larger ones, are turning more and more to computerisation of their clerical procedures.

Reason? _____

Clue? _____

9 A quorum must usually be present at formal meetings, e.g. Annual General Meetings, meetings of shareholders.

Reason? _____

Clue? _____

10 Certain items appear on the agenda of many regular meetings, e.g. any other business and date of next meeting.

Reason? _____

Clue? _____

✦ Removing reasons

1 Read the following passage and use it to complete the table below:

In the name of safety, gangways between desks should not be blocked with boxes, files or wastebins as employees may trip over them causing injury. Filing cabinet drawers should be closed immediately after use, or the cabinet may become unbalanced and topple over. Torn or frayed floorcovering could cause a person to fall, so it should be repaired or replaced. Office doors should be locked and windows secured at the end of the day. This will prevent burglars from breaking in. To avoid a fire hazard electrical appliances should be unplugged and switched off at the end of each day.

SAFETY PRECAUTION	REASON
1 Do not block gangways between desks with boxes, files or wastebins.	_____
2 _____	_____
3 _____	_____
4 _____	_____
5 _____	_____

(NB: Retain consistency of expression by using verbs at the start of each item in column one.)

2 Read the following passage and use it to complete the table below:

> When transcribing recorded dictation assess the size of each document before typing it so that the correct size of paper can be chosen. To avoid making unnecessary errors and having to type the document again, always check any doubtful points in the dictation with the dictator. If there is any doubt about spelling, look up unfamiliar words in a dictionary.
>
> Letters required urgently by the dictator should be typed and returned to him first, so that the document can be dealt with quickly. Letters cannot be signed with grammatical errors, so make sure they are grammatically perfect. To avoid having to insert the paper back into the typewriter to correct errors, always proofread carefully before removing work from your typewriter.

RULES FOR TRANSCRIBING	REASON
1 Assess the size of each document before typing it.	_____
2 _____	_____
3 _____	_____
4 _____	_____
5 _____	_____

✦ Counting the words

Summary assignments normally state the number of words to be used. This will usually be expressed in one of two ways:

1 *Use no more than 160 words*
   In this case, do not exceed 160 words. 150–160 will normally be accepted, but anything less than 155 will be penalised.

2 *Use approximately 160 words*
   Here, 155–165 will not be penalised.

What to count

When counting the number of words used, do not count the words in the heading or any numbers used in your display. Sub-headings, however, should be included in your word count.

Will the examiner check?

An examiner with many scripts to mark will know approximately how much space your summary should take up on your answer sheet. He/she will be able to see if yours looks too long or too short.

If you indicate that you have used the precise number of words instructed (perhaps a white lie?) then the examiner may just spot that it looks too long or too short, and will double-check.

If you do not indicate the number of words used, you will also be penalised.

The best option is to try to stick within the word limit and always include it at the end in brackets.

A worked example of a short summary

There are many ways in which summaries can be handled, and many different final versions which could all be quite satisfactory. However, it may be helpful to take a look at the various stages involved in just one method of producing an effective summary.

Step 1   Read through the text carefully.

Step 2   Highlight important words and phrases, by using the method of circling shown here, by underlining, or by using a highlighter pen:

```
Summarise the following passage using approximately
50 words.


    A lot of (personal contact) is associated with
(secretarial work) - contact with people (inside)
(the company,) eg fellow employees, juniors,        } eg (omit)
management, other departments, as well as
clients and other people (outside the company.)
Being (able to communicate well) with people is
therefore a most (important aspect) of the
secretary's role.  The nature of a secretary's
job means she is in (constant communication) with
many people (in her own company,) and she is
(expected to treat all office personnel,) from      } eg (omit)
senior management to the junior mail clerk,
(with the same amount of respect.) Tact,        ✓  (personal
diplomacy, a pleasant disposition, friendliness ✓  qualities)
and helpfulness are some of the (invaluable)
(qualities) a secretary needs when dealing with
people (outside the organisation.)  When in
contact with such people, either by telephone } addition (omit)
or in person, the secretary, as a
(representative of her company,) is expected to
(reflect a good image) of the organisation she
represents (at all times.)

(148 words)
```

Step 3   Having double checked that nothing in the original has been overlooked, produce a first draft.

Step 4   Noting that too many words have been used in the first draft, again highlight key words and phrases. Make notes about how it can be reduced still further, and where words can be altered.

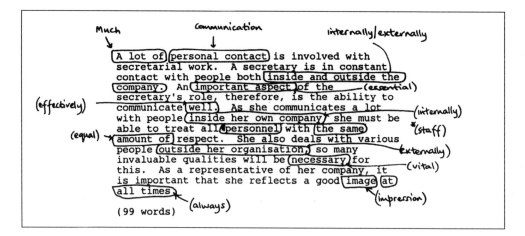

Step 5   Produce your first summary.

```
Secretarial work involves much communication
with people both internally and externally.
It is, therefore, essential to acquire
effective communication skills.

Inside the company, the secretary should treat
all levels of staff with equal respect.  When
dealing with people outside, many personal
qualities are vital.  A good impression of the
company must always be reflected.

(54 words)
```

✦ Guidelines for writing summaries

1   Read the instructions carefully and determine what is required in your summary. Maybe only a certain theme from the passage needs to be picked out, or perhaps it should all be summarised. Whatever, many students produce very good summaries, but lose marks because they have not done what the instructions requested.
2   Read the passage through carefully twice – the importance of this reading period cannot be over-emphasised. You really need to 'think yourself into the theme' of the passage and ensure a complete grasp of the topic before continuing.
3   After checking the instructions again, go through the passage highlighting the information which should be included in your summary.

4 Re-check what you have highlighted in case you have missed something or highlighted something incorrectly.

5 Make a rough draft from your highlighting, using your own words and avoiding the language of the original passage wherever possible.

6 Check your draft carefully against the original, making sure that you have not left out anything of importance, or added anything which is not relevant.

7 Write out the summary in its final form. Take every possible opportunity to rephrase in an attempt to cut down on the number of words used.

8 Count the words used, and if necessary make some more amendments to keep within the limit prescribed.

9 Read your summary through carefully to check for grammatical, punctuation or spelling errors.

✦ Business summaries

The summaries we have looked at so far have been 'continuous prose', i.e. a straightforward paragraph or two. However, the recent trend is towards realistic summaries, summaries to suit a specific purpose. Virtually any type of presentation could, therefore, be required. It is important that the instructions are studied carefully so that you pick out only the information required in your summary, and that you display it appropriately.

Here are some examples of different types of business summaries which you could be asked to produce:

Advertisement/notice

Obviously an advertisement or notice should be presented suitably. Items should be centred to attract attention. Perhaps points can be listed, with sub-headings. Use capitals and underscoring to add to effect.

Checklist

Enumeration is required in any checklist. Perhaps an introduction is necessary also. Take care with consistency of expression, so that all points on the checklist follow the rule of grammatical parallelism. (A useful word-saving ploy here is to use verbs at the start of each point.)

Handout/information sheet

Sub-headings may be appropriate, as well as numbered points. Again, take care with consistency of expression

Notes for a speech

For reference when making a speech, again enumeration would probably be easier to follow, perhaps also with subheadings for different aspects of the main theme.

NB: There can be no hard and fast rule to say 'Oh it's a handout – I must do it like this', or whatever. The instructions will tell you for what purpose your summary is to be used. After reading the passage carefully, and double-checking the instructions, careful thought should be given to using the most suitable format.)

Covering memo

When instructed to compose a business summary of the type discussed, it may be relevant for a covering memo to be written to the person who requested it. Your memo should be short and state the source of the material which has been used.

Example:

```
SAFETY IN THE OFFICE

As requested, I have made a summary of the article which appeared
in the May edition of 'Business Digest' for its inclusion in the
next issue of the staff newsletter.

I hope you find this satisfactory.

Enc
```

A worked example of a business summary

As with any assignment, it must be remembered that no two people will produce identical summaries, yet many could be suitable for the purpose intended. However, this worked example of a business summary is given to illustrate the principles and procedures involved in effective summarising.

Step 1
Read the instructions carefully, marking the important points.

> Your employer is giving a (talk) entitled "Running your own Business" at a local club. She says to you, "Will you please [list] the [main points] about being your own boss and the (misconceptions) people have about it from this leaflet? It will (help me in giving my talk.)
>
> Use approximately 120 words for your summary.

Step 2
Consider a suitable format. Your summary is to be used by your employer as reference when giving a talk about 'Running Your Own Business'. Your employer stresses she wants a list of the 'main points' as well as 'misconceptions'. These two terms give you a clue as to sub-headings which could be used. Also important here is the word 'list' – obviously your employer does not want to read from a script, so continuous prose will not be suitable. A list will be easy to refer to, and your employer will be able to expand on each point, thus making her talk sound very natural.

Step 3
Read the passage carefully several times, highlighting the important points.

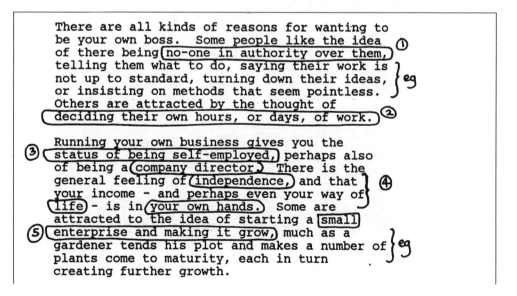

> There are all kinds of reasons for wanting to be your own boss. Some people like the idea ① of there being (no-one in authority over them,) telling them what to do, saying their work is not up to standard, turning down their ideas, } eg or insisting on methods that seem pointless. Others are attracted by the thought of (deciding their own hours, or days, of work.) ②
>
> ③ Running your own business gives you the (status of being self-employed,) perhaps also of being a (company director.) There is the general feeling of (independence,) and that } your income - and perhaps even your way of ④ (life) - is in (your own hands.) Some are attracted to the idea of starting a [small] ⑤ (enterprise and making it grow,) much as a gardener tends his plot and makes a number of } eg plants come to maturity, each in turn creating further growth.

If you are your own boss, say some people, work is so much more pleasant. You can get someone else to do the less interesting jobs ⑥ and you are not bogged down in annoying details. Work becomes easier, too, because you can get someone else to do the more difficult tasks.

Many others want to set up a little business of their own to occupy their spare time, and ⑦ as a pleasant way of earning extra money from work they like doing.

These are just a few of the reasons commonly given. Some have good sense behind them; others are based on completely false ideas. Most contain some element of truth which gets magnified out of all proportion and seized upon without it being borne in mind that there are other points to consider as well.

end of 'benefits'

lead-in to 'misconceptions'

As with so much else in life, running an enterprise of your own entails disadvantages as well as advantages. It is surprising how rarely people stop to consider in real detail just what the drawbacks are, yet this is an essential first step for anyone thinking about whether it is even practicable for him to be his own boss.

← misconceptions

An important reason why there is such glamour about being in charge of your own business is that when you are working for someone else, many of the petty irritations of life, as well as the chore of often having to get down to work that you do not feel like doing at that particular time, become associated with being an employee. There is a feeling that, if only you were your own boss, life would immediately become infinitely pleasurable and free from irksome detail.

This is almost entirely misleading. Many of the little annoyances probably have nothing to do with being an employee: being interrupted when you have at last immersed yourself in some disagreeable task, missing the bus when you are in a hurry, feeling tired or in other ways not really up to working hard at the moment, and so on. These occur just as much when you are your own master. In fact, they tend to happen much more often, while at the same time, their effects can be far more upsetting.

eg (omit)

There are very real drawbacks to running your own business, though for the right kind of person, immeasurable benefits also.

Step 4

Produce a rough draft or notes from the original, referring to the instructions again to ensure you are picking out what is required.

Step 5

Go through your draft/notes and make marginal notes regarding amendments/synonyms/rephrasing. Remember that your summary should be expressed in your own words wherever possible.

MAIN POINTS *(Benefits)*

- No-one to give you instructions *(answer to no/one)*

- Choose own hours/working arrangements *]– link?*

- Self-employed status – director? *accountable?*

- Independent, responsible for own income/life *self-reliant?* *company/business*

- Satisfaction from seeing enterprise grow *pleasure* *simple?*

- Less interesting work – other people also more difficult work *laborious?* *} Delegation!*

- Business occupies spare time – earn money too *create income*

MISCONCEPTIONS

vital

Few consider all details – essential first step.

Being the boss seems glamourous – thinking that life would be better if no mundane chores, no annoyances, like employees – wrong! *annoyances*

Irritations also when you are boss – more often? Effects more upsetting! *far-reaching?* *disagreeable?*

CONCLUSION *consequences*

Consider drawbacks carefully. *(disadvantages)* If right for you – immeasurable benefits. *rewards?*

limitless/ countless?

Step 6

Produce your final summary by linking up the notes into full sentences. Count the words. If necessary, make further amendments. Make sure your summary reads smoothly and is correct in spelling and punctuation. Finally, ask yourself if your summary is a satisfactory condensed version of the original, and also if your summary could be used for the purpose mentioned in the instructions.

Step 7
Don't forget to produce a brief covering memo for summaries of this nature.

M E M O R A N D U M

To   Mrs Eileen Starr, Managing Director

From Sharon Tan

Ref   GS/ST

Date 12 July 19--

RUNNING YOUR OWN BUSINESS

I have summarised the leaflet you gave to me,
listing the main points about being your own
boss, together with misconceptions. This is
attached.

I hope this helps you in giving your talk next
week.

Sharon

Enc

RUNNING YOUR OWN BUSINESS

BENEFITS

1   You have no-one to answer to, and have
    self-employed, maybe director, standing.

2   You make your own choices, including
    working hours.

3   You are self-reliant, accountable for
    your own income.

4   You obtain pleasure from seeing your
    company grow.

5   Delegation is possible - of the simple
    and the laborious jobs.

6   It can fill your spare time and create
    income from work you enjoy.

```
MISCONCEPTIONS

1   Some do not consider the drawbacks - a
    vital preliminary step.

2   Some feel life would improve without
    the aggravations often encountered as an
    employee.

    However, most of such aggravations occur
    to employers as well as employees, but
    with more disagreeable consequences.

CONCLUSION

Consider the disadvantages carefully.
If it is for you, the rewards are
limitless.

(115 words)
```

✦ Assignments

1   You work for Collectibles plc. Mrs Janet Broadbent, Personnel Manager, has been concerned about staff training and has asked you to complete this table using the notes below. Include any courses to be attended in the next few weeks, but indicate this. Mrs Broadbent has made some notes.
(LCCIEB EFB1 style)

Mrs B – all courses except Auctions (not worried because John has done Auction Training, also Ken who has also completed Finance Training).

Susan been to Dolls and Health & Safety Training but Roger has only attended Autographs. Ken trained for Stamp History at the same time as Karen – she has been to all 3 Management courses.

Roger and John both going to Health & Safety Training next month, when Susan will be attending the Autograph session.

Karen is attending a course on Doll's History right now.

STAFF TRAINING

Staff	Knowledge of Contents			Management		
	Stamps	Dolls	Autographs	Auctions	Health and Safety	Finance
Mrs B						
John						
Susan						
Roger						
Ken						
Karen						

2 As part of a college project, you have just interviewed Harold Weston, Course Director of Aurora Management Consultancy Group. The following is a verbatim record of the information he gave you in answer to your questions.

Use the information to complete the diagram.

I have overall responsibility for all the courses offered by the Aurora Management Consultancy Group. My three assistants are very valuable though – James Lee runs the part-time courses, Keith Chan is responsible for intensive courses and Rita Wong deals with in-company training.

The secretarial work is dealt with by Wendy Roberts – she reports to the Administration Manager, Yong Wai Kee. Wai Kee also supervises the Security Chief, Graham Voon.

The Chief Executive of the Group is Dr Dean Franks – he's quite a tough cookie, but I guess he has to be. His PA is Prema Viswanath and she seems to be able to handle him OK.

I suggest you should talk to Ganesh Karuppiah about marketing matters. He's in charge of that area. Individual areas are taken care of by Frank Dupont (Western Europe), Jim Smith (UK and Southern Europe) and there's also our new man Donnie McLellan in charge of Scotland and Northern Ireland.

Legal matters – you should talk to Sham Hassan – she's the Company Secretary so she's expert in all things legal.

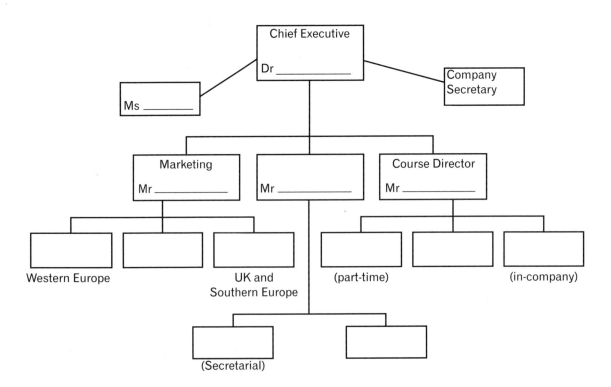

3   You work in the Travel Section at Minton Engineering Group, 46 Tower Avenue, Hong Kong, telephone 45223456. The Marketing Director, Ong Hee Huat, is going to Singapore on Wednesday 22 June. Study this note from him and complete the hotel booking form.

Thanks for booking my flight to Singapore. Please book me in at the Sheraton Towers – I'll check in as soon as I arrive (early) rather than go straight to our regional office.

I'll stay in the hotel until Sunday morning – my friends will collet me and I'll stay at their home until I fly back here the following week.

In the hotel I'll need space to work and entertain so please book an executive suite with sitting room.

(LCCIEB EFB1 style)

HOTEL BOOKING FORM

Please complete in block capitals

City	
Hotel	
Guest	
Mr/Mrs/Miss/Other	
Company	
Address	
Telephone	
Arrival	
AM/PM	
No of nights	
Room	
Rate	
Date	

4   You work for Aurora Golf Clubs, a company which owns 5 golf clubs in England. On 29 May you answer a telephone call from Mr James Milton. Below are your notes of the telephone call. Use these notes to complete the standard complaint form.

Visited Player Golf Club yesterday at 9.00 am with 4 business colleagues.
Difficult to find entrance as no sign on the main road.
Many staff rude and unhelpful.

Whole place untidy, even the greens. Two trees had fallen on the fairways — no attempt was made to remove them.

Hired a set of clubs — 2 had damaged handles.

Helped by very civil girl in Reception but would like to shoot the waiter!

Restaurant cold and food unappetising.

Unlikely to visit again.

Colleagues found the club expensive and poor quality.

Mr Milton's tel no: 0181 330 2349

(LCCIEB EFB1 style)

AURORA GOLF CLUBS
COMPLAINT FORM

Name .... Tel No ....

Date of visit .... Time ....

Club visited ....

1 General comments
   Reception area ....

   Reception staff ....

2 Equipment
   Equipment hired ....

   Condition ....

3 Course
   Comments on Fairways ....

   Comments on Greens ....

4 Restaurant
   Food ....

   Staff ....

Any other comments ....

....

....

Name of person recording complaint ....

Date ....

---

5 You are secretary to the Principal of a secretarial college and the Principal feels the following article contains useful points for students who will be leaving shortly, in preparing them for job interviews. Make a suitable summary for the Principal to issue to teachers for them to use in class discussion. Use no more than 70 words.

Interviews – experiences which some people love, and some hate. Whichever category you belong to, a few tips should be borne in mind to ensure interview success.

In nearly all meetings, the first impression is that which makes the strongest impact on new acquaintances, be they colleagues, friends or other associates. If that goes wrong, it may be impossible to correct. Secretaries are often seen as status symbols, so an employer would prefer a smart and presentable person to fulfil this role. Not many employers would be impressed by a provocative evening-type dress and hair tossed seductively, and it certainly would not be everyday office attire, so plan your wardrobe carefully. Personal freshness is also important, particularly when under stress. You must consider the effect you may have on the people around you. If you have ever stood next to someone on a bus whose personal 'aura' makes you rush to get off before your stop, then you know what I mean. Give your teeth a good going-over too, to make sure they sparkle and that your breath smells fresh. Long tapering nails also wouldn't be able to whizz across a keyboard if you are asked to do a typing test, so give yourself a good manicure and ensure your nails are attractive.

The evening before the interview, get all your clothes ready so as to avoid a panic and not being able to decide what to wear. Make sure your hair is clean and shining too. A rumbling tummy is a sure sign of nerves, so avoid embarrassment by having a hearty breakfast. Nerves can often make your nose run too, for no apparent reason, so be sure to carry tissues. If you are wearing tights, make sure you carry a spare pair in case you damage them on the way to the interview.

Before you walk into the interview room, take a few deep breaths to calm your nerves – always a useful calming technique. And when you walk in, smile! Don't get carried away so that your smile looks forced, but be as natural as you can. Be friendly in the interview itself, and it will make it easy for the interviewer to conduct the interview. However nervous you feel, sit in as relaxed a manner as you can, and don't keep twitching nervously, with your fingers, with the strap of your handbag, with your skirt hem, or whatever. Look at the interviewer directly and don't avoid eye contact or it will not give a good impression. When answering questions, avoid using 'yes' or 'no' – they tell an interviewer absolutely nothing and result in a very dull interview. Try to answer as fully as possible, without going off the mark.

Remember that the aim of an interview is to allow the interviewer(s) and the interviewee to get to know each other in a short space of time in order to decide quickly if it would be possible to work together. it is not intended to be like entering the torture chamber. Relax – and try to enjoy it!

6 All the secretaries in your organisation use audio transcription, as the employers prefer not to use shorthand dictation. In informal talks with many secretaries personally, you know there is a considerable amount of frustration because of poor audio dictation technique by their employers. You recently came across the following article in a secretarial magazine, and feel it includes helpful advice for employers on effective audio dictation techniques. You decide to summarise it as a checklist for employers to follow when dictating, and to send it to the editor of the staff magazine asking him to consider it for inclusion in the next issue. (Use approximately 100 words.)

Using dictation machines saves considerable time, as the secretary does not need to be present, thus it leaves the secretary free to deal with her other responsibilities while the boss dictates his correspondence. But how many secretaries out there continually bang your head against the office wall in frustration because the boss has coughed loudly in your ear? Does your boss mumble, talk too loudly occasionally and then almost whisper? How many times have you rewound and listened to an unfamiliar word 20 times and just wished the boss had the sense to spell it out?

Well maybe your boss is an admirable Accountant or a marvellous MD, but good dictation technique requires considerable practice. I hope this advice will be helpful – perhaps you can casually put it on your boss's desk with his coffee in the morning, but don't admit where it came from of course!

Before starting dictation, it is essential to be organised. All the necessary papers should be to hand. Otherwise you'll get frustrated and start scrambling about in the midst of dictation and it will be especially infuriating for your secretary if you forget to switch off the mike during this process!

Interruptions will affect your train of thought during the dictation so try to time your recording when you know you have some time free and do it in a room which is free from noise.

Once these preparations have been made, you're off. Before starting dictation on each piece of correspondence, do state the exact nature of the document, e.g. 'short letter', 'long report', etc. Also give an indication of the number of copies which will be required. This type of information is invaluable to your secretary as to the correspondence to be transcribed.

As for the dictation – the microphone is not a lollipop, so don't try to eat it! Hold it two or three inches away from your mouth. If you hold it too close, your speech will be blurred; too far away and you won't be heard at all. Don't mumble into the mike, but try to ensure your speech is clear. And please don't go like a bull at a gate – a secretary will not thank you if you dictate at 50 miles an hour!

When you have dictated the first sentence or so, listen to it again by playing back the recording, so that you can make any necessary adjustments – the sound may be too high or too low, so it's much better to correct it at this point than deafen your secretary later!

If the volume's OK, then go ahead. We all need to pause for thought now and again, so when you find it necessary to do so, or when the phone rings, remember to switch off the mike. Your secretary doesn't want to listen to a few minutes of nothing, or to a conversation with your wife about what's for dinner!

Wherever you can, try to include a mention of new paragraphs, and give clear instructions to your secretary regarding headings and any items which need to be numbered.

Your secretary will also need to clarify things with you every few minutes if you don't spell out personal names, place names, foreign names – anything which she may be unfamiliar with. Numbers too – prices, sums of money, percentages, etc.

When you've successfully reached the end of a document, mark the length of the document on the index slip – this will be a valuable reference tool for your secretary on the size of paper to use for the correspondence.

Finally, make sure you keep any letters, memos, reports, files and other relevant documents connected with the dictation in a special pile, and pass all this to your secretary with the recording. In this way all the information she needs will be just where she can find it, and she won't need to bother you with queries.

If you follow the above advice, it should save your secretary much frustration – and a happier secretary makes your life easier too, doesn't it?

Happy Dictating!

7 After reading the following assignment carefully, study the answer given. Discuss what is wrong with it, and rewrite the answer more appropriately.

You have been asked to give a talk at a secretarial seminar on the secretary's duties in connection with meetings, and the text of your speech is printed below. You have also been asked for a one-page summary of your speech for inclusion in the seminar booklet which delegates will keep for future reference. Using an appropriate format make your summary in not more than 150 words.

Meetings form an essential part of business life and, as secretaries, our role is to ensure that they are organised and administered efficiently, and that all the paperwork is dealt with correctly. I would like to talk to you today on the various things we have to think about when preparing for meetings, and the documentation involved.

Once it has been agreed that the meeting will take place on a particular day there are many practical tasks you should attend to. First of all make sure you enter the date of the meeting in your boss's diary and your own. This will, of course, avoid the risk of a clash of appointments at a later date. Then check the venue for the meeting, and if there is a regular room make sure it is available. This may be the company's own board room, or in the case of a departmental meeting perhaps you will use the manager's office. You then need to prepare and circulate the notice of meeting and agenda. If you will turn to page 41 of your seminar booklet you will see examples of the wording and layout of the notice and agenda.

(NB: Discuss from examples printed in seminar booklet page 41.)

Any additional documents for distribution, such as reports, statistics, etc., should be circulated with the notice and agenda, so that members may become thoroughly familiar with their contents prior to the meeting. Remember also to make additional sets of such documents – isn't it always the case that someone forgets to bring their copies on the day of the meeting, and we end up having to get extra copies for them at the last minute! If you take extra copies to start with, you will avoid this last-minute rush.

In consultation with your Chairman you should then produce a draft of the Chairman's agenda which he may amend as necessary. The Chairman's agenda is a little more detailed than the ordinary members' agenda. It is for use only by the Chairman, containing extra notes for his own reference in helping him to conduct the business of the meeting efficiently.

(NB: Discuss Chairman's agenda from page 42.)

So much for the preliminary documentation, what about other matters? If you have a regular caterer, a provisional order should be made for refreshments at this stage, which will be confirmed when the number of participants is known nearer the date.

Any equipment which may be required at the meeting should be arranged, including making sure any visual aids required will be available if necessary. (Does anyone require the overhead projector, spirit pens, video recorder, etc.?)

Place names should be prepared if these are needed to identify the participants at the meeting. Obviously these will not be necessary at a departmental meeting where everyone knows everyone else, but at more formal meetings they may be useful.

Once these provisional arrangements have been attended to, you can more or less relax until the day of the meeting itself. Then you will need to make sure everything is organised as efficiently as possible, using a bit of the foresight we are supposed to develop as secretaries. First of all arrange the meeting room, attending to such things as seating arrangements, water and glasses, writing paper and pencils, and ashtrays. Any documents to be used during the meeting should be laid out on the table. Spare copies of the agenda and minutes of the last meeting should be at hand, as well as the official minute book and any other reports which I mentioned earlier. You should also check that any equipment and accessories required are in the right place and in working order. You don't want your boss to switch on the OHP during the meeting only to find the bulb has blown, or for him to write on a transparency only to find the spirit pen has run out!

Next reconfirm that refreshments will be served at the appropriate time, and give any last-minute instructions regarding the number of members attending the meeting.

The switchboard and receptionist should also be given a list of participants at the meeting, together with instructions for diverting their calls as necessary. Perhaps a colleague will be called upon to take all calls, or the switchboard operator herself may be required to take messages. Whatever the arrangements, make sure the relevant people know what is required of them.

If you are attending the meeting as secretary, gather your own paperwork together with suitable materials to take down the minutes. Ensure that you have your own and your boss's diaries available to check details of appointments when future dates have to be arranged during the meeting. Finally place a 'meeting in progress' notice on the door. This will ensure no one walks in and disturbs the progress of the meeting. I will not mention anything about Minutes here because my colleague will be discussing that with you in detail later in the programme.

Arranging meetings can be a bit of a headache – collating all the reports and material for the meeting, making sure all the documentation is issued at the appropriate time, and all the various other matters which we have to attend to. But if you think them through logically, step-by-step, and use the summarised checklist which I have included in the seminar booklet, you can ensure that nothing is overlooked.

So whether you are organising your first meeting or your fiftieth, I wish you success.

COMPREHENSION

By the end of this section you should be able to:

❑ choose synonyms for given words

❑ identify the meaning of words from the context

❑ calculate how marks are allocated in comprehension questions

❑ develop effective techniques to answer comprehension questions.

No communication in our business or private life can take place successfully without comprehending. Any assignment we undertake in any aspect of our studies is an assignment in comprehension. Most examiners and assessors would comment that many questions are badly answered because candidates do not answer the question which has been set – they do not fully understand what is required before answering the question.

Comprehension is tested every time we read or write. Most errors in previous units of this book will have resulted from not having read a question properly, and fully understood it, before attempting an answer. The importance of careful and thorough reading cannot, therefore, be over-stressed.

It is most unlikely that you have not studied comprehension exercises before now. We all know what comprehension exercises require – a passage has to be read and then questions based on the passage must be answered.

The importance of using a dictionary has to be emphasised. Occasions will arise when you are not familiar with a word used in a passage. Always look up unfamiliar words immediately, and relate the dictionary meaning to the contextual use of the word.

In view of the importance of vocabulary work, preliminary exercises are provided in this unit on the meanings of words in context, followed by a look at the types of question asked, how to word and display your answers and how marks are allocated.

✦ Using a dictionary

Comprehension is all about understanding. That is why use of a dictionary is so important, to ensure understanding. Use a dictionary if necessary to fill in the blanks in the words below. You should choose a word which could be used to replace the phrases in italics.

1 My boss is always *finding fault* with anything and everything in my work.
(f _ _ t _ _ i _ _ s)

2 Since the company recruited a new Accountant, the accounting and book-keeping records seem to have *gone from bad to worse*.
(d _ _ _ r _ _ r _ _ _ d

3 I understand Personnel haven't decided on a replacement for the MD's Secretary, but Laura and Jackie are *in the running*.
(c _ _ t _ _ d _ _ g)

4 I felt like a *fish out of water* on my first day at work. I knew no-one at all.
(m _ _ _ _ t)

5 If I work hard at all these exercises, I'm sure I'll *make the grade*.
(s _ _ _ _ _ d)

6 You must *bring home* to Lesley that she cannot leave it until the last week of term before she starts work on her integrated project.
(c _ _ v _ _ _ e)

7 You must be honest with yourself and others – don't try to *gloss over* the truth.
(c _ _ c _ _ l)

8 Stella is always *assuming superior airs*, but she's really no better than the rest of us.
(p _ t r _ n _ _ _ _ g)

9 John has been the *main person* behind the formation of the new company.
(m _ _ _ _ _ m _ _ d)

10 When my car's engine is cold, it goes *in fits and starts* until it warms up.
(j _ _ k _ _ y)

✦ Grammatical precision

When choosing the meaning of a word mentioned in a passage, care must be taken not to alter the meaning or change the tense. You must make sure your answer fits exactly in the passage in place of the stated words or phrases.

Example: He *intentionally* left the fire door open.
Incorrect: on purpose/deliberate
Correct: deliberately

In each sentence below, one word is italicised. From the choices given, choose one word which could replace it.

1 This electronic typewriter is going to be *superseded* by a new model.
a) replace   b) replaced   c) replacing   d) replaces

2 Do you remember the *halcyon* days we spent whiling away the hours on Rawa, our paradise island off the east coast of Malaysia?
a) tranquil   b) tranquillity   c) tranquiliser   d) tranquilising

3 My boss is always making *insinuations* about a pay increase, but I've still not had confirmation.
a) hint   b) hints   c) hinted   d) hinting

4 If my son is *contumacious*, I always send him to bed without supper.
a) disobey   b) disobeyed   c) disobedient   d) obedient

5 Don't forget to have your work permit *abrogated* before you fly home.
a) cancel   b) cancels   c) cancelled   d) cancelling

6 It's a woman's *prerogative* to arrive a few minutes late for a date.
a) privilege   b) privileged   c) privacy   d) private

7   Linda is a *peripatetic* author – she has been all over the world while writing her first novel.
    a) travel   b) travelled   c) travelling   d) traveller

8   A secretary has to perform quite a lot of *esoteric* duties in her job.
    a) specialist   b) specialise   c) specialised   d) special

9   I need a *corroborator* to back me up or I'll be in big trouble, even though it's not my fault.
    a) support   b) supporter   c) supporting   d) supported

10   My boss is always very *irascible* over the tiniest mistake in my work.
    a) irritate   b) irritable   c) irritant   d) irritability

✦ Contextual clues

Very often the meaning of an unfamiliar word can be identified from the context. In the following sentences:

a) choose one word from the choices given to replace the nonsense word which is in italics.
b) unjumble the word in italics to make a synonym for the word you chose to replace it.

Example: I have to act as the *idyaremrinet* between my boss and his callers.
             Answer: go-between
             Synonym: intermediary

1   Don't be a victim of *crotinarspation* – you should not put off until tomorrow what you could do today.
    a) dilettante   b) dilapidation   c) dilatoriness

2   Suzanne has those *nitane* qualities which make her perfect for the job
    a) inert   b) inhuman   c) inborn

3   A letter which is written in a *genniscodencd* tone will not give the recipient a very good impression.
    a) courteous   b) patronising   c) polite

4   If any of the company's rules are *lovetiad* you will receive a verbal warning in the first place.
    a) disobeyed   b) followed   c) obeyed

5   Since the new Chairman was appointed, the company has grown substantially and become very *orpserpuso*.
    a) unsuccessful   b) successful   c) profit-sharing

6   Drinking too much coffee at night causes *mosainin*.
    a) caffeine   b) sleeplessness   c) tiresome

7　The disciplinary matter is held in *yebacean* for the Manager to make a decision when he returns tomorrow.
　　a)　awaiting　　　　　b)　suspension　　　　c)　suspense

8　If you want to change your lunch hour, you must obtain the *conitans* of your manager first.
　　a)　appendix　　　　　b)　deprecation　　　　c)　approval

9　The new secretary shows a lot of *togismanna* towards me, but I don't know what I've done to upset her.
　　a)　resentment　　　　b)　friendship　　　　c)　contentment

10　When the fire bell rings, employees must leave the building and report to their *gestideand* safety officer.
　　a)　nomination　　　　b)　nominated　　　　c)　nominal

✦ Types of answer

Most comprehension questions ask for a certain type of answer:

- ✦ Who? (a person)
- ✦ When? (a time)
- ✦ Where? (a place)
- ✦ Why? (a reason)
- ✦ How? (a method)
- ✦ What? (a thing/idea)

Example:　Question: In what year did Henry Ford produce his first motor car?
　　　　　Question type: When?
　　　　　Answer required: A time

In the following questions, what type of question is asked, and what type of answer is required?

1　Which sister wrote the book *Wuthering Heights*?
　　Question type: _____
　　Answer required: _____

2　Give one reason for the drop in prices of computers.
　　Question type: _____
　　Answer required: _____

3 What did Lisa's boss find was the most convenient time for dictation?

Question type: _____

Answer required: _____

4 What are the peak advertising hours on television?

Question type: _____

Answer required: _____

5 Mention one item of equipment which could help Janice with her tasks.

Question type: _____

Answer required: _____

6 In what way do Pam's methods differ from those of the other secretaries?

Question type: _____

Answer required: _____

7 Suggest one reason why some people collect stamps.

Question type: _____

Answer required: _____

✦ Giving opinions

Some comprehension questions require the candidate to state someone's opinion. It could be one of three people whose opinion is required:

1 The author's
2 The candidate's (based on the passage)
3 Someone else's (someone else mentioned in the passage)

If no one else is mentioned, you should give the author's opinion.

Example: Question: How will the new technology affect the secretaries mentioned?
Answer: Give the author's opinion, as in the passage, regardless of how much you know about the subject.

Decide whose opinions are required in the following questions:

1 Do you agree with the author that shorthand will never be completely redundant?

Whose opinion? _____

2 State two advantages of facsimile transmission mentioned.

Whose opinion? _____

3   Mention two of the factors upon which the choice of method of communication is dependent.

Whose opinion? _____

4   Why is Great Britain thought to be the ideal market for the products mentioned?

Whose opinion? _____

5   Mention three ways in which the secretary in the passage considers information technology has changed her role.

Whose opinion? _____

✦ Wording and displaying answers

An examiner often has hundreds of scripts to mark. A little extra thought in presenting your answers neatly will put him/her in a much better mood than will a paper which looks messy and has arrows everywhere.

As with other aspects of your communication course, presentation of comprehension answers is very important. Bear in mind the following guidelines:

1   Do not waste time writing out the questions on your answer sheets. The examiner is well aware what questions have been set.
2   Unless the instructions state otherwise, answers should be expressed in complete sentences, not in note form.
3   Your answers must be grammatically correct and suitably punctuated.
4   It is worthwhile following the pattern suggested by the wording of the question.

Study the following examples:

1   Why are bank notes advantageous over coins?
    Bank notes are advantageous over coins because ...

2   Why did the workers go on strike?
    The workers went on strike because ...

3   What impression does the writer give you of ...?
    The impression the writer gives me is ...

4   Which fact best illustrates the ...?
    The fact which best illustrates the ... is ...

5   Mention two ways in which ...
    Two ways in which ... are:
    a)   ...
    b)   ...

6   Why did the writer think ...?
    The writer thought ... because ...

7   How was ... understood in the past?
    In the past ... was understood as ...

8   Name four qualities essential for ...
    Four qualities essential for ... are:
    a) ...
    b) ...
    c) ...
    d) ...

9   Which sentence in the passage shows most clearly the ...?
    The sentence which shows most clearly the ... is '...'

10 In your own words, what do you think is meant by the expression '...' ?
    I think this expression means ...

✦ Marks awarded for comprehension questions

One way of judging whether a lot or a little is required of any question is to refer to the number of marks awarded. Some students write half a page in answer to a 2-mark question, and two lines in answer to an 8-mark question. Obviously that cannot be right!

Comprehension questions need careful consideration. You should check carefully the number of marks allocated to each question and bear this in mind when looking for and writing out your answers.

Very often questions ask for reasons, advantages, arguments, effects. Remember in such cases that the number of marks allocated will be divided equally between the number of reasons, advantages, etc., which you give.

For example, a 6-mark question may mean there are three reasons, with 2 marks for each. An 8-mark question may mean there are four advantages, with 2 marks for each, and so on.

There can be no hard and fast rules. All I say is be aware that examiners do not usually award marks *ad hoc*. There is generally a strict marking scheme to which they work. Wording your answer in close relationship with the marks available should be remembered at all times.

Remember, too, that marks are probably awarded for neatness and presentation.

✦ Guidelines for comprehension

1   The importance of careful and thorough reading cannot be over-emphasised. Concentrate carefully and read the passage through once. Then read through the questions. On your second reading of the passage, it should be possible to identify areas to which certain questions refer.

2   Make a note in the margin of the passage as a cross-reference to the question number concerned. In some comprehension passages, questions are posed so that they work logically through the text, but this is not always the case.

3   Answer the questions one by one, tackling them in the order in which they are printed if possible.

4   Use your own words rather than those used in the passage wherever possible.

5   Take particular note of the number of marks allocated to each question. This gives you an idea of how much is required in your answer, and how much detail is necessary.

6   Base the wording of your answer on the wording of the question. This also helps to reinforce in your mind the question which is asked.

7   When you are required to give definitions of words or phrases, be sure your answer is in the same part of speech. If a noun is given, your answer should be a noun, etc. Be careful when consulting a dictionary because often more than one meaning is provided – be careful to choose the right meaning which matches the meaning of the word in the passage. Do not copy dictionary definitions out 'wholesale' – use your initiative to rephrase accordingly.

8   Your handwriting should be legible and your expression as correct as possible. Present your answers neatly, with question numbers clearly shown. Marks can be lost because of poor presentation and untidy work.

✦ Assignments

1   Read the following passage carefully.

LUXOR HOTELS AND CONFERENCE FACILITIES

Our company name stems from the day when the founder, George Meredith, was staying in Luxor and planning a conference to be held in Singapore. He decided to set up his own business and began with one hotel in 1989. Today there are Luxor hotels in more than 100 countries around the world. The biggest, with 600 rooms, is in Chicago and the smallest, with 100 rooms, in Perth, Western Australia. There are no hotels with fewer than 100 rooms. All Luxor hotels in the USA have at least 250 rooms whereas European hotels prefer smaller units. Over 66% of Asian hotels have more than 300 rooms.

Quality is emphasised at all Luxor hotels. They are all decorated annually, all fittings are regularly checked and any worn furniture is immediately replaced. In 1992 alone, 5000 litres of paint were used in Singapore and about 50% of the carpets were replaced in our hotels in China. During 1994, 1000 beds were replaced in Cape Town by new ones imported from Canada. In 1996 every conference centre in Asia replaced its video facilities with the newest German equipment. By 2001, half the video facilities in all European hotels will have been updated.

Staff training is paramount at Luxor hotels. The largest hotels have a training manager and smaller ones are grouped together for training. All staff from senior managers to bar staff and reception staff attend training sessions annually. The quality of their work is assessed at monthly meetings with their line managers.

From the very beginning, Luxor's conference trade has developed at great pace. In 1990 there were three conferences with just 200 delegates, but by 1995 there was at least one conference every week of the year and almost 10,000 people attended. Subjects ranged from international trade to private meetings of national sports bodies. One of the strangest topics for a conference was plankton farming. This was attended by 700 delegates from around the world – half the number who were at the Chicago conference on whales in Lake Michigan in 1994.

Luxor Hotels and Conferences continues to grow and we look forward to the future with confidence and anticipation.

Indicate whether these statements are true or false. Quote a few words from the text to support your answers.

a) There are 100 Luxor hotels.
   True/False
b) All meetings held at Luxor hotels are concerned with business.
   True/False
c) In 1995 50 conferences took place.
   True/False
d) Every Luxor hotel has a training manager.
   True/False
e) 40% of Asian hotels have 250 rooms.
   True/False
f) George Meredith attended a conference in Luxor.
   True/False
g) 700 delegates visited a place called Whales in Lake Michigan.
   True/False
h) Half the carpets in China's hotels are new.
   True/False

i) All Luxor hotels have at least 100 rooms.
   True/False
j) Seventy per cent of the video equipment in European hotels will be changed in 2001.
   True/False

2 Read this passage and then answer the questions which follow. Use your own words as far as possible.

> To please his son, John Wilson recreated the wood and pea netting goal he had first made as a boy. He then saw the huge potential for a portable goal that could be packed away in a bag and used anywhere – beach, lawn or field.
>
> Funding came from remortgaging his home in Sheffield and from a government grant. Using John's patented design, a local plastics company then produced goals that were strong, easy to assemble, safe, virtually impossible to knock over and yet light enough for children to carry and erect. 'ITSA Goal' (Inter Trading Sports Associates) was now in business.
>
> *The first half*: John's initial plan to sell the goals via sports shops was dashed when retailers told him there was no market for a product costing £125 when cheaper, albeit inferior, portable goals already existed. John turned to the Football Association who agreed to test the product, liked it and gave it official approval. Luck then took a hand. The FA was talking to Coca-Cola about a Youth Development project for small team games for which John's product was ideal. John calls the resulting deal a win win win situation.
>
>> 'Coca-Cola buys regularly from me in bulk at a discounted price. I sell the goals – Coca-Cola "Big Red Bag" branded – to schools and football clubs. I target through leaflets and other literature and word-of-mouth. Customers benefit from the discounted price. I return the money from the sales to Coca-Cola who also get the brand name displayed nationwide.'
>
> *The second half*: John generously stresses the role that Midland has played in helping him over the years. John felt he lacked sound financial advice. The Midland Branch Manager for Rotherham met that need.
>
>> 'He restructured the whole financial side of the company and helped me with planning. Funding the business through my mortgage wasn't sensible. Taking a business loan with the house as security was far more tax efficient.'
>>
>> 'The Bank Manager also introduced me to a good accountant. For me, this was the major cultural change, realising that an accountant needn't just be someone who comes in and tots up the figures at the end of the year. Now we monitor the situation constantly and can plan accordingly.'

Today, with a £1/2 million turnover and growing and all John's loans cleared, ITSA Goal's own factory produces goals and other soccer related equipment for schools, clubs and individuals throughout the UK and Europe. No question about it, John has scored with this cracking idea.

Reproduced courtesy of John Wilson, ITSA Goal and Midland Bank plc

a) How did John Wilson please his son? (2)
b) Explain 'the huge potential for a portable goal'. (2)
c) Explain 'John's initial plan to sell the goals via sports shops was dashed.' (2)
d) Why was John's plan 'dashed'? (2)
e) How did John finance this project initially? (2)
f) How did the Bank Manager help John? (4)
g) What happened when John took on a good accountant? (6)
h) What does Coca-Cola gain from the business? (4)
i) What does John mean by a 'win win win' situation? (2)
j) Explain the following phrases used in the passage:
   i) cheaper, albeit inferior (2)
   ii) other soccer related equipment (2)

Total: 30 marks

3 Read the following passage, then answer the question which follow.

AROMATHERAPY

Aromatherapy involves the use of essential oils from plants. These oils are very *potent* and to understand their benefits you need to know what they are, and how they work in aromatherapy.

An essential oil is a delicate fluid which forms the fragrance of a plant or flower. It can be stored in the stem, leaves, roots or bark, depending on the plant. Although called oil, it doesn't actually resemble one in texture, but is a highly scented and extremely potent liquid.

The powerful *aroma* of essential oils can affect the way we feel. Experts say the reason for this is that their aroma is 'transported' from nerve cells in the nose to the part of the brain which is concerned with emotion. Therefore, different oils are often used to help relieve anxiety and stress, and to *alleviate* depression.

It has been proved that essential oils have a great ability to penetrate the skin. Once absorbed into the blood stream, different ones seem to have an 'affinity' with different organs in the body.

Essential oils are regenerative as well as antiseptic, and therefore help the skin to heal faster. Lavender, for instance, is excellent for treating acne, boils, burns and eczema, whereas tea tree oil is good for spots, pimples and insect bites.

You need to smell pure undiluted essential oils to appreciate their potency and they should never be used *neat*. Eucalyptus and peppermint, for instance, can irritate the skin if applied undiluted.

Essential oils are beneficial in various ways, so it is important to choose the right one.

(Extract from *Prima* magazine, London)

a) Explain the meanings of the following words, as used in the passage:
   i) potent
   ii) aroma
   iii) alleviate
   iv) neat
b) Where do the oils used in aromatherapy come from?
c) How does the aroma of these oils affect us?
d) What would happen if eucalyptus was applied to the skin neat?
e) With which oil should insect bites be treated?

4 ACUPUNCTURE

Acupuncture – needle-therapy – hails from China. According to traditional Chinese medicine, good health depends on the body's ability to maintain a state of inner balance. In acupuncture the needles are used to restore balance and so cure illness.

Bodily harmony, or health, is said to be the result of a balancing act between two opposing forces known as Yin and Yang. Yin represents soft, feminine qualities. Yang hard, masculine qualities.

Good health also relies on the smooth flow of the body's life-force or vital energy known as Chi. Emotional upsets, poor diet, overwork and stress can disturb the even flow of Chi and lead to illness. The vital Chi circulates along a network of invisible channels called Meridians.

Treatment involves stimulating various defined points along the Meridians by planting needles in them. This strengthens Chi, and restores the equilibrium of Yin and Yang. These points are known as acupuncture points.

Sometimes described as 'acupuncture without the needles', acupressure uses light fingertip pressure. In Shiatsu – the Japanese version – heavy pressure is involved too.

(Extract from *Prima* magazine, London)

a) Briefly explain the three forces on which the Chinese believe good health relies.
b) What are Meridians?
c) Briefly explain how acupuncture works.
d) How does acupressure differ from acupuncture?

5 Read the following passage, then answer the questions that follow.

MINERALS – ARE YOU GETTING ENOUGH?

The weather's boiling, you've been running around, you're in a bit of a lather and suddenly an *excruciating* cramp hits you. Such heat cramps are caused by losing sodium when we perspire – just one of the effects of not having enough of an essential mineral in the system.

Minerals are the poor relations of vitamins. Few of us know just which minerals we need (and which we should avoid), how much we need and which foods they are found in. It gets more confusing, because if you eat too much of one mineral, such as iron, it might cause you to absorb less of another such as zinc. Even worse, minerals such as lead can be positively bad for you. And excessive aluminium has been linked with Alzheimer's disease.

So just what are these elusive substances? Minerals are metals which occur naturally in the soil and are absorbed into the plants and animals we eat. If we don't get enough of these minerals, we feel run down. At worst, this can cause mineral *deficiency* illnesses such as anaemia.

Many of us could be low in certain minerals – especially if we eat an unbalanced diet, or one high in refined food. Refining often means *extracting* the most wholesome part of the food. White bread, for example, contains less minerals than wholemeal bread because the wheatgerm and bran are removed.

Although the cells in our body naturally contain *minute* amounts of minerals, they are used up as our cells become worn out. As the body is not very good at storing minerals (apart from a little calcium, phosphorus, magnesium and iron), it is vital we have enough in our daily diet.

There is considerable *controversy* over whether or not we need to take supplements. If you continually eat on the run and you know you're not having a balanced diet, then a supplement can only do you good. But do you need a supplement if you're eating a balanced diet of mineral rich liver, meat, fish, dairy produce, wholegrains, fruits and vegetables?

Traditional nutritionists say that a balanced diet will give you all the nutrients you need. Others believe that the use of pesticides which poison the soil, pollution and food processing mean that many of our foods no longer contain enough minerals.

Whatever the truth, taking a supplement will do you no harm – provided you take only the recommended dose. Taking a higher dosage can be positively harmful. Too much iron can prevent you absorbing zinc, and if you take excessive amounts of magnesium, you'll get a bout of diarrhoea!

(Extract from *Prima* magazine, London)

a) Explain the meaning of the following words, as used in the passage:
   i) excruciating
   ii) deficiency
   iii) extracting
   iv) minute
   v) controversy
b) What causes heat cramps?
c) Briefly explain what minerals are.
d) Why do certain people not have enough minerals?
e) Which minerals is the body good at storing?
f) Would supplements of minerals be harmful to someone who eats a balanced diet?

6 Read this passage and then answer the questions which follow. Use your own words as far as possible.

PROFILE OF ANITA RODDICK

I started The Body Shop in 1976 simply to create a livelihood for myself and my two daughters, while my husband, Gordon, was trekking across the Americas. I had no training or experience and my only business acumen was Gordon's advice to take sales of £300 a week. Nobody talks of entrepreneurship as survival, but that's exactly what it is and what nurtures creative thinking. Running that first shop taught me business was not financial science; it's about trading – buying and selling. It's about creating a product or service so good that people will pay for it. Now 22 years on, The Body Shop is a multi-local business with 1650 stores in 47 countries, trading in 24 languages across 12 time zones. And I haven't a clue how we got here!

It wasn't only economic necessity that inspired the birth of The Body Shop. Women, when they want to earn a livelihood, usually earn it through what they are interested in or what they are knowledgeable about. *I had a wealth of experience to draw on.* I travelled, and I spent time in farming and fishing communities with pre-industrial peoples. My travels exposed me to body rituals of women from all over the world. Also the frugality that my mother exercised during the war years made me question retail conventions. Why waste a container when you can refill it? And why buy more of something than you can use? We behaved as she did in the Second World War – we re-used everything, we refilled everything and we recycled all we could. The foundation of The Body Shop's environmental activism was born out of ideas like these.

I am aware that success is more than a good idea. It is timing too. The Body Shop arrived just as Europe was going 'green'. The Body Shop has always been recognisable by its green colour, the only colour that we could find to cover the damp, mouldy walls of my first shop. I opened a second shop within six months, by which time Gordon was back in England. He came up with the idea for 'self-financing' more new stores, which sparked the growth of the franchise network through which The Body Shop spread across the world. The company went public in 1984. Since then I have been given a whole host of awards, some I understand, some I don't, and a couple I think I deserve.

The Body Shop and I have always been closely identified in the public mind, undoubtedly because *it is impossible to separate the company values from my own personal values* and issues that I care passionately about: social responsiveness, respect for human rights, the environment and animal protection. But I must point out that The Body Shop is not a one-woman show – it is a global operation with thousands of people working towards common goals, engaged in their own livelihood, and franchisees running their own businesses.

The Body Shop is always on my mind, in one way or another. Whether it be in a state of delight or frustration. The relationship I have with The Body Shop is one where I sometimes can't tell the difference between stress and enthusiasm.

Reproduced courtesy of The Body Shop International PLC

(a) Why did Anita Roddick start The Body Shop? (2)

(b) What did she learn from her first shop? (4)

(c) Anita Roddick says 'I had a wealth of experiences to draw on.' Summarise these experiences. (6)

(d) Give two reasons to suggest why 'green' is important to The Body Shop. (6)

(e) What does Anita Roddick mean when she says 'It is impossible to separate the company values from my own personal values.' Try to explain these values in your own words. (8)

(f) How would you sum up how Anita Roddick feels about The Body Shop? (4)

Total: 30 marks

7 Read this passage carefully and then answer the questions which follow. Use your own words as far as possible.

Reproduced courtesy of British Telecommunications plc from BT's Annual Review and Summary Financial Statement 1998

THE COMMUNITY OPPORTUNITY

Companies do not exist above and beyond the societies in which they operate; they are part of those societies. They are *'citizen companies'*, with all the rights and responsibilities that citizenship brings. BT is determined to make an imaginative and effective impact in all the communities in which we conduct our business. Some 90% of members believe that companies have at least some responsibility to the community. We are proud to accept that responsibility.

BT is committed to helping people in need and at risk *to improve their quality of life* through our Community Partnership Programme. With a budget of around £15 million a year for working with community causes, this programme is the largest of its kind in the UK. But it is not just about good citizenship. We also believe it is *good business*. Seventy per cent of the general public say that the contribution a company makes to the community could affect their buying decisions.

This is why *we are careful that all our involvement is reputation-enhancing*. After all, a good reputation means that governments will want us in their countries, customers will want to buy from us, shareholders will want to invest in us, skilled people will want to join us, and our employees will be proud to work for us.

Our community partnership activities throughout the UK are themed around access and communication. We place particular emphasis on education and training, the improvement of communication skills, support for people with disabilities, and the involvement of BT people.

In the last year we have put in place a programme to enable charities and voluntary groups to make more effective use of communications technology. As part of this, we are collaborating with the charity One World On Line to offer training and support for small charities to help them run their own Internet sites.

But it's not just about encouraging people to talk and listen. BT is bringing the benefits of the new technology it is developing to the people who need it most. For example, BT and the Anchor Trust are developing remote health monitoring to help older people continue to live independently.

More than 80 million people in the UK have some form of hearing loss, and BT is helping to address their communications needs. All our public payphones are fitted with inductive couplers to help hearing aid users and we have been working with the Royal National Institute for Deaf People (RNID) to improve deaf people's access to arts venues around the country.

Typetalk, the national telephone relay service run by the RNID with funds from BT, enables 20,000 deaf or speech-impaired customers to communicate via a textphone. BT will also be one of the corporate sponsors of the millennium celebrations, not just at the Millennium Dome in Greenwich but throughout the country. We want to make a contribution that will *touch everyone's lives* in the year 2000, so we will be launching 'Mill-e-Mail' – a free electronic mail address service, which means that no-one need ever be out of touch.

A comprehensive set of reports is also being published that describe BT's social, environmental and technological interactions with society. Through these reports, we aim to *stimulate a wider debate* into how BT can contribute to an improved quality of life for all.

(a) What does the writer mean by 'citizen companies'? (4)

(b) Why does the company believe that it is 'good business'? (4)

(c) Explain 'we are careful that all our involvement is reputation-enhancing'. (4)

(d) Describe BT's work with charities and voluntary organisations. (8)

(e) How is BT helping to celebrate the millennium? (4)

(f) Explain the following phrases as used in the passage:
   i) to improve their quality of life (2)
   ii) touch everyone's lives (2)
   iii) stimulate a wider debate (2)
   Total: 30 marks

8 Read this passage carefully and then answer the questions which follow. Use your own words as far as possible.

WAKE UP TO POLLUTION

'Don't choke Britain' is about persuading people to forget the car and wake up to better ways to get around. This local authority-led initiative aims to raise public awareness about the damage to our environment and health caused by increased traffic congestion and pollution.

Embracing many local initiatives throughout June, the Don't Choke Britain Campaign urges people out of their cars and onto bikes, buses, trains and pavements.

Midland Mainline has a raft of travel options which complement the vision of a less car-orientated future. Its latest offer is Door-to-Door, where two, three or four people can catch an off-peak train to London and back from as little as £39 for the group. A pre-booked taxi to and from the station is included in the price.

'Until people are offered a cheaper and more convenient alternative, such as Door-to-Door, they will continue to take the car – whether it's all the way to London or just to the station,' says Midland Mainline's Product Manager, Chris Lyons.

Perhaps the most ambitious scheme is the proposed development of an East Midlands Parkway Railway Station, close to the M1 motorway. As Chris Lyons says, 'Midland Mainline are looking hard at taking more responsibility for *our customers' real journey* from their front door to their final destination, not just the journey from station to station. For example to make getting to airports easier, we are looking to develop competitively priced tickets that combine rail transport on Midland Mainline with other modes of transport. Combining the various travel options in one straightforward offer will make travelling to the airport by public transport much more attractive.'

Clearly, *co-ordinated public transport* is the way forward if a cleaner, greener Britain is to be achieved. Midland Mainline's services take a sizeable chunk of traffic off the M1 and that's good news for the environment. But is it realistic to think that *hardened car users* can be coaxed away from their steering wheels?

'No-one says it's going to be easy,' says Chris Lyons. 'But if the products are right and backed up with a reliable, good quality service, then it's possible.'

Using the car has its own problems, not least of which is traffic jams, incessant road works and the prospect of heavyweight measures to curb driving such as motorway tolls, reduced access to town centres and higher taxation.

Constant improvements to Midland Mainline's services such as greater frequency, new products and better customer service are definitely persuading more and more people to use the train.

Reproduced courtesy of Midland Mainline

(a) What does the writer mean by 'Don't Choke Britain'?
     What is the purpose of the 'Don't Choke Britain' campaign? (4)
(b) Explain the sentence 'Midland Mainline has a raft of travel options which complement the vision of a less car-orientated future.' (2)
(c) Describe the Door-to-Door scheme. (4)
(d) How can the planners make it easier for people to get to airports? (4)
(e) What are the problems facing car users? (6)
(f) Explain the following phrases:
     i)   Embracing many local initiatives (2)
     ii) Perhaps the most ambitious scheme (2)
     iii) our customers' real journey (2)
     iv) coordinated public transport (2)
     v)   hardened car users   (2)

     Total: 30 marks

9   The Personal Assistant to the Far East Division's Chairman is to give the opening address at a secretarial seminar, and she has submitted a draft of her speech to you. Read it carefully and answer the questions which follow.

    In the days of illiterate kings and barons, when most dealings were conducted verbally through intermediaries, the job of 'secretary' conjured up a picture of someone employed by the rich and powerful as a private ear, intent upon the concealment of dirty linen. However, take heart. By the late Middle Ages the word 'secretary' had gained in status, referring to one whose office it was to write for another, especially one who was employed to conduct correspondence, to keep records.

    So the written word became the chief medium of communication, and when the Victorians launched the newest 'profession' in the widest sense of the word – commerce – with all its attendant record-keeping, and invented the Penny Post, the business letter as we know it was born.

From that point the phenomenon has been developed to a high degree; indeed, doubtless far too many such letters are written now, causing literally tons of paperwork to be produced, processed and stored every working day. Hence secretaries have really come into their own and not just as transcribers of letters. For as busy decision-makers in all spheres, be they MPs, surgeons, barristers, bankers, civil servants or business executives, cannot write all their letters out by hand, equally they cannot make every single telephone call, book all their own appointments or keep track of all their file copies. So they need someone to bail them out. Someone who will give a reliable and sensible back-up service, will hold the strings, acting as a base or nerve-centre in the hectic flow of events, and can be trusted to handle all information passing before them in an adult and serious fashion. In other words, guess who?

A 'secretary' can now signify anything from a thigh-booted, nail-polishing dolly who sits behind a typewriter thinking about her boyfriend and waiting for 5 pm, to the *high-flying and terrifying paragon who can speak five languages, take shorthand at 300 wpm while piloting a VC10 and run a press reception for 1000 before breakfast*. At its most accurate the word denotes those who occupy the area between these two – that small army of quiet and efficient persons whose job it is to deal with their employer's day in manner both discreet and reliable. These people are the present answer to a solid, lasting and not inconsiderable demand and it would be hard to see how they could be *superseded*. Until some bright spark invents a machine that can think as well as take messages, compose and produce individual letters, keep a vague employer to his schedule, remember everything from the year dot and make drinkable coffee, secretaries are the best alternative.

So far so good. A job to be done and a female workforce who can do it. But why can we do it? I think for the very reason that we are female. Because there will always be a large sphere of work for which I believe women are temperamentally better suited than men. Really effective secretarial work demands imagination; putting yourself in another person's place and thinking for them. And women have on the whole always been better equipped to do this. A recent movement has initiated heated debate about the comparative roles of the sexes, in the wake of which have come opportunities hitherto unheard of for women to prove themselves equal to a man's world. And some are clearly more than equal, revealing formidable ability, drive and stamina in many important areas. Certainly these prominent women will continue to focus attention on changing attitudes to their sex, but they will not alter the fundamental nature of the ordinary, timeless female capacities and strengths. The debate will go on, but it will not change the fact that women by and large have more patience, attention to detail, self-control and imagination – that is, the qualities that make, *inter alia*, a good secretary.

You might say 'anyone who has mastered all this and still has some energy left deserves to go places – upwards'. As I have said before there certainly are women in very senior, stimulating and deeply rewarding jobs who started out as secretaries and who made the transition with resounding success. But for the rest of us, the question must be asked 'where are we going?'

For the *status quo* is showing signs of exciting development. The much-heralded silicon chip technology is clearly here to stay and is surely removing all the drudgery which has been built into secretarial work – the filing, the checking, the tedious garnering of information. But because such technology cannot make decisions, the thinking part of the secretary's job – the administration, the coordination, the arranging and confirming, the *liaision* with people – must be thrown into relief, expanded and endowed with a new status. Result – streamlined version of an old classic: that position which is often at the very centre of power, carries a sizeable amount of responsibility, calls for the exercise of the highest level of expertise and represents really caring work, putting to good use the feminine capacity for being a buffer state, a partner and full supporting cast. Surely there is quite a good job to be made of all that?

Well, here we are. We have been taught to take shorthand (and sometimes we can even read it back!) and to type. The same broad aims and much the same problems concern us all. How to create order out of chaos, how to raise or foster the public image of the company, how to bring the best out of the people and the crises. And how about when we don't really understand the technicalities of the work we are dealing with – or no-one ever thinks we need encouragement – or is there just too much work?

Well, you can take a deep breath and get cracking – with the aid of a philosophical acceptance of what you probably can't change, some firm priorities held well in view, a degree of skill, and a few well-tried life saver tips – which is what this two-day seminar is all about. I hope you enjoy it and I wish you luck!

(Adapted from *Super Secretary* by Sally Denholm-Young, published by Settle Press, London)

a) Explain the meaning of the following, as used in the passage:

   i)   superseded
   ii) *inter alia*
   iii) status quo
   iv) liaison

   (4 marks)

b) To what phenomenon is the writer referring when she says '… the phenomenon has been developed to a high degree'? (4 marks)

c) The writer refers to a 'secretary' in one context as '... a terrifying paragon who can speak five languages, take shorthand at 300 wpm while piloting a VC10 and run a press reception for 1000 before breakfast ...' Explain what you think her meaning is, in your own words, simply and clearly. (6 marks)

d) Why does the writer believe the secretarial workforce is made up mainly of women? (6 marks)

e) To what 'transition' is the writer referring when she says '... who have made the transition with resounding success'? (4 marks)

f) What effects is new technology having on the role of the secretary now? (6 marks)

(Total: 30 marks)

Appendix

✦ Breakdown of examination questions by topic

This illustration shows the major documents which you may be required to produce in the examinations shown:

Unit	4–6 Business letter	11 Sales/circular letter	7 Fax message	8 Memorandum	9 Report	10 Meetings documentation	12–13 Press release	12 Article	14 Notice or advertisement	15 Leaflet or information sheet	17 Complete a form or label a diagram	17–18 Design a form or questionnaire
Pitman English for Business Communications Level 1	✓		✓	✓							✓	
Pitman English for Business Communications Level 2	✓	✓	✓	✓			✓	✓				
Pitman English for Business Communications Level 3	✓	✓	✓	✓	✓	✓	✓	✓	✓	✓		
LCCIEB English for Business First Level	✓			✓							✓	
LCCIEB English for Business Second Level	✓	✓	✓	✓			✓	✓	✓	✓		
LCIEB English for Business Third Level	✓	✓	✓	✓	✓	✓	✓	✓	✓	✓		
RSA Communication in Business Stage I	✓		✓	✓					✓	✓	✓	
RSA Communication in Business Stage II	✓	✓	✓	✓		✓			✓	✓		✓

✦ Assessment

In Business English examinations there are often no right or wrong answers – only those that are businesslike, appropriate and accurate. Assessment will usually take into consideration various factors like language, content, layout, tone and style.

General guidelines

- Use a new page for each answer. Show the number clearly in the margin.
- When handwriting answers leave a line space between paragraphs just as you would when typing and avoid cramping.
- Align correctly when using numbered items.
- Use capitals or underlining consistently.
- Ensure that your handwriting is legible.
- Go easy on the liquid correction fluid.
- Check for accuracy in grammar, spelling and punctuation – and then check again!

Business documents

- Display business documents correctly and consistently, using the same style when handwriting documents as you would if typing them.
- Include all mechanical details, e.g. letterhead, reference, date, subject heading, sender's name, title, enclosures.
- Number continuation sheets appropriately.
- Use a tone appropriate to the reader/sender/purpose.
- Insert names, places, dates, etc., to add realism to answers.
- Structure documents logically, rearranging information provided – but make a plan first.

Comprehension

- Explain clearly and concisely, in your own words where possible.
- Consider the contextual meanings when definitions are required.
- Consider the marks available for each question.

Completing forms or other documents

- Read the instructions carefully and do what is asked.
- Pick out the relevant words or phrases from the question.
- Read the headings on the form or other document carefully so that you understand the details you must find to complete the document.
- Write neatly and legibly in the appropriate space.
- Double check all the details to ensure accuracy.

Summarising

+ Consider the purpose for which the summary is to be used.
+ Use a suitable format.
+ Use your own words wherever possible.
+ Do not use short note form unless instructed to do so.
+ Consider the word limit.
+ Include a covering memo when appropriate.

✦ Examination papers

Computer reference to be entered on Answer Book: 398116

(TIME ALLOWED - TWO HOURS)

You have TEN minutes to read through this question paper before the start of the examination.

All questions are to be attempted.

English and mother-tongue dictionaries and electronic spell-checkers may be used.

The mark allocation for each question is given and you are advised to take this into account in planning your work.

Attention should be paid to clear, neat handwriting and tidy alterations.

Answers will be assessed on layout, content, use of English and effective communication in the given situation.

Information obtained from one question may be used in answering another.

Please start each answer on a new page.

NOTE: This question paper includes a form (Question 3). When you have completed the examination, make sure that this form is inserted in your answer book.

NO EXTRA FORMS WILL BE PROVIDED.

Printed by

© RSA 1998
Registered as a charity

CIBI (March 1998)

H30 0398
116/0198/450

GENERAL INFORMATION APPLICABLE TO ALL QUESTIONS

(Information obtained from one question may be used in answering another.)

Tiger Security UK specialises in safeguarding premises, personnel and property. It also offers a safe collection, storage and delivery facility for valuable goods of all kinds. The firm has several branches throughout the country and its headquarters are in Liverpool.

You work as a clerical assistant to the general manager of the Caldon branch situated at 18 - 26 Fastnet Road, Caldon, CN1 5QB, telephone number 01529 583959, fax 01529 583956. The manager's name is Mr Alec Dean.

Your duties include the day to day running of the general office, answering the telephone and dealing with enquiries. Ms Shami Ibadan is in charge of accounts and Mr James Hawksworth supervises drivers.

1   Writing a letter

SITUATION

A letter has been received from a prospective customer regarding the collection, storage and delivery of valuable family heirlooms. The letter is in Appendix A on page 5.

Alec comes into your office and says to you:

"We've had a letter from Mrs Carlson. She isn't on the phone so we can't ring her. I'll need to go and see her to give her some help and to discuss her needs.

"I'll go next Tuesday, 17 March, at about 10.30 am. I hope the time and date will suit her. She won't open the door to strangers so tell her that I shall use one of the company's small vans. She will be able to recognise it quite easily."

ASSIGNMENT

Using the information above and referring to the letter from Mrs Carlson (Appendix A on page 5), write the letter for Alec to sign. Assume that you will use the firm's headed notepaper but observe the conventions of a business letter.

(20 marks)

2   <u>Writing a memo with a reply slip</u>

SITUATION

A fax has been received from head office. It has been decided that the larger type security vans will be replaced by smaller, but much more efficient vehicles, which have first class communication systems. The new vans also have a very complex locking system.

All drivers will need instruction in operating these vehicles. James Hawksworth says to you:

"Will you do a memo to go to all drivers, please? One of the new vans will be brought over from head office on 14 April and will be here with an instructor for the next four days.

"All drivers will need about half an hour of instruction on the technology but not in driving - the new vans have power steering so they are very easy to drive.

"Put a reply slip at the bottom of the memo. I want the drivers to give me a time and date when they will be available between 10.00 am and 4.00 pm, April 14, 15, 16, and 17 inclusive. I want their replies by 10 April so that I can organise the time efficiently. We'll need full names, the registration number of present vehicles and signatures, please."

ASSIGNMENT

Write the memo with a reply slip according to James's instructions.

(20 marks)

3   <u>Completing a form</u>

SITUATION

This morning, Alec has visited a customer and obtained details of the goods she wants collected, stored and delivered. He has made a set of notes and has asked you to complete the necessary form. The customer's name is Mrs Norris. Her address is 139 Redwood Road, Caldon, CN4 5HR. Her telephone number is Caldon (01529) 291736.

ASSIGNMENT

Using Alec's notes (Appendix B on page 6) and other information in this question paper, complete the form on page 7.

(15 marks)

4   Drafting an advertisement

SITUATION

Your office is getting busier and both Alec and Shami think that extra help is needed. Shami would like some help with her work and Alec thinks a school leaver who could be trained would be very useful. The position will be full-time. The person appointed would be working with you for most of the time and would share your duties.

Alec says to you:

"Will you draft an advertisement for the local press for an office junior, please? Qualifications in Maths and English are essential. We want someone with a pleasant personality and who will have a flexible approach to our work - they also need to be patient with telephone enquiries. You will be training them in office skills and Shami will do the accounts side.

"The going rate for a school leaver is around £5,000 a year. Ask for replies in writing please. Don't give our telephone number."

ASSIGNMENT

Using the above information and any other relevant information in the question paper, draft the advertisement. For this question you may ignore margins to make the best use of the space available. Do not use colour.

(20 marks)

APPENDIX A

The Beeches
Middleton Lane
Hasteley
Nr Caldon
CN6 9PQ

Tiger Security UK
18-26 Fastnet Rd
Caldon
CN1 5QB

11 March 1998

Dear Sir

I want to send some family heirlooms to my son in Cornwall but I can't get out of the house because I have arthritis. I don't have anyone to pack for me and I wouldn't let anyone into the house if I didn't know them anyway.

I have to go into a home at the end of March - I'm 91 you know! - and I want to get these valuable things off as soon as I can. If you can help me I can pay you - I do have the money. Could you come next week?

I'm not on the phone but I never go out because I cannot walk very far. Ring the bell until I answer the door, I'm a bit deaf.

Yours hopefully

Clara Carlson (Mrs)

APPENDIX B

Alec's Notes

Details of Goods from Mrs Norris

		Value
1 - Painting 75cms x 40cms	-	£20,000
1 - Georgian Silver Teapot	-	£650
1 - Gold Watch (Hunter)	-	£500

Collection on March 18th

To: Mr Keiron Norris
"Tower House"
Cadwallader
Cornwall
CL2 7AH

The telephone number for Mr Norris is 01732 597993

Deliver on April 10th

Details of costs and payment

Cost of storage will be £55

Mrs Norris wants to pay cash

Price for collection and delivery will be £200.00
Total cost will be £255.00

To be used when answering Question 3.
Please detach this sheet and place it in
your answer book.

Insert here:

Centre Number:
Candidate's Name:

TIGER SECURITY UK

PLEASE USE BLOCK CAPITALS WHEN COMPLETING THIS FORM

Address of branch _____

Name of customer _____

Address _____

Telephone number with STD code _____

Details of goods for collection and value

_____

_____

_____

Are goods to be stored?   YES/ NO * _____
*Delete as necessary

Date of collection _____

Goods to be delivered to: Name   _____

Address _____

Telephone number with STD code _____

Date for delivery _____

Total amount to pay _____ Method of payment _____

Customer's signature _____

Any other details and/or information _____

_____

Date of completing form _____

Member of staff completing form

M
A
R **216** **COMMUNICATION IN BUSINESS**
STAGE II
FRIDAY 13 MARCH 1998

Computer reference to be entered on Answer book: 398216

(TIME ALLOWED - TWO AND A HALF HOURS)

You have TEN minutes to read through this question paper before the start of the
examination.

All questions are to be attempted. They should be answered in the order in which they
appear.

Please start each answer on a new page.

The mark allocation for each question is given and you are advised to take this into account in
planning your work.

Answers will be assessed on layout, content, use of English and effective communication in
the given situation.

English and mother-tongue dictionaries and electronic spell-checkers may be used.

Information obtained from one question may be used in answering another.

CIBII (March 1998)

H32 0398

GENERAL INFORMATION APPLICABLE TO ALL QUESTIONS

(Information obtained from one question may be used in answering another.)

You are employed as an Administrative Officer by the Banfield Housing Association. Its address is Welling House, 18 Bishop's Way, Banfield, BD3 4XA. The telephone number is 01932-448866 and the fax number is 01932-733933. Housing associations own, manage and maintain properties for rent. The Banfield Housing Association owns three estates, Merryworth, Bidden and Yardley. It has contracts with general builders and specialist firms for the maintenance work on its properties. It has a staff of 22 under the Chief Executive, Mrs Anita Bridger.

You have various duties. They include dealing with queries and problems of tenants of the Association's houses and flats, liaising with firms working on properties, and assisting the Association's professional staff. You are also the Secretary of the Consultative Committee which exercises general oversight of the Association's work.

1   Writing a letter

SITUATION

The Association is carrying out work to improve the kitchens in Borthwick Terrace on the Yardley estate. The houses date from the 1930s. New sink units are being fitted, together with extractor fans to improve ventilation.

This morning you received a letter of complaint from Mrs Johnson, one of the more difficult tenants. You telephoned the builder, Mr Reg Moss, whose comments were characteristically forthright. Mrs Johnson's letter and Mr Moss's comments are in Appendix A on pages 5 and 6.

When the Association gave notice of the work to be done it warned tenants to plan ahead and to cooperate with the builder.

ASSIGNMENT

Write a tactful but firm reply to Mrs Johnson, covering relevant points in her letter. Give a gentle hint as to how she might be more cooperative. Tell her when it is planned to complete the work. You can assume that you have the Association's headed paper. Sign the letter yourself.

(20 marks)

2   <u>Composing a notice and agenda for a meeting</u>

SITUATION

The Banfield Housing Association Consultative Committee meets at monthly intervals, usually at 6.30 pm, on the last Friday of the month, in the Conference Room of Welling House. It comprises representatives of various interests on the three estates and of the local authority, and professional staff of the Association.

It is chaired by the Chief Executive. She tells you: "I have several items for the next agenda. We must discuss play facilities at Bidden following the petition. We also need members' views about safer access to Dean Bancroft Primary School when the road is improved. Several people want to bring up re-cycling - whether the collection points at Yardley are in the best places - we've had some complaints. Mark Wilson will report on the refurbishment programme. Put these items on the agenda please, with the usual items, plus any others requested by members. Make sure members know the meeting will start at 7.00 pm - there's no way I can be back from my afternoon meeting that day by 6.30 pm. I did mention it last time but they may have forgotten."

In your file you have two items - see Appendix B on page 7.

ASSIGNMENT

Prepare the notice and agenda. The wording of agenda items should be brief but informative.

(20 marks)

(OVER)

3   Designing a form

SITUATION

Sometimes tenants with disabilities apply to have adaptations to their homes. Adaptations are special fittings to help people to live independently. For example, in the last four months the Association has put in grab rails for a man with arthritis, provided an outside telephone bell for a deaf woman, had a front door ramp installed and allocated a wider garage for a wheelchair user, and arranged a transfer to a ground-floor flat for a blind man and his guide dog.

So far, each change has been made after discussions with the tenant, the general practitioner (doctor) and the contractor doing the work. It has been realised that quicker decisions could be made if the Association had all essential details available, including the doctor's opinion, as soon as an application is made for an adaptation or exchange of the property.

The Chief Executive asks you to design a form for this purpose. She explains: "We shall need full details of the tenant, the family (if any), existing accommodation (we know the property in general but may not know of recent changes inside it), what is wanted, what causes difficulty in the present house or flat, and details of the disability. Then we shall need a statement of the applicant's present condition from the doctor. Applicants could also get an occupational therapist's opinion or they might prefer us to arrange that. By the way, we need to get signed consent for us to make any further enquiries of any doctors who have treated the applicant. Would you design the form please? Encourage people to apply as soon as they feel a need - that will enable us to help them in a planned way instead of having to do things in a rush."

ASSIGNMENT

Design the form, using two pages of your answer book.

(20 marks)

4   Preparing a fact sheet

SITUATION

Tenants who forget essential tasks or leave things in the house or flat when they move cause problems. You and your colleagues have recently talked about this in detail. A transcript of the conversation is contained in Appendix C on pages 8 and 9.

Your colleagues liked your idea of a fact sheet, which could be sent to tenants who are about to move.

ASSIGNMENT

Prepare the fact sheet as suggested. Select relevant points from the conversation (Appendix C on pages 8 and 9). Express them briefly, in positive terms and in an orderly sequence. Give the fact sheet a suitable title. Use one page of your answer book. Pay particular attention to spacing and clear layout.

(15 marks)

APPENDIX A

---

37 Borthwick Terrace
Banfield
BD7 9RZ

12 March 1998

Dear Sir or Madam

I have just had your builder in to do my new sink unit and fit the extractor fan. It has not done me any good. The doctor says I must take things calmly and not get in a state but how can I with all this going on? He was here nearly all day yesterday and I couldn't get to the cooker so I had no dinner and with diabetes it is important that I eat on time. When he left, he left a big hole in the wall and I could see the sky through it. The fan he put in first made a loud humming noise and he said he would change it. What about the gate he broke with his ladder? When will it be repaired? I shall get all the dogs in the area in my front garden. At my age I can't cope with all this. I want to live in peace. Mrs Andrews next door says he did her kitchen in one day. Some people get all the luck. What are you going to do about it?

Yours faithfully

Ann Johnson

Ann Johnson (Mrs)

(OVER)

APPENDIX A (continued)

Mr Moss's comments to you on the telephone:

"I ought to get double rate for working at Mrs Johnson's. She is an ungrateful so-and-so. She finds fault with everything. Her sink unit took longer than all the others because she hadn't cleared out the cupboard underneath and then I found that water had leaked into it. There was rot underneath and I had to replace some floorboards before I could start to put in the new unit.

"I made the hole for the extractor fan and fitted it but she didn't like the noise so I've ordered another make. I offered to board up the hole. There's a flower bed outside the window and she said: 'Don't you dare tread on my daffodils' but I would have had to, so in the end she told me to leave it.

"All the time I was there she kept asking me when I would finish. I'm down to go back and complete the job on Friday of next week and I shall be glad to see the last of it. I plead guilty to breaking the gate - I'll repair that at the same time. I've ordered the wood. I offered to clear the way to her cooker but she told me just to get on with the job.

"As for Mrs Andrews at number 35, everything was ready and clear for me there - and I got cups of tea and delicious chocolate cake. That lady is an excellent cook."

APPENDIX B

Note - March Consultative Committee

Mr Shah, one of the members, wants the Committee to discuss whether the Association can press for a footbridge over the railway at Wilton Lane, Merryworth. He says children have been seen using the crossing by the stile as short cut. People fear there could be accident. He is also contacting local Councillors.

Letter from Mrs Schmidt

```
                                    9 Willow Terrace
                                    Banfield
                                    BD9 2RR

                                    10 March 1998


Dear Sir or Madam

I understand you do the agenda for the
Consultative Committee.  As you may know, I have
just been elected as the new tenants'
representative for the Yardley estate.  I should
like to bring up the lack of sufficient garages
on this estate.  I expect you are aware of the
problem.

I look forward to meeting you at the March
meeting.

Yours faithfully


Helga Schmidt


Helga Schmidt
```

APPENDIX C

Transcript of staff conversation about moving

Bill: It's strange what people forget. One family left an expensive telephone answering machine plugged in. They got half-way to their new place some distance away, then remembered and came back, each blaming the other.

Lucy: They don't see things because their minds are on their next home. Someone left all the sandwiches. People often forget to tell the gas and electricity firms. Then they get annoyed when they are billed for what the next tenants have used. One family with an elderly relative who needed frequent visits from the nurse forgot to tell her they were moving - you'd think they would tell the doctor's practice.

Kevin: There was a bit of a disaster in my last job. The tenant moved in the middle of a cold spell and didn't turn off the water. The house was empty for several days and the pipes froze and burst. A passer-by noticed water streaming out of the front door. There was a lot of damage which had to be put right before the next tenant could move in.

Ibrahim: I had a man who forgot to arrange for his mail to be redirected and he had a lot because he was chairman of this and secretary of that, quite a figure in the local community, and the house was empty for a while, and then among all this accumulation of mail when we sent it to him there was a Premium Bond prize notification.

Theresa: I get really annoyed at the rubbish some people leave - anything they don't want! It must be a depressing sight for the next tenants.

Lee: And sometimes the house might be clean and tidy but then you glance in the loft and it's full of junk. Or you go to the garden shed and it's full. One family forgot to shut the windows and a cat got in and produced five kittens - no doubt she was looking for peace and quiet.

Mary: I thought the cat had been left behind once. I had gone to check the house and there was this frantic mewing and scratching at the back door. I phoned the family. They had remembered the cat. They let it out at the new house and that was the last they had seen of it - three days before. The cat had lost weight but soon recovered. It is sometimes a good idea to get some medication for an animal who might become disorientated or frightened by a move.

June: It's a good idea to feed an animal as soon as you arrive at the new place. What annoys me is when people strip the house or flat of fittings which don't belong to them. Light fittings which were supplied with the house are a favourite, but I have known even kitchen units removed.

Mark: And what about the awful Do-It-Yourself efforts that greet the next tenants? One tenant had tried to move a radiator which was in the way of something. He had replaced the piping with flexible piping and drilled holes all over the place. It was downright dangerous. We had to have it repaired at considerable cost before the next tenants could move in - and of course the DIY enthusiast had to pay up for all the damage he had caused.

Candidate: I had to waste time recently when tenants moved out as arranged but did not return the keys and did not leave a forwarding address (which I had assured them would be kept confidential). Do you think we might produce a fact sheet of all the points you have mentioned? Then we can give it to tenants before they move. They could then check that each task has been done.

<table>
<tr><td>
ENGLISH FOR BUSINESS COMMUNICATIONS

LEVEL 1
</td></tr>
</table>

This paper must be returned with the candidate's work, otherwise the entry will be void and no result will be issued.

No   **EL-NBC 11**
      50134

CANDIDATE'S NAME ....
(Block letters please)

CENTRE NO .... DATE ....

Time allowed: *1 hour 30 minutes*
                       (plus 15 minutes' reading time during which no
                       writing will be allowed).

*Answer **ALL** questions. All answers must be written in ink, typed or word processed.*

Your answers should be written on separate sheets of paper except for Task 4. The answer to Task 4 should be written on the form in the question booklet. Make sure your name appears on each sheet of paper used.

*Answers to **ALL** tasks will be assessed for language and content. Two tasks only will also be assessed for layout. This will be indicated on the task.*

———————

FOR EXAMINER'S USE ONLY

TASK 1	TASK 2	TASK 3	TASK 4	TOTAL
25	25	25	25	100

SITUATION

You are the Administrative Assistant (AA) to Jinit Singh,
Personnel Manager of Bentak Products, PO Box 2288, Nakuru.

Jinit Singh will not be coming into the office until later and has
left the following in your in-tray.

Task 1 *(Your answer will be assessed for layout.)*

AA

The word processor operators are having problems changing over to the new Fontplus WP system after using our very basic one for so long. I phoned Star Training Ltd late yesterday. I enquired about 2 places for a 3-day course in 2 weeks' time. Please write to book this – state the dates required – confirm cost – state which system to be learned.

Ask for details of the accommodation.

I'll sign the letter when I get back.

JS

WORD PROCESSING - 1, 2 OR 3-DAY COURSES

Courses held to clients' requirements at any time

Don't let your staff learn your new WP system by trial and error or long drawn-out day-release or evening classes

Systems offered: *Perfectionprint*
Supertype Princess
Fontplus

One-day course: *Ksh 4250 per person*
Two-day course: *Ksh 7500 per person*
Three-day course: *Ksh 10500 per person*

If required, accommodation can be arranged at modestly-priced hotels.

STAR TRAINING LIMITED
69-75 Main Street
NAIROBI

(25 marks)

Task 2 *(Your answer will be assessed for layout).*

Respond to this note by carrying out the instructions.

AA

Please write a memo to Mrs Smith, the Word Processing Office Supervisor. Tell her about the arrangements we've made for Fontplus training (refer to letter to Star Training Ltd). Details of accommodation have been requested. Ask her to choose 2 people – they will need to pass on what they learn to the others. Course fees and accommodation will be paid direct by us. Other reasonable expenses can be claimed.

JS

(25 marks)

<u>Task 3</u>

You have received the following telephone message from Mr Singh. Carry out his instructions.

MESSAGE FOR

M ✓   **AA**

WHILE YOU WERE OUT

M.... Jinit Singh

Of..

Telephone No ....

Telephoned	✓	**Please ring**	
Called to see you		**Will call again**	
Wants to see you		**Urgent**	

Message: ....Accounts Vacancy – Interviews at Mombasa Branch

Please fax Bill Macdonald in Mombasa. Send names of candidates – give
interview times (half hourly interviews from 10.00am) – next Friday. You
have already got the full list of candidates – we'll only interview those
ticked. The Chief Accountant confirms he will interview with Bill and Jinit.
Request BM to acknowledge receipt of fax.

Taken by ....Eunnah (Reception)

<u>Accounts Vacancy - Candidates</u>

Peter Malik ✓
Joseph Gichuyhi
Anna Wu ✓
Manjit Kaur ✓
Simon Njuguna
Pearl Karamba
Jackson Banda ✓
Brenda Mbena

(25 marks)

Task 4

Respond to the letter from Blandish Limited.

BLANDISH LIMITED

27 Independence Way
Nairobi

Tel: 227439   Fax: 227440

Bentak Products
PO Box 2288
Nakuru

Dear Sirs

Lucy Belen has applied for a post as a Personal Secretary in this firm. We understand that she was employed by you from 1992 to the present and would be grateful if you would supply a reference as soon as possible.

Yours faithfully

I. Thuo

Isaac Thuo
Personnel Officer

AA
Please refer to Lucy's record card and complete the standard letter form. JS

RECORD CARD			
Name: **LUCY BELEN**			
Joined company: **21 MARCH 1992**			
Job: **WP OPERATOR**			
	Good	Satisfactory	Poor
Attendance		✓	
Punctuality	✓		
Standard of work	✓		
Qualities: honesty	✓		
reliability	✓		
helpfulness		✓	

Task 4 (continued)

Candidate's Name: ....

BENTAK PRODUCTS
PO Box 2288
Nakuru

....

....

....

....

Dear ....

I refer to your letter requesting a reference for ....

I trust the details given under the following headings provide the information you require.

Length of service and position held: ....

....

....

Standard of work: ....

....

....

Personal qualities: ....

....

....

I have no hesitation in recommending .... for the post
applied for.

Yours ....

Jinit Singh
Personnel Manager

(25 marks)

END OF EXAMINATION

ENGLISH FOR BUSINESS COMMUNICATIONS

LEVEL 2

No   **EL NBC 12**
     50142

CANDIDATE'S NAME ....
(Block letters please)

CENTRE NO .... DATE ....

Time allowed: 2 hours.
                (plus 15 minutes' reading time during which no
                writing will be allowed).

Answer **ALL** questions. All answers must be written in ink, typed or word processed.

Your answers should be written on separate sheets of paper. Make sure your name appears on each sheet of paper used.

Answers to **ALL** tasks will be assessed for language and content. Two tasks only will also be assessed for layout. This will be indicated on the task.

—————————————

FOR EXAMINER'S USE ONLY

TASK 1	TASK 2	TASK 3	TASK 4	TASK 5	TOTAL
20	20	20	20	20	100

SITUATION

Light Waves Ahead is a small commercial radio company with
a station in Blantyre and another in Harare. Its main source of
income is from advertising on the air by local firms. You are
Personal Assistant (PA) to Mr Moses Banda, the General
Manager.

<u>Task 1</u> *(Your answer will be assessed for layout.)*

Respond to the note from Moses Banda.

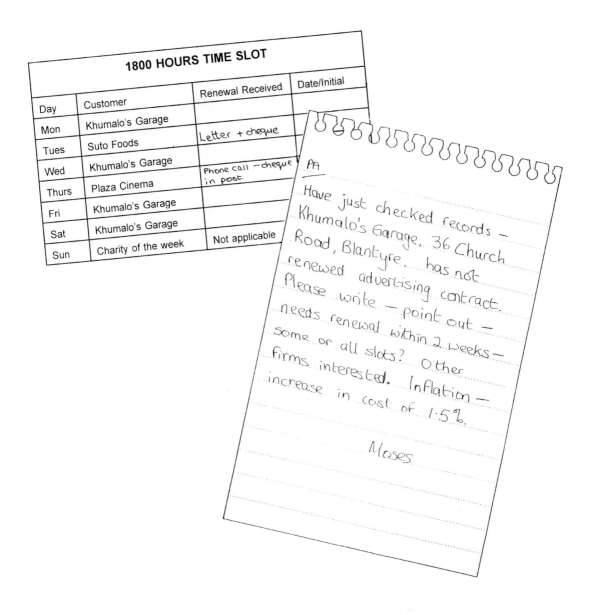

1800 HOURS TIME SLOT

Day	Customer	Renewal Received	Date/Initial
Mon	Khumalo's Garage	Letter + cheque	
Tues	Suto Foods		
Wed	Khumalo's Garage	Phone call – cheque in post.	
Thurs	Plaza Cinema		
Fri	Khumalo's Garage		
Sat	Khumalo's Garage		
Sun	Charity of the week	Not applicable	

PA

Have just checked records –
Khumalo's Garage, 36 Church
Road, Blantyre, has not
renewed advertising contract.
Please write – point out –
needs renewal within 2 weeks –
some or all slots? Other
firms interested. Inflation –
increase in cost of 1.5%.

Moses

(20 marks)

Task 2   *(Your answer will be assessed for layout.)*

Deal with the following as requested.

PA

I'm looking for extra programmes for the morning of Tuesday 5th. Please write and circulate a memorandum to Heads of Department noting the times which need filling and asking for details of suggested programmes, including titles and estimated cost. The information needs to be on my desk by Friday morning.

Thanks. Moses

DRAFT TIMETABLE

Tuesday 5 - am

6.00 am	News.
6.30	Advertisement break.
6.35	Question Time.
7.00	Advert break.
7.05	The Money Market.
7.30	Advert break.
7.35	?
8.00	Advert break.
8.05	Farming Today.
8.30	Advert break.
8.35	?
9.00	Advert break.
9.05	Listeners' Letters
9.30	Advert break.
9.35	?
10.00	Advert break.
10.05	The Woman in White (drama).
10.30	Advert break.
10.35	The Woman in White (continued).
11.00	Advert break.
11.05	?
11.30	Advert break.

(20 marks)

Task 3

Please respond to the note from Lois Shava.

PA.

Help! I am trying to get this series together (very short of time). Moses suggested that you might write this for me if I gave you the basic information. Alice Limula — Blantyre High School 1965-70 — later studied English Literature at Cambridge University in England — programme starts 15th of next month — set in nineteenth century — Limula spent five years in America after Cambridge — entitled Corn from the Desert — time of broadcast 8.15pm — about three generations of farmers — rags to riches theme.

Sorry it's a bit confused. I know you will sort it out.

Thanks   Lois Shava

Malawi News
17 Uhuru Street
Blantyre
Malawi

Head of the Drama Department
Light Waves Ahead
45 Freedom Avenue
Blantyre
Malawi

Dear Sir

Corn from the Desert

We understand that you are shortly broadcasting a new drama series written by Alice Limula.

As Miss Limula was educated in Blantyre we would be interested in printing a short article (about 100 words). Perhaps you would like to submit this to the News for inclusion in next week's edition.

Yours faithfully

J Gwenzi

Jeremiah Gwenzi
Editor

(20 marks)

Task 4

Action the following.

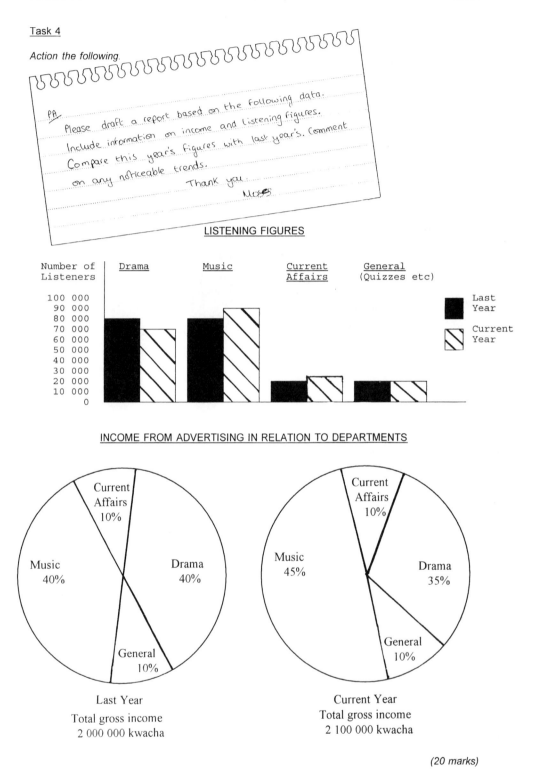

PA,

Please draft a report based on the following data. Include information on income and listening figures. Compare this year's figures with last year's. Comment on any noticeable trends.

Thank you.

Moses

LISTENING FIGURES

INCOME FROM ADVERTISING IN RELATION TO DEPARTMENTS

Last Year
Total gross income
2 000 000 kwacha

Current Year
Total gross income
2 100 000 kwacha

(20 marks)

Task 5

Act on the reminder note.

REMINDER

Tapes for "Corn from the Desert"
not back from editing. Fax
our station in Harare. - Needed
by Friday — programme going
out next Monday on life of
Alice Limula. Extracts from "Corn
from the Desert" needed for this
programme. Ask if any other
information available on tape
about her. Use courier - speed/
safety.

(20 marks)

END OF EXAMINATION

Index

Comments made about the third edition of *Communication for Business*

Also written by Shirley Taylor:

The Secretary in Training

A practical and comprehensive workbook containing all the fundamental theory of office procedures and secretarial duties. Suitable for classroom and home-based study, with students encouraged to show how much they know before undertaking further research. It is user-friendly and designed with both students and lecturers in mind. ISBN 981-223-3105 Pbk

Practical Audio Transcription

This succinct introduction to audio transcription enables students to attain basic audio transcription competency in approximately 12 hours. The main theory points are covered with plenty of practice material included for the student to gain competency. A C60 cassette containing graded practice exercises is available for departmental use. The cassette contains all instructions, allowing students to work through the programme at their own pace, making it suitable for full-time, part-time students and students in open learning workshops and in the workplace. ISBN 0-582-35698-9 Pbk Cassette ISBN: 0-582-35699-7 Csd

Also published by Longman:

Business Administration by Pauline Foster is a single student-centred text covering the basic principles of Business Administration at level 2. It provides thorough coverage of this area, using case studies and revision questions to reinforce the theory being taught. ISBN 0-582-36864-2 Pbk

Contemporary Word Processing by Jacqueline Appleton is an ideal text to cover the Text Processing module of the new RSA Certificate in Administrative and Secretarial Procedures. It is also a core text for all students taking courses involving word processing, text production and keyboarding at foundation and intermediate level for all examining bodies. ISBN 0-582-31272-8 Pbk

For more information about these and other titles, or to order a copy, please contact:

Steve James
Pearson Education
Further Education and Study Guides Division
Edinburgh Gate
Harlow
Essex
CM20 2JE

Telephone: 01279 623437   Fax: 01279 623266   e-mail: steve.james@awl.co.uk

Visit our on-line catalogues at:
http://www.awl-he.com